W0098041

COMCAVE.COLLEGE®

Hallert 1
Tel: 0231 72525-0
Fax: 0231 1262822

44227 Dortmund
www.comcave.de
info@comcave.de

CCNR003285-000315

Lehr- und Handbücher zu Sprachen und Kulturen

Herausgegeben von
José Vera Morales und Martin M. Weigert

Bisher erschienene Werke:

Arabisch
Waldmann, Wirtschaftswörterbuch
Arabisch-Deutsch · Deutsch-Arabisch

Chinesisch
Kuhn · Ning · Hongxia Shi, Markt
China. Grundwissen zur erfolgreichen
Marktöffnung
Liu · Siebenhandl, Einführung in die
chinesische Wirtschaftssprache

Englisch
Ehnes · Labriola · Schiffer, Politisches
Wörterbuch zum Regierungssystem
der USA · Englisch-Deutsch,
Deutsch-Englisch, 3. Auflage
Fink, Wirtschaftssprache Englisch –
Zweisprachiges Übersetzer-Kompendium
Fink, EconoTerms A Glossary of
Economic Terms, 6. Auflage
Fink, EconoTexts I, 3. Auflage
Fink, EconoTexts II, 2. Auflage
Guess, Professional English, 4. Auflage
Königs, Übersetzen Englisch – Deutsch
O'Neal, Banking and Financial English,
2. Auflage
O'Riordan · Lehniger, Business 21 –
Modernes Wirtschaftsenglisch kompakt
Schäfer · Galster · Rupp, Wirtschafts-
englisch, 11. Auflage
Wheaton · Schrott, Total Quality
Management
Zürl, English Training: Confidence in
Dealing with Conferences, Discussions,
and Speeches

Französisch
Jöckel, Training Wirtschaftsfranzösisch,
3. Auflage
Lavric · Pichler, Wirtschaftsfranzösisch
fehlerfrei – le français économique
sans fautes, 2. Auflage

Italienisch
Haring, Wirtschaftsitalienisch

Macedonia, Italienisch für Alle
Macedonia, Wirtschaftsitalienisch,
2. Auflage
Macedonia, Made in Italy

Polnisch
Milińska, Übersetzungskurs Polnisch-
Deutsch und Deutsch-Polnisch

Russisch
Baumgart · Jänecke, Rußlandknigge,
2. Auflage
Fijas · Tjulnina, Wirtschaftsrussisch –
Wörterbuch Band I: Deutsch-Russisch
Fijas · Tjulnina, Wirtschaftsrussisch –
Wörterbuch Band II: Russisch-Deutsch
Jänecke · Klemm, Verkehrslexikon,
Deutsch-Russisch · Russisch-Deutsch
Rathmayr · Dobrušna, Texte schreiben
und präsentieren auf Russisch

Spanisch
Jöckel, Wirtschaftsspanisch – Ein-
führung
Padilla Gálvez, Wirtschaftsspanisch-
Wörterbuch Spanisch-Deutsch ·
Deutsch-Spanisch
Padilla Gálvez, Wirtschaftsspanisch-
Lexikon Spanisch-Deutsch ·
Deutsch-Spanisch
Padilla Gálvez · Figueroa de Wachter,
Wirtschaftsspanisch: Textproduktion
Padilla Gálvez, Wirtschaftsspanisch:
Marketing
Schnitzer · Martí, Wirtschaftsspanisch –
Terminologisches Handbuch, 3. Auflage
Schnitzer u. a., Übungsbuch zu
Wirtschaftsspanisch, 2. Auflage
Vera-Morales, Spanische Grammatik,
3. Auflage

Tschechisch
Schmidt, Deutsch-tschechisches Wörterbuch der Betriebswirtschaftslehre

Business 21

Modernes Wirtschaftsenglisch kompakt

An understanding of the business world
in the 21st century

A course and reference handbook
Recommended for UNIcert® 3 and 4 Business
English modules, LCCI and TOEIC

Frances O'Riordan

and

Doris Lehniger

R. Oldenbourg Verlag München Wien

Die Deutsche Bibliothek - CIP-Einheitsaufnahme

O'Riordan, Frances:
Business 21 : modernes Wirtschaftsenglisch kompakt ; an
understanding of the business world in the 21st century ; a course
and reference handbook recommended for UNIcert 3 and 4 business
English modules, LCCI and TOEIC / Frances O'Riordan and Doris
Lehniger. – München ; Wien : Oldenbourg, 2002
   (Lehr- und Handbücher zu Sprachen und Kulturen)
   ISBN 978-3-486-25907-0

© 2002 Oldenbourg Wissenschaftsverlag GmbH
Rosenheimer Straße 145, D-81671 München
Telefon: (089) 45051-0
www.oldenbourg-verlag.de

Gedruckt auf säure- und chlorfreiem Papier
Gesamtherstellung: Books on Demand GmbH, Norderstedt

ISBN 978-3-486-25907-0

Mission Statement

Our mission in writing *Business 21* was:

- To provide a handbook for students at third level institutions and people working in the business world who wish to understand more about general concepts of business and the accompanying business terminology.

- To help the user survive in an increasingly complex and jargon rich business environment.

- To assist readers in following business and economic affairs.

- To offer a comprehensive reference material for instructors of Business English who may wish to develop a more thorough understanding of the subject matter in their field.

- To help prepare students who may wish to study abroad at third level institutions in English-speaking countries.

The authors both have a business and academic background with extensive experience in teaching students at universities and other language institutions in Germany and abroad.

Business21 has been recommended as course material for the **UNIcert® Level 3** and **4** subject-related modules.

It is also suitable for this purpose for the

- London Chamber of Commerce and Industry **(LCCI)** Examinations
- Test of English for International Communication **(TOEIC)**.

A short note on UNIcert®

UNIcert® is a system of certification increasingly used by universities in Germany. It aims to standardise the grades awarded by universities for various levels of modern language competence, to promote a greater degree of comparability between university language course programmes and thus to provide a certificate which is valid and acceptable also beyond the university context, as an indication of practical foreign language ability as required by academically trained personnel.

For more detailed info visit the homepage:
http://rcswww.urz.tu-dresden.de/~unicert

Contents

SECTION II: TAXATION

Introduction

> *Just when you think you've graduated from the school of experience, someone thinks up a new course.*
>
> Mary Waldrip

This material is a result of detailed classroom experimentation combined with feedback from students, business academics and managers.

It is targeted at an **upper-intermediate** to **advanced** audience. This would include everyone from the average reader to the student at a third level institution to people working and teaching in the business world.

The reader can simply refer to the 14 units and their subsections to obtain an overview of the main concepts and ideas which underpin the whole field of business.

In particular we have decided to focus on the background information necessary in understanding the content of the world's most widely read international news media on business and finance.

The book Business 21 attempts to explain general business concepts. The reader should be aware, however, that it is written in an **Anglo-American** business context and variances in terminology and interpretation may occur from country to country.

The material in the book is accessible and written in a readable style.

An extensive English-German vocabulary list is provided in each unit in order to assist the reader in understanding the contents and to further language acquisition.

Each unit contains comprehension questions to check understanding plus additional discussion points to allow students in a classroom situation to practice the language.

In addition **Internet links to each unit** are provided at:
http://rcswww.urz.tu-dresden.de/~business/

Instructor's Notes

A combination of autonomous and instructor assisted acquisition is recommended as the appropriate mix for teaching this book.

Each unit can be used independently and the instructor can focus on those units necessary for his/her particular target group.

As the contents of the unit may present some complications the detailed vocabulary lists serve to assist those who require more support in reading and understanding effectively.

The material also allows instructors the freedom to include more case studies, videos and other materials tailored to their individual classroom preferences.

Suggested approaches:

The standard approach is for students to read the units as a homework assignment and answer the comprehension questions in class. It is advisable that the vocabulary list of each unit be read through before proceeding with the text corpus.

Reading aloud can be practiced in a classroom environment whenever students experience pronunciation difficulties.

The next step is the **discussion**. The students use the vocabulary learnt in the unit as a basis for expressing their ideas more precisely in commenting on current business and economic issues. The provocative points in the Discussion Forum offer the opportunity to create lively debate.

Another possible approach, especially with the longer units, is to get students to prepare (either at home or in the class) one or more sections of a unit as appropriate and then introduce them to the class.

This can be supplemented by the material recommended in the continuously updated **Internet Link** pages:

http://rcswww.urz.tu-dresden.de/~business/

Alternatively students may be asked to do their own Internet searches which can form the basis of **presentations** and discussions. This can be developed into various individual/pair/team **projects**. The projects can be presented at a **(mini) conference**. Instructors can also, via students' assignments, build up a collection of supplementary materials from these sources.

Other media sources, of course, may also be used to 'tie-in' with the units, linking the material with current developments in the business world.

Business and economic affairs in **publications** such as The Economist, Business Week, The Financial Times, The Wall Street Journal, Newsweek, Time, Business Spotlight and other English language media are highly appropriate.

Authentic company materials such as annual reports, newsletters, general PR material, and contracts can also be integrated. This material is easily available on the Internet.

We strongly recommend instructors to combine this reading material with a variety of **audio and visual** sources. Useful authentic resources here include the business reports on BBC, CNN and NBC TV (all three are also available online), company videos as well as standard Business English video/DVD materials.

Another approach towards the Discussion Forum is to integrate **writing** by asking students to choose one or more of the discussion points for essays or other written assignments

Self-study

This book can be used equally well by individuals as an effective and efficient guide to learning, linking and applying important business concepts for use in everyday life.

It is particularly suitable as a self-study material for those working in the business world such as banking, insurance, and for those preparing to study at third level institutions in English-speaking countries.

The reader will appreciate the approach followed in explaining general concepts and related business terminology. The units can be used independently.

An extensive vocabulary list avoids the necessity of specialist dictionaries. It is recommended to read the vocabulary before commencing with a unit.

The comprehension questions after each section serve as a useful revision tool.

> The authors welcome any suggestions and criticisms on the book. Please email **business21@mailbox.tu-dresden.de**

Acknowledgements

The authors would like to thank the following individuals from the academic and business world:

Many thanks to **Martin Weigert** at Oldenbourg - *All good things come to those who wait.*

Anna Boujevitch for the layout and design.

Ursula Birke
Christel Matzke
Klaus Nitzsche
Sven Riddell
Norman Rosendahl
Professor Walter Schmitz
Professor Bernd Voss
Annekathrin Witzmann
(all Dresden University of Business and Technology, Germany)

Siobhan Dalrymple
Professor Klaus Gommlich
(Kent State University, USA)

Stephen Gilroy
(Hong Kong Shanghai Bank PLC)

Michael Peter
(Capital Markets, Deutsche Bank AG, Germany)

Anthony Fitzpatrick
Robert Sweeney
(Entrepreneurs in Ireland and Germany)

Paul Taylor
(Managing Director, UK Office, Northwest Coatings Corporation, USA)

Venera Ibragimova
Lilia Ismagilova
Dina Phatkulova
(Moscow State University of Commerce Ufa Institute, Russian Federation)

A very special thanks to the Advanced Business English students of the Winter Semester 2000/01 and the Summer Semester 2001 for reviewing and offering their perspectives on the material.

Alejandra Donado
Andreas Bähn
Andreas Recknagel
Anja Nagel
Anne-Maria Gehlhar
Arnold Lange
Audrey Laffitte
Bastian Lettenwitsch
Benoît Petit
Berit Jähnigen
Bernd Hegwein
Björn Kunze
Camille Gignier
Catherine Horn

Gerd Schnabel
Hanka Rothe
Heiko Leipold
Hendrik Augustin
Henry Weiß
Holger Waldhausen
Holger Winkler
Irina Stoyanova
Iris Langhans
Isabelle Gil
Jan Tannenberger
Jana Matschewski
Jana Richter
Jana Vollmer

Michael Bertrand
Michael Lutzenberger
Nico Kersten
Nora Handwerker
Petra Teresiak
Ralph Rummler
Robert Wauer
Roland Wunderlich
Romi Fiedler
Sandra Paschke
Sascha Kornek
Sebastian Haubold
Simone Krantz
Stefan Eitze

Celine Chantepy
Charlie Knapp
Christelle Fernbach
Christian Thombansen
Christobal Mora
Dana Goller
Daniel Queißer
Diana Forner
Diana-Maria Hempel
Dorit Schöne
Elodie Siellermann
Erik Reips
Erwan Salembier
Falk Semmler
Felix Finger
Franz Döscher

Javier Perello
Jerôme Mutelet
Jochen Schaefer
Jörg Elzemann
Julia Lehmann
Juliane Gölz
Katherina Gondermann
Kerstin Creutz
Kevin Hay
Kristian Kappel
Lars Hübner
Lars Kirsten
Lars Wolf
Marco Weimann
Marie-Pierre Touzé
Markus Fischer
Melaine Escoffier

Stefan Heimann
Stefan Immisch
Stefanie Wagner
Stefen Liebernickel
Steffen Kottwitz
Stephan Menzel
Susanne Arlt
Susanne Schubert
Sven Friedrich
Thoralf Wagner
Till Theegarten
Tobias Oertel
Tobias Rothbart
Ulrich Goedicke
Wolfram Bauer
Yvonne Bethage

The authors and publishers also wish to thank the following organizations:

BBC Online
Czech Oil Refineries
CNN Europe
IBM (UK)
National Broadcasting Corporation
The Economist Newspaper Limited, London
The Financial Times Newspaper Limited
The New York Times Company
The Times Newspaper Ltd.
The Wall Street Journal

SETTING THE SCENE – THE BIG PICTURE

> *When I was young, I thought that money was the most important thing in life; now that I am old, I know it is.*
>
> *Oscar Wilde*

FOCUS This unit provides a very general introduction covering the development of economic activity. Key concepts of the business world which will be discussed more fully in later units are also introduced.

1.0   TRADING

Life in Stone Age times was relatively simple and relatively short. The simple needs for food, clothing and shelter were satisfied from what could be hunted, grown or made by oneself, i.e. self-sufficiency in a **subsistence** economy.

However, in the Bronze and Iron Ages, people began to specialize in producing a limited number of items. This **division of labour** led to the development of *trade* (buying and selling) as they exchanged their surplus for other items that they required. The first system was known as **barter**, i.e. the exchange of goods for goods. Problems with barter were the coincidence of wants and the difficulty in valuing commodities.

To overcome these problems **money** was introduced as a medium of exchange. Items such as shells, teeth and precious metals were used before people finally got round to producing coins and notes.

Money was a major improvement in that it was a:

- **Medium of Exchange** – allowed goods and services to be bought and sold
- **Measure of Value** – used to price goods and services
- **Store of Value** – could be saved
- **Means of Deferred Payments** – when goods were bought on credit the amount owed could be measured using money

It was also:

- **portable** – easily carried
- **durable** – lasted a long time
- **divisible** – divided into smaller amounts, i.e. units of 1, 5, 10, 100, etc
- **easily recognizable**
- **uniform in quality**

Money is **legal tender** in that the native notes and coins, i.e. unit of currency of each country, must be accepted in payment for goods and services. Today we may be looking at the end of money with the advent of e-money in its various forms.

Goods or tangible items and **services** or intangible items were produced because people had **needs** (to survive in life, i.e. food, water, clothing, shelter, etc) but also **wants** (to improve their standard of living, i.e. quality of life).

As consumers resources are scarce or limited, choices have to be made on how best to spend money. The price system that we have on Planet Earth operates through the inter-action of the forces of supply and demand. **Supply** may be defined as the quantity of a commodity which firms are prepared to *sell* at a given price, while **demand** is the quantity of a commodity which consumers are prepared to *buy* at a given price. A **market** can be defined as a set of arrangements by which buyers and sellers are in contact to exchange products, i.e. goods or services.

 Explain the development of trade.

2.0   PRODUCTION

Specialization and the **division of labour** led to manufacturing eventually becoming divided into assembly lines and other processes leading to the mass production of goods. This was the one of the main achievements of the Industrial Revolution in 18th century Britain.

2.1   The Factors of Production

In order to produce goods and services, four essential resources referred to as the **factors of production** are required. These are:

Land – which refers to any factor of production supplied by nature, i.e. areas used to construct buildings, and to natural resources such as minerals, crops, animals and climate. While the supply of land is fixed, the quality can be improved via fertilizers, drainage and irrigation.

Labour – is the economic activity directed towards the production of wealth. This consists of skilled, semi-skilled and unskilled workers and is in turn dependent on the education, training and experience they receive.

Capital – refers to any form of man-made wealth which can be used to produce additional wealth. In the normal sense it means money used to start a business.

Human Capital (Enterprise) – is that form of human activity which supplies the initiative necessary for setting up and organizing the other factors of production and taking the risks involved. The entrepreneur's objective is to make a profit.

The **production** process itself can be considered under three main headings – primary, secondary and tertiary industries.

- *Primary* production consists of the extractive industries from the natural environment, i.e. mining, fishing, forestry and farming. These primary products form the raw materials necessary for secondary production.

- *Secondary* production refers to the manufacturing and construction industries, which convert raw materials into finished products.

- *Tertiary* industries provide services and are often referred to as **commerce** and **direct services**.

    Explain the factors of production.

2.2   Commerce

Commerce consists of trade and commercial services and assists the process of **domestic** (home) or **foreign** (international) trade. It may be defined as the area that deals with the buying and selling of goods using **channels of distribution** through the **manufacturer, wholesaler** and/or **retailer** on to the **consumer**.

Services to trade include banking, transport, communications, insurance and warehousing.

Direct (personal) services look after people's general health and welfare, for example, doctors, teachers, police services and entertainers.

    a. *What is commerce?*
    b. *Present the following diagram as a summary of what has been covered so far.*

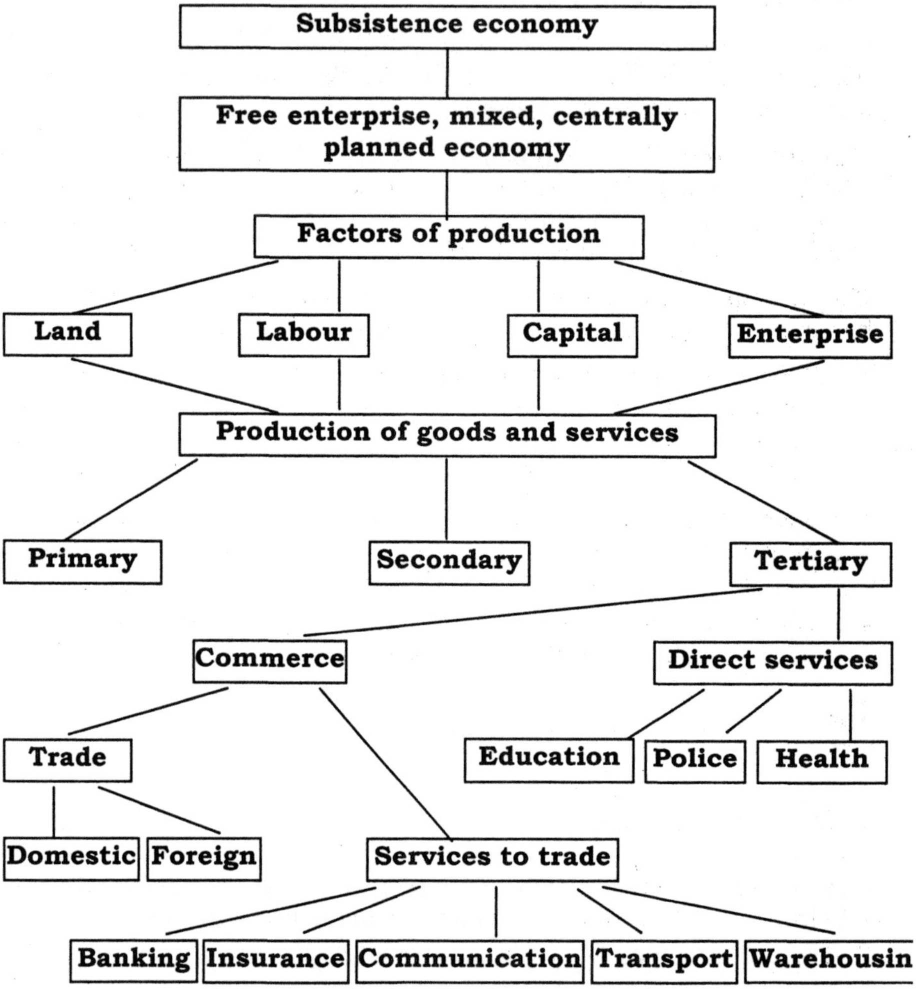

```
                    ┌─────────────────────────────┐
                    │     Subsistence economy      │
                    └─────────────────────────────┘
                    ┌─────────────────────────────┐
                    │ Free enterprise, mixed,      │
                    │  centrally planned economy   │
                    └─────────────────────────────┘
                    ┌─────────────────────────────┐
                    │    Factors of production     │
                    └─────────────────────────────┘
      ┌──────┐    ┌────────┐        ┌─────────┐     ┌────────────┐
      │ Land │    │ Labour │        │ Capital │     │ Enterprise │
      └──────┘    └────────┘        └─────────┘     └────────────┘
             ┌──────────────────────────────────┐
             │  Production of goods and services │
             └──────────────────────────────────┘
   ┌─────────┐          ┌───────────┐            ┌──────────┐
   │ Primary │          │ Secondary │            │ Tertiary │
   └─────────┘          └───────────┘            └──────────┘
          ┌──────────┐                    ┌─────────────────┐
          │ Commerce │                    │ Direct services │
          └──────────┘                    └─────────────────┘
   ┌───────┐                  ┌───────────┐ ┌────────┐ ┌────────┐
   │ Trade │                  │ Education │ │ Police │ │ Health │
   └───────┘                  └───────────┘ └────────┘ └────────┘
 ┌──────────┐┌─────────┐   ┌──────────────────┐
 │ Domestic ││ Foreign │   │ Services to trade │
 └──────────┘└─────────┘   └──────────────────┘
 ┌─────────┐┌───────────┐┌───────────────┐┌───────────┐┌────────────┐
 │ Banking ││ Insurance ││ Communication ││ Transport ││ Warehousin │
 └─────────┘└───────────┘└───────────────┘└───────────┘└────────────┘
```

3.0   ECONOMIC MODELS

Economic systems have developed from the primitive **subsistence economy** mentioned in the opening paragraph above and nowadays operate according to one of three recognized models:

A **free enterprise economy** is one in which the economic decisions are made by private individuals, some of whom own the factors of production. This capitalist system type of economy is often referred to as a market economy, free enterprise or laissez-faire system. The USA is a classic example.

A **centrally planned economy** is one where all decisions are taken by the government, which also claims ownership of the factors of production. This is often referred to as a controlled, command or socialist economy. An example was the former USSR. North Korea is a current example.

A **mixed economy,** commonly referred to as a social market economy, aims to have the best of both of the other two kinds of economies, i.e. some elements of central planning and state ownership coupled with free enterprise. Countries of the European Union provide examples of this although the current tendency is to develop towards a free enterprise economy.

 Describe the different types of economic models.

4.0   INTRODUCTION TO ECONOMICS

All of the models mentioned above are covered by the subject known as **economics**. This is a science or body of knowledge which is concerned with the fundamental problems that face the human race – that of satisfying the infinite wants of mankind with the limited resources available. This involves making decisions on how these resources are used and how the wealth derived from these resources is distributed. Economists usually divide the science into two distinct parts – microeconomics and macroeconomics.

Microeconomics focuses on that part of the economy which consists of consumers collected into households at one end of the scale and producers operating as firms at the other, with both linked by the price or market system. In other words, it studies the behaviour of individual consumers, firms and markets.

Macroeconomics is the study of how the larger parts of the economy function, i.e. it looks at the economy as a whole. It deals with the government, the banking system, how foreign money is earned and transferred, how economic development is achieved, and how tools of measurement are used in the economy.

Unit 2 focuses on the evolution of economic science.

 Differentiate between micro and macroeconomics.

5.0   POPULATION

Trends in population are important for the business world in determining markets and changes in these markets.

Population refers to the number of people living in a particular area. The population of a country can be measured by a **census**, which is important for government planning in the areas of housing, education, transport, health care and other facilities.

Factors influencing the **size of population** are the birth, death, fertility, reproduction and net emigration (leaving) plus immigration (entering) rates. The number of people of varying ages depends upon the birth and death rates – currently Western Europe is feeling the effects of an ageing population. A country can be **overpopulated**, **underpopulated** or have an **optimum** or ideal population, which makes the most efficient use of a country's resources of land, labour and capital.

The **sex distribution** (number of males and females) plus **age distribution** coupled with the **geographical distribution** showing a move from **rural** (the countryside) to **urban** (towns and cities) areas and **conurbations** (continuous built up areas linking several towns around main cities) are other factors that need to be considered for economic planning. The future will demand more **geographical mobility of labour** with people moving to different areas in search of work.

 Explain the link between population and the world of business.

6.0   KEY CONCEPTS OF BUSINESS

We define a **business** as an organization concerned with producing goods or supplying services to be sold to the general public. A person setting up a business is referred to as an entrepreneur. The entrepreneur takes many risks; he/she may lose a lot of capital if the business fails, but if it is successful a lot of money can be made; this is referred to as **profit.**

The people who purchase goods or services are known as **consumers.** An entrepreneur must be aware of what the consumers' needs and wants are before setting up in business. **Market research** is used to achieve this, giving the businessperson vital information on whether the product will sell or not, - this is, like **advertising,** an important element of **marketing.**

The entrepreneur has a variety of options on how to organize the business. (S)He can set up as a sole trader, or form a partnership or company. The **sole trader** is the owner of the business and has to do the decision making and assume all the risk, i.e. is fully liable, alone. On the other hand, the businessperson retains all profits. A **partnership** is less risky in that two or more persons are required in order to start, so more people invest and risks and profits are shared.

A **company** must be registered with the Registrar of Companies and has **investors,** called **shareholders,** who pool money together so that the business has sufficient funds available to purchase machinery and materials to produce goods. Credits and other financial services are provided by a **bank** or other **financial institutions.**

The shareholders hope for a share of the profits, referred to as the **dividend.** The amount of money entering the firm must at least match the amount going out so that its debts are paid and the business remains solvent.

If the business goes bankrupt the shareholders may lose their investment, but they enjoy **limited liability**, which means they cannot lose a penny more than they invested in the first place.

Larger companies may sell their shares to the general public by getting themselves quoted on the Stock Exchange. Such companies are known as **public limited companies (PLC or plc)** and their shares can then be bought and sold on a regular basis to the general public - examples include IBM, General Electric and Siemens. In contrast shares from **private limited companies (Ltd)** are not normally traded on the Stock Exchange - these are often small family or medium-sized enterprises where the shares can only be sold with the agreement of the other shareholders.

When a business is established it employs people in various capacities. An entrepreneur will employ **management** to run the specialist areas of the business, for example a **human relations manager** to look after staff recruitment and training and maintain relations with the **trade unions**. Other departmental managers may include accounting, marketing or production.

It is important that every organization insures its personnel against accidents and its premises and stock against theft and fire. This will involve taking out **insurance; a premium** is paid to the insurance company and the conditions are stated in the insurance **policy**.

Once a year **tax** has to be paid to the state, which in capitalist economies tends to interfere as little as possible in economic affairs thus allowing the concept of supply and demand to determine the market.

The concepts that have been introduced in this section will be explored in more detail in the various units throughout this book.

Summarize the most important types of business units.

Discussion Forum

a. *What are the effects of an ageing population in Western Europe?*
b. *The only thing that is permanent in the business world is change. Discuss current and future trends.*

VOCABULARY

A	
advertising	Werbung, Werbeindustrie
achievement; to achieve	Errungenschaft, Leistung; erreichen, erzielen
to acquire; acquisition	erwerben; Erwerb
B	
barter	Tauschhandel, Kompensationsgeschäft
C	
census	Volkszählung
channel	Kanal
to claim	beanspruchen
coincidence	Zusammentreffen, Übereinstimmung
commodity	Ware
conurbation	Ballungsgebiet, Conurbation
crop	Feldfrüchte

D

to defer	verschieben, aufschieben
demand; to demand	Nachfrage; Forderung; fordern
to derive from	(sich) her~/ableiten von
debt	Schulden
distribution; to distribute	Vertrieb, Verteilung; vertreiben, verteilen

E

enterprise; entrepreneur	Unternehmen, Unternehmer

F

to facilitate	ermöglichen, erleichtern
fertility; fertilizer	Fruchtbarkeit, Fertilität; Düngemittel
forestry	Forstwesen

H

human relations manager	Personalchef

I

item	Ding, Posten
infinite	unendlich
insurance	Versicherung
to interfere	sich einmischen
irrigation	Bewässerung

L

laissez-faire	Laissez-faire (wirtschaftl. Liberalismus)
legal tender	Gesetzliches Zahlungsmittel
liability	Haftung

M

measure; to measure	Maß, Maßnahme; messen

P

partnership	Personengesellschaft, Teilhaberschaft
to pool	zusammenschließen, vereinigen
precious	kostbar
premises	(Geschäfts)Grundstück, ~gebäude
private limited company (Ltd)	Gesellschaft mit begrenzter Haftung
public limited company (plc)	Aktiengesellschaft

R

recruitment; to recruit	Rekrutierung
to refer to as	bezeichnen als
retailer	Einzelhändler
registrar/register of companies	Handelsregisterführer, Handelsregister

rural	ländlich
S	
scarce	knapp
shareholder	Aktionär
self sufficiency	Selbstversorgung, Autarkie
shelter	Unterkunft
shell	Muschel
sole trader	Einzelunternehmer
store	Speicher, Lager(bestand)
subsistence economy	Subsistenzwirtschaft
supply	Angebot, Versorgung
surplus	Überschuss
T	
tax; to tax	Steuer; besteuern
theft	Diebstahl
trade union	Gewerkschaft
to transfer	übertragen
tangible	greifbar, sachlich
U	
urban	städtisch
W	
want	Bedürfnis, Wunsch
warehousing	Lagerung
wealth	Reichtum
wholesaler	Großhändler

A BRIEF LOOK AT THE HIGHLIGHTS IN THE EVOLUTION OF ECONOMIC SCIENCE

> *Q: How many economists does it take to change a light bulb?*
>
> *A: None. If the light bulb needed changing the market would have already done it.*
>
> *Anon*

FOCUS This unit has been especially compiled for anybody seeking an understanding of the historical development of the world of economics and how famous theoretical geniuses like Adam Smith and Karl Marx fit in.

1.0 Introduction
2.0 Mercantilism
3.0 The Physiocrats
4.0 The Classical Economists
    4.1 Adam Smith
    4.2 David Ricardo
    4.3 John Stuart Mill
5.0 The Classical Dissenters
    5.1 Thomas Malthus
    5.2 Karl Marx
6.0 The Keynesian Theory
7.0 More Recent Theories and Ideas

1.0   INTRODUCTION

The word *economics* is derived from the Greek *oikonomikos*, which means skilled in household management.

The economic problems experienced in the past and today remain the same.

- How do we decide what to produce with the limited resources available to society?

- How do we ensure stable prices and make full use of our resources?
- How do we provide a better standard of living for society today and tomorrow?

One can go back as far as one likes in history and still find prominent, intelligent individuals writing about wealth and the state. Early philosophers and theologians like Aristotle (384-322 BC) and St. Thomas Aquinas (1225-1274AD) were two such figures but they made no permanent contribution to economic thought as we understand it, mainly because the societies in which they lived were very different from the modern state.

An economist is an expert who will know tomorrow why the things he predicted yesterday didn't happen today

Anon

This timeline diagram gives a quick overview of the highlights of economic thought which will be discussed in the following sections.

Timeline of Economic Schools

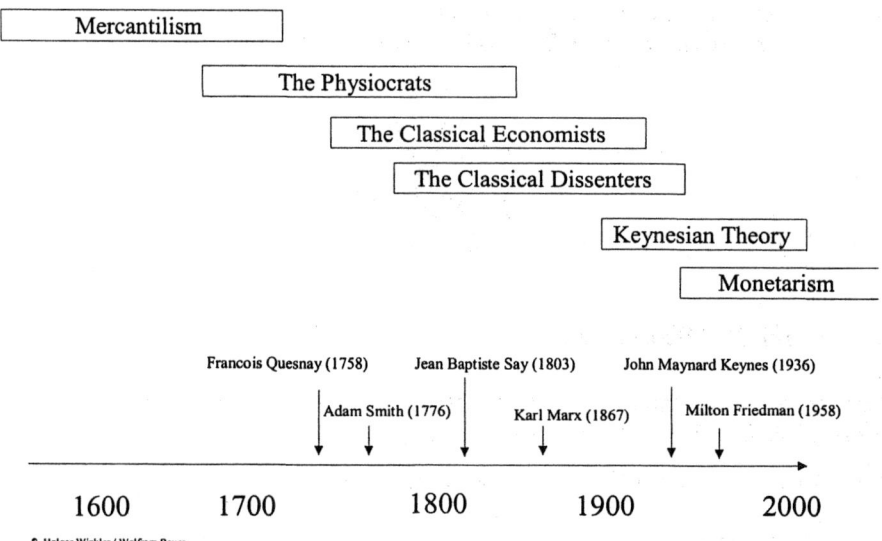

© Holger Winkler / Wolfram Bauer

2.0 MERCANTILISM

The beginning of economics, as we understand it in the modern sense, came in the sixteenth and seventeenth centuries with the development of the school of thought which we call mercantilism.

This was an economic philosophy focusing on commerce and industry adopted by merchants and statesmen. There were two main ideas in their doctrine:

- Some state intervention to achieve harmony and economic well-being among the various groups that make up society is essential.
- The state must do all it can to ensure a favourable Balance of Trade (an excess of exports over imports) and a good flow of precious metals (money in this period took the form of gold and silver).

Mercantilism represented the elevation of commercial interests, and especially trade, to a key area in the national policy of a state. Important Mercantilists included Jean Bodin and Colbert from France and the British Mercantilists John Hales and William Petty.

3.0 THE PHYSIOCRATS

The next school of economists to emerge was that of the physiocrats ('rule of nature'), a group of philosophers from France in the second half of the eighteenth century, of whom one of the most famous was a doctor, Francois Quesnay.

Their main doctrine was that mankind, like everything else that exists, is governed by natural laws and is only capable of achieving the greatest level of happiness when these laws are followed. In the economic sphere they regarded self-interest as the natural tendency of man because according to them economic laws are derived from the laws of nature. Therefore, the state should abolish all laws which interfered with such freedom. They opposed the Mercantilist policy of promoting trade at the expense of agriculture because they believed that agriculture was the sole source of wealth in an economy.

It is interesting to note that at this early stage, the greatest of economic arguments had emerged: the physiocrats believing in 'laissez-faire' (leave things alone) - the basis of free enterprise, and the mercantilists recommending varying degrees of state control.

4.0   THE CLASSICAL ECONOMISTS

The age of classical economists was born with the emergence of the market system, first in Britain and then in Continental Europe and America in the latter half of the eighteenth century. New explanations and theories about society and commerce were being developed by the great changes that were sweeping through the community. Home and foreign trade were expanding rapidly, banking and credit mushrooming and new machines and methods were revolutionizing industrial and agricultural production.

All countries undergoing this economic ferment experienced a population explosion and huge fortunes were made by individual traders, companies and nations.

The classical economists are the most important group of economists because the greater part of modern economics is based on their theories. They were not in agreement about everything - in particular, they had varying opinions about the ultimate economic fate of mankind - but they developed a method of thinking about economic problems which is substantially unchanged today.

The founder of the classical school, which is still relevant in our 21st century, was Adam Smith.

4.1   Adam Smith (1723-1791)

Smith is regarded as the father of modern economics. An Oxford graduate, and lecturer in moral philosophy at Glasgow and Edinburgh universities, Smith wrote a book titled *An Inquiry into the Cause of the Wealth of Nations (1776)*. In it he explained how vast fortunes were being made by entrepreneurs, how the market economy operated, and what the benefits of economies of scale in production were.
He also stressed the importance of the factors of production (see Unit 1), rather than money.

In addition he formulated theories about how the state should behave. Like the physiocrats he believed in laissez-faire; unlike them he didn't believe that only agriculture was productive.

Smith saw the market system acting as an invisible hand, which leads people to pursue their own self-interests, and which also unintentionally produces the greatest benefit for society as a whole in contrast to state intervention as the best regulator.

4.2   David Ricardo (1772-1823)

Ricardo produced works that were very largely a refinement and development of Smith's theories. Unlike Smith, whose book is full of practical examples and comments on current affairs, Ricardo's economics is highly theoretical. Indeed his great achievement is that of being the first to develop a complete system of economic theory.

He is mainly remembered for his theory of comparative advantage which basically states that each country should specialize in those goods which it can produce more easily than other countries, i.e. at the lowest opportunity cost. It can then trade its surplus of those goods to other countries. The result is that a far greater quantity of all goods will be available than would otherwise be the case.

He also believed that the landlord class were enriching themselves at the expense of society and he campaigned tirelessly in the British Parliament and in print for free trade.

4.3   John Stuart Mill (1806-1873)

Mill wrote *Principles of Political Economy*, which was essentially a survey of all the accepted economic theory of his time. He believed in a moderate amount of state intervention to redistribute wealth and a mild version of socialism but was opposed to Karl Marx's ideal of a communist state because of the danger to the rights and freedom of the individual.

Another important economist from this school was Jean-Baptiste Say, a French economist, who published *Traité d'Economie Politique* in 1803, in which he outlined a principle which classical economists afterwards called Say's Law. This principle, stated simply, was that supply creates its own demand.

5.0   THE CLASSICAL DISSENTERS

Thomas Malthus and Karl Marx were two of the most famous classical dissenters or opponents of the classical economists.

5.1   Thomas Malthus (1766-1834)

Malthus with his theory on population alarmed his contemporaries by stating that population increased more rapidly than food production with the inevitable result being famine. His theory was flawed in the short term, as he did not foresee the American food exports from the prairies. His conviction that the population would rise as the standard of living increased was also incorrect. However, his theory of population still looms over us as the greatest economic problem of our time.

5.2   Karl Marx (1818-1883)

Marx was an intellectual economist who found fault with the free enterprise system of economics. He saw that there were large pockets of unemployment that grew worse as industrialization and economic development increased. He saw that workers, without whom production would not be possible, received minimal rewards for the contribution of their labour compared with the profits gained by entrepreneurs.

He foresaw that the capitalist economic system would lead to the growth of large monopolies, overproduction and eventually a collapse of the economic system as happened, albeit limited, in the 1930s. He failed, however, to foresee the development of trade unions and his prediction of continuously growing unemployment and deepening crises did not ultimately prove accurate.

Marx's essential theory was that all production belongs to labour because workers produce all value within society. At some point the workers would organize and through revolution overthrow the old order and establish a dictatorship of the proletariat controlling all the factors of production.

He did bring into prominence the business cycle and his economic system, in which change is an essential part, is more realistic than the rather static systems of the classical economists. Finally, in pointing out the connection between economics and the social system, he was introducing an idea whose full implications have still to be worked out.

Marx's views were expressed in his two great works, the *Communist Manifesto* and *Das Kapital (Capital)*.

Capitalism, Socialism and Communism Explained

Capitalism is the system of economic organization, which focuses on business enterprise for private profit. Private property and open markets are key characteristics. The spirit of capitalism is acquisition of money income, achieved by the sale of products or services on an increasingly global market.

Socialism, which came to prominence in the 19th and 20th centuries, is essentially a planned economic system characterized by government ownership and operation of all major industries but which allows private ownership in less important areas of industry such as restaurants, shops and other small enterprises. Variations of socialist ideas can even be traced back to Plato's Republic and Thomas More's Utopia. Socialism was regarded by the Bolsheviks under Lenin (who adopted the name Communist Party after the 1917 October Revolution) and other former socialist states as the first step towards the final objective of communism.

Communism, is a planned economic system in which private property is eliminated and all citizens share the benefits of the common wealth according to their needs. All the factors of production and production targets are controlled by the state in a classless society.

6.0   THE KEYNESIAN THEORY

John Maynard Keynes (1883-1946)

In the first quarter of the twentieth century economists were, on the whole, concerned with clearing up the details of classical economic theory. They did not seem to be aware, however, that there was one great flaw in macro-economic theory, namely that it did not have any way of accounting for recession.

John Maynard Keynes (pronounced like 'canes'), civil servant, Cambridge professor, government financial adviser and negotiator, in his massive 1936 published work *The General Theory of Employment, Interest and Money* explained how recessions happen and how they may be avoided.

His main theory is that an economy needs to be regulated, otherwise there will be booms and recessions. It is the duty of the government to step in and, by varying its own expenditure, make sure that there is enough spending to give full employment without inflation. His greatest influence is that he helped the mixed economy (see Unit 1) to come into being.

Keynes' theories have been taken up, amended and adapted by various economists ever since.

    a. What are the main economic problems?
    b. Summarize the main concepts in the evolution of economic science.
    c. Outline in detail the concept of laissez-faire.
    d. Differentiate between socialism and communism.

7.0   MORE RECENT THEORIES AND IDEAS

Economic theories are constantly changing. While Keynesian theories dominated economic policymaking in the decades following World War II, by the end of the 1960s inflation and poor productivity forced economists to seek out new solutions.

The most important theories and ideas developed were:

Game Theory which is a branch of applied mathematics used to analyze certain situations where there is an interplay between parties that may have similar, opposed or mixed interests. In a typical game, decision-making 'players', who each have their own goals, try to outsmart one another by anticipating each other's decisions.

Game theory was originally designed by the Hungarian-born mathematician John von Neumann and his colleague Oskar Morgenstern, a German-born economist, to solve problems in economics. Their book *The Theory of Games and Economic Behaviour* (1944) observes that economics is much like a game in which the players anticipate one another's moves and that it therefore requires a special kind of mathematics which they coined game theory.

Monetarism is the theory that inflation is caused by an excess quantity of money in an economy and the complete belief in the efficiency of free market forces. The theory was developed by the economist Milton Friedman, who won the Nobel Prize for his theories. Monetarism can be seen as a counter revolution to Keynes.

Control of the money supply is the main, if not only, determinant of a nation's economy. Monetarists believe that management of the money supply can decide recession or growth and they dismiss fiscal policy (government spending and taxation) as ineffective.

Rational Expectation Theory says that people make good use of information that is available today and can generally guess the future correctly. It also argues that the market's ability to anticipate government policy actions limits the effectiveness of these actions.

Crucial in this theory is the belief that government can ultimately do nothing substantial to change the autonomous workings of the economic system and should not introduce laws that interfere in economic activities, (e.g. bringing in a minimum wage). Limited government fiscal and monetary measures in the economy are sufficient.

Supply Side Economics is more like the Classical Economists' approach believing in economic growth as the fundamental cornerstone for improving society's material well-being. It emphazises cutting income tax, reductions in unemployment benefits and weakening the power of organized labour.

Other policies include investment subsidies, lower government spending, retraining workers, various government measures to develop young people's skills and encourage the long-term unemployed back into the labour force. This was the economic style favoured by Margaret Thatcher in the UK and Ronald Reagan (although he increased military spending) in the USA during the 1980s, often referred to as Thatcherism and Reaganomics.

Most states today try to mix supply and demand oriented theories.

A study of economics usually reveals that the best time to buy anything is last year.

Anon

 Explain two recent economic theories.

Discussion Forum

a. *Less government and more of Adam Smith's invisible hand in the economy is better. Discuss.*
b. *Capitalism is the exploitation of man by man. Communism is the exact reverse. Discuss.*
c. *What were the reasons for the collapse of the socialist states of Eastern Europe?*
d. *Is capitalism the only realistic economic model for the 21st century?*

VOCABULARY

A	
to abolish	abschaffen
abundant	reichlich
to account for	erklären
achievement	Leistung, Errungenschaft
acquisition	Erwerb
affluent	wohlhabend, Wohlstands-
albeit	wenn auch , obgleich
to amend	ergänzen
to anticipate	vorhersehen
B	
balance of trade	Handelsbilanz
to be aware	sich (einer Sache)bewusst sein
beyond	über etw. hinaus (gehend)
boom	Aufschwung
to bring into prominence	in den Vordergrund rücken
C	
civil servant	Staatsbeamter
to coin	hier: nennen
competition	Konkurrenz
contemporaries	Zeitgenossen
conviction	Überzeugung
crucial	entscheidend, äußerst wichtig
D	
to dismiss	abweisen, ablehnen; entlassen
dissenter	Abweichler
to derive	ableiten, herleiten
duty	Pflicht
E	
economies of scale	Größenvorteile, Economies of Scale
emergence	Entstehen, Aufkommen

to encourage	ermutigen, motivieren
entrepreneur	Unternehmer
eventual	schließlich
excess	Überschuss
expectation	Erwartung
expenditure	Ausgaben
F	
famine	Hungersnot
fault	Fehler
to favour	favorisieren
ferment	Gärung, Veränderung
fiscal policy	(konjunkturorientierte) Finanzpolitik
flawed	fehler-/mangelhaft
fortune	Vermögen
I	
inevitable	unvermeidlich
inquiry	Untersuchung, Erkundigung, Anfrage
to interfere	eingreifen, sich einmischen in
interplay	Zusammenspiel
L	
labour force	erwerbstätige Bevölkerung
labour	Arbeitskraft
laissez-faire	Laissez-faire, (wirtschaftlicher Liberalismus)
to loom	(bedrohlich) schweben
M	
money supply	Geldvolumen
to mushroom	sich rasch entwickeln
N	
negotiator	Verhandlungsführer, Unterhändler
O	
objective	Ziel, Zweck
opportunity costs	Opportunitätskosten, auch Alternativkosten
to outsmart	überlisten, austricksen
to overthrow	stürzen
P	
pockets of unemployment	Gebiet mit hoher Arbeitslosigkeit
poverty	Armut
precious	wertvoll
prediction	Voraussage

R	
to refer to as	bezeichnen als
to reverse	umkehren
reward	Entgelt, Belohnung
S	
squalor	Schmutz, Elend
subsidy	Subvention
sufficient	ausreichend
supply price	Angebotspreis
supply side economics	Supply Side Economics, angebotsorientierte Wirtschaftspolitik
surplus	Überschuss
survey	Überblick
T	
tax	Steuer
theory of comparative advantage	Theorie der Komparativen (Kosten)Vorteile
to trace back	zurückverfolgen
trade union	Gewerkschaft
U	
ultimately	letztlich
unemployment benefit	Arbeitslosengeld, Arbeitslosen- unterstützung

THE STRUCTURE OF BUSINESS – PRIVATE AND PUBLIC ENTERPRISE

> *There are three types of companies:*
> *Those who make things happen.*
> *Those who watch things happen.*
> *Those who wonder what happened.*
>
> *Philip Kotler / Gary Armstrong*

FOCUS This unit covers the different types of businesses, which have developed in the private and public sector to supply the wide variety of goods and services, which consumers want to buy.

1.0   INTRODUCTION

The various requirements of setting up business have led to the development of different types of business organizations. The **private sector** or **private enterprises** are the terms used to describe all businesses, which are owned by individuals or groups of individuals and essentially run for profit.

Public sector or **public enterprises** are owned and controlled by the government or local or municipal authorities and run for the benefit of the country.

2.0   THE PRIVATE SECTOR

Let us first examine the main types of enterprise found in the private sector.

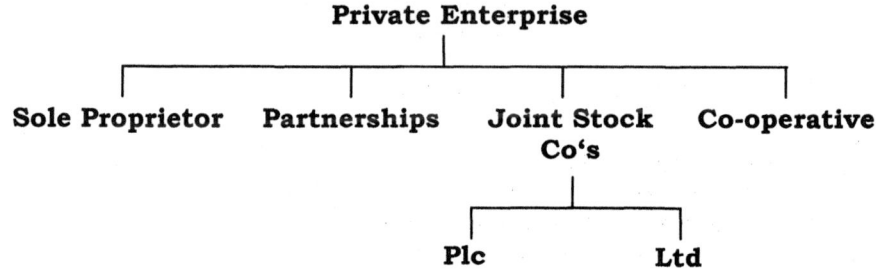

2.1   Sole Proprietor/Sole Trader

The title clearly means that there is only one owner of the enterprise, although there can be, of course, many employees. Typical examples would be a hairdressing salon, newsagent or boutique.

A sole trader can finance the business using personal funds, borrowing from friends or receiving funds from a financial institute. The legal requirements are very few in most countries:

- registering of name and business
- registering for tax
- obeying health regulations
- obeying safety at work regulations

The one-person business has, obviously, many advantages and disadvantages and whether it can survive in the modern business world depends very much on the character and ability of the individual involved.

Advantages

- few legalities
- little paperwork
- owner makes own decisions
- flexibility
- convenient to the public, i.e. long opening hours especially in USA, UK.
- profits not shared

Disadvantages

- *unlimited liability* – the owner is liable for all the debts of the business, even to the extent of losing his/her own private property
- no opportunity for consultation and shared decision-making
- unsocial or unfriendly hours due to late opening times, working at weekends and during holiday periods
- lower profits due to size
- difficult to raise capital
- difficult to benefit from bulk discounts

2.2   Partnerships

In the U.K. partnerships are governed by the Partnership Act of 1890. This law defines a partnership as the relationship between persons carrying on business in common with a view of making a profit. In addition, limited partnerships must abide by the Limited Partnership Act 1907. A minimum of two partners is enough to create a partnership.

Partners usually draw up a **deed of partnership** in the manner of a legal contract, although there is no obligation to do so. If there is no deed the partnership is known as **partnership at will** and difficulties arising are resolved under the 1890 Partnership Act. A deed of partnership, however, takes precedence over the Act.

The deed may contain the following:

- nature of the business
- place of business
- date of commencement of partnership
- capital contributions of each partner
- accounting methods employed
- profit and loss sharing ratio
- salary, where applicable, paid to each partner
- procedures for *dissolution* (winding-up of the business). A partnership may be dissolved by one partner retiring or dying, by agreement, by court order, at the end of a period of time, i.e. fixed term, or on completion of the venture.

Partnerships are usually found in the accounting business, in law firms and in medical practices.

Types of partner and partnership

In a **general partnership** all the partners play an active role in the business, are liable for the debts of the firm and receive a full share of the profits.

A **limited partnership** has partners who are only liable for their share of the capital invested. However, there must be at least one general partner who assumes general liability.

A **joint venture partnership** is set up to undertake a specific venture, such as a pop concert.

A **sleeping (dormant/silent) partner** is a partner who invests capital but unlike an active partner is not involved in running the business.

A **quasi partner** is one who retires from the business but leaves capital in the business as a loan.

A **junior partner** is usually a newcomer to the business and has limited rights and privileges. S(H)e often receives a salary rather than a share of the profits but may become an active partner over time.

When unlimited partners are *jointly and severally liable* for the debts of the business, it means that each unlimited partner is jointly and severally, i.e. individually, responsible for the entire debts of the business, even including his/her own private assets.

Advantages	Disadvantages
<ul><li>more capital than sole proprietor</li><li>consultation may produce better decisions and service</li><li>new partners can join</li><li>easy to form</li></ul>	<ul><li>unlimited liability (except for limited partners)</li><li>no separate *legal identity*, i.e. the partnership does not exist separately from the individual partners who constitute the business.</li><li>disagreements may occur to the detriment of the partnership</li><li>capital for expansion may be limited</li><li>difficulties with continuity – i.e. if a partner dies the partnership can be negatively affected.</li></ul>

> **Goodwill** is particularly important in a sole trader or partnership business - it is difficult to define – but it is associated with the reputation, location and good service of an enterprise, e.g. a restaurant with a good name for food and friendly and efficient service.

   a. *What are the differences between sole traders and partnerships?*
   b. *Differentiate between a general and limited partnership.*

2.3 Joint Stock Companies

Joint stock or limited liability companies came into being in the 19th century side by side with the rise in economic growth. The adjective 'joint stock' comes from the fact that originally traders pooled their stock of goods in selected ventures to exploit certain markets.

2.3.1 Overview

A **joint stock company** or **limited company** can be defined as an association of people who contribute their money to a common fund to be used in some business venture and who share the profits and losses of the concern.

A company, therefore, comprises a group of shareholders investing money into a common fund to produce goods or services with the aim of seeing their share value rise and receiving a portion of the profits, known as a dividend. The money the shareholders contribute is known as share capital.

There are two main types:

- **Private limited company** or **limited liability company (LLC) in the US**
- **Public limited company** or **corporation (US)**.

2.3.2 Types of Capital

The **capital** of a company can be broken up as follows:

Authorized registered capital - The *maximum* amount of money that can be raised from the public as stated in the Memorandum of Association (see 2.3.4) and the prospectus.

Issued capital - The segment of the capital which the company has decided to issue to the public for subscription. It can be equal to or less than the authorized capital but never greater.

Subscribed capital - The amount of the issued capital purchased by the general public.

Called-up capital - The amount of money the company requires to call in, i.e. requests to be paid, immediately to cover investment in the business and to pave the way for growth and profitability.

Paid-up capital - The amount of the called-up capital for which shareholders have actually paid.

A company has a responsibility to its **stakeholders** who consist of:

- customers
- shareholders
- suppliers
- the government
- employees
- the general public
- the environment

    a. Explain what a joint stock company is.
    b. Compare and contrast the different types of capital.

2.3.3 Characteristics of Joint Stock Companies - Ltd and PLC

Private Limited Company (Ltd)	**Limited Company (PLC or plc)**
• A minimum number of shareholders is needed for the formation of this business unit.	• There must be a certain number of shareholders for formation (more than for a private limited company).
• Shares cannot be issued to the public and are not quoted on the Stock Exchange.	• Finance is raised by issuing shares to the general public which are bought and sold on the Stock Exchange.
• Business can commence on receipt of a Certificate of Incorporation.	• A Trading Certificate from the Registrar of Companies is necessary after incorporation.
• Not normally required to publish its annual accounts or hold a statutory meeting - depending on the turnover,	• Accounts must be audited and published annually.

number of people employed and whether it is in the interest of the public.

- In private companies shares are held by a small group of people, usually connected with the business, e.g. family business firms. The shares are bought and sold with the agreement of the other share-holders.

- A public company issuing new shares at any time must grant its existing members the first option to buy; this is called **pre-emption** rights.

2.3.4 Formation of a Joint Stock Company

The company must register with the Registrar of Companies and submit certain documents including:

- the Articles of Association (Bylaws - AE)
- the Memorandum of Association (Certificate of Incorporation)
- a statement of the authorized or nominal share capital
- a list of those who have agreed to become directors of the company
- the directors' written consent to act as directors of the company
- a declaration of compliance with the Companies Act.

Additional Stages in Forming a Public Company:

- issuing of a prospectus
- employing of an *issuing house* (a financial institution which handles issues of shares on behalf of companies)
- applying to the Stock Exchange for permission to deal on this market
- issuing shares

NOTE: For prospectus, classes of shares, etc. see Unit 5 on the Stock Exchange.

Important Documents in the Formation of a Company

The **Articles of Association** refer to the *internal* constitution of a company and set out its rules and regulations. It gives information on such issues as the rights of the shareholders, the powers of the directors and the holding of meetings.

The following is included:
- amount of authorized share capital and its division into different classes of shares

---

- procedure for issuing shares and the voting rights attached to the different classes of shares
- procedure for calling shareholder meetings, e.g. A.G.M.
- procedure for electing and replacing directors
- power and duties of the directors
- procedure for winding-up the company
- auditing procedure for company accounts

The **Memorandum of Association** sets out the relationship of the company to the general public and clearly defines what the powers of the company are. It includes:

- name clause stating the name of the company followed by the abbreviation 'Ltd' or 'plc'
- the objectives of the company – these specify what the company intends to do
- a statement that the liability of the members is limited
- a statement of the amount of the share capital - Stamp Duty is payable on this
- the signature of each founding subscriber, as well as the number of shares s(he) is purchasing
- location of the registered office of the company. This is where all legal documents are sent.

If everything is in order, a Certificate of Incorporation will be issued, making the business a separate **legal entity,** meaning it has a life distinct from that of its shareholders and will be incorporated under the Companies Act. This means it can continue to exist after the death of a shareholder, it can sue and be sued, etc. Being incorporated means that the organization has now the status of a 'company'.

A plc will also need a Trading Certificate.

2.3.5 Advantages and Disadvantages of Joint Stock Companies

Companies have a number of advantages and disadvantages over sole traders and partnerships:

Advantages
- limited liability – the investors can only lose the amount they have invested in the company, they are not liable for the company's debts.

Disadvantages
- there are more legal formalities involved in forming a company than in other business units
- profits must be shared between all the shareholders

- the company can raise large amounts of capital through the issuing of shares.
- the company has a separate legal identity of its own
- continuity is assured
- separate legal existence from its shareholders

- public companies must publish their accounts
- activities are restricted to those stated in the Articles of Association
- profits are liable to corporation tax

a. Compare and contrast private and public limited companies.
b. Outline the steps in the formation of a joint stock company.
c. Differentiate between the Articles and Memorandum of Association.

2.3.6 Organizational Structure of Public Limited Companies

The Board of Directors

In small companies the board of directors - the management committee of a company - often own more than 51% of a company and have control. In larger companies directors are not allowed to hold shares, so ownership and control are separate. The board of directors is headed by the **chairperson** whose functions are to make sure meetings are properly convened in accordance with standing orders (rules formulated for the conduct of meetings).

The functions of the board are:

- to appoint the managing director who will run the company on a daily basis
- to appoint one of its members as chairperson of the board
- to declare dividends
- to approve the annual accounts
- to provide a good return on shareholders' investments
- to appoint senior management such as the financial controller or the marketing manager
- to borrow funds on behalf of the company from financial institutions
- to make decisions on mergers or takeovers
- to discuss whether to go public if the company is private
- to decide the company's major objectives or goals
- to analyze strategies that might help to achieve these objectives. When a particular strategy is chosen, it becomes company policy.

- to ensure that a statutory meeting is held after the company is established and an **Annual General Meeting (AGM)** or **Annual Stockholders Meeting** (AE) is held once a year.

Executive director members of the board are members who also work in the company, usually in a managerial position. Finance and marketing managers are the staff members most likely to become board managers. **Non-executive directors** on the other hand are 'outside' or part-time directors. They are often famous persons, e.g. Margaret Thatcher, Bill Clinton.

The **managing director** ensures that the company operates in accordance with the board's wishes and runs the company efficiently on a day-to-day business. This person is also often referred to as the **Chief Executive Officer (CEO)**. In smaller companies the managing director often takes the responsibilities of the chairperson of the board as well.

The title **president** refers to managing director or CEO in the USA, in the UK it is the title sometimes given to the most senior executive or former managing director or chairman in a public company as an honorary position.

In Germany there is a **supervisory board**, or controlling body, usually elected by the shareholders and the employees of the company, which in turn elects and supervises a board of management.

The **company secretary** has statutory and administrative duties. (S)He is responsible for:

- ensuring that proper books are kept and statutory annual returns are made to the Registrar of Companies
- sending notice of board meetings to directors, and notice of general meetings to shareholders
- recording minutes of these meetings
- keeping an up-to-date register of all shareholders
- managing pension funds and insurances
- overseeing personnel and accounting

  a. *Explain the functions of the chairperson and board of directors.*
b. *What is the role of the managing director/CEO and the company secretary?*

The Role of the Auditor

To control fraud and financial misreporting every company is obliged to appoint an **auditor** who must be an accountant or a firm of accountants.

His/her duties are:

- to ensure that proper books are kept
- to check that the trading, profit and loss accounts and balance sheet are prepared correctly from the books of the company
- to report on the company's affairs to the shareholders and state whether (s)he is satisfied or not with the manner in which the accounts were prepared
- to check the existence of all shares and bank statements
- to make a report at the AGM

 Why are auditors required?

2.3.7 Companies in Difficulty

The company itself, a director, creditors or a government minister may appoint an inspector to look into the workings of any company, particularly if wrongdoing is suspected.

An **examiner** may be appointed by the courts to see if a company can be saved or if it must be liquidated. (S)He has full powers to examine all documents and take over the board's functions and make an interim and a full report.

A company can be wound-up:

- compulsorily (by the courts) or
- voluntarily (by its members or creditors)

The commonest form of winding-up is the so-called voluntary liquidation by creditors.

It is **voluntarily** wound-up by the shareholders or creditors if:

- it is insolvent (i.e. if its liabilities are greater than its assets)
- a special resolution is passed
- it is taken over
- it was set up for a specific time or its purpose has expired

It is **compulsorily** wound-up by the courts if:

- it is insolvent
- a special resolution is passed
- it didn't commence business within a year
- there is an insufficient number of members, this number varies from country to country

If a company is to be wound up it is handed over to a **liquidator**, who liquidates all assets, calls all the creditors together and distributes the assets as appropriate:

- to cover the costs of liquidation
- to pay preferential creditors, e.g. taxes, outstanding wages and salaries
- to pay secured creditors, e.g. the bank
- to pay unsecured creditors, e.g. suppliers

Any remaining funds are then divided among the shareholders. The company is then wound up, i.e. ceases trading.

It is not always necessary to liquidate a company. When a company only defaults on its repayments to the debenture holders, a **receiver** may be appointed by the court so that they are paid.

When the receiver is appointed, the board resigns and the receiver decides either to keep the company running, to sell it or to liquidate it.

If the debenture holders are paid off and the company is still trading, the receiver will then return the company to its board of directors.

Note that a liquidator always winds up a company whereas a receiver does not.

Differentiate between a receiver, a liquidator and an examiner.

2.4   Co-operatives

A **co-operative** is an autonomous group of people who jointly (collectively) own and democratically control a business.

Co-operatives are an egalitarian form of business organization with limited liability– examples are retail shops and creameries. Many have, because of the era of the big firm and fierce competition, converted themselves into plcs.

The co-operative movement had its origins in the small cotton towns in Lancashire, England. The Welshman, Robert Owen (1771-1858), is often referred to as the father of the co-operative movement. Guidelines were developed, which still govern the thinking and conduct of co-operatives today.

These are:

- Open membership – anyone can join
- Democratic control – one person, one vote
- Limited return on capital
- Surplus (profit) to be distributed
- Cash sales only – no trade credit
- Neutral on political and religious issues

A German example of a co-operative in the 1830s was the option of placing deposits with a co-operative organization known as Raiffeisen. This concept became very popular leading to the establishment of a bank.

A **building society** is a co-operative banking enterprise financed by deposits on which interest is paid and from which mortgage loans are advanced for the purchase of land and/or property. This was the original function of this type of business unit – today a wide range of financial services including banking, investment, insurances, foreign exchange, etc is offered.

A **credit union** is similar to a co-op; it consists of a group of people with a common objective who club together to accept the members savings and use these savings to grant loans to members at reasonable rates of interest.

 Explain the origin and concept behind co-operatives.

3.0   THE PUBLIC SECTOR

This refers to enterprises such as public corporations, government departments and local authorities.

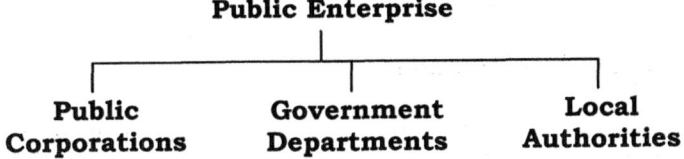

Public Enterprise

| **Public Corporations** | **Government Departments** | **Local Authorities** |

3.1   Public Corporations

The essential features of public corporations are that the assets have been established or taken over by the state, so that the industry is owned, managed and controlled by the state. Railways and water and power utilities are often public corporations.

Reasons for their existence:

- provision of essential services, e.g. postal service
- fill gaps left by private enterprise, e.g. bus services in rural areas
- national security
- to complete projects for which the financial requirements are too great to be met by the private sector, e.g. building new rail networks and dams
- to develop natural resources, e.g. forestry
- to avoid economic chaos, e.g. where a bank or insurance company has gone bankrupt
- provide employment
- to promote economic development in the private sector, e.g. government agencies that are set up to attract foreign investors

Negative features:

- abuse of monopoly position
- inefficient, overstaffed and underfinanced
- may incur losses and require subsidies that raise the public debt, which in turn increases the level of taxation and borrowing
- high charges
- poor quality management

Nationalization is the process whereby the government takes control of a private enterprise. e.g. British Rail in the 1940s (privatized again in the 1990s).

Deregulation is a regulatory trend where public corporations, instead of being privatized, are subject to competition thereby losing their monopoly position, e.g. the US postal service.

Privatization involves the selling off of public companies to private enterprise, e.g. Deutsche Telekom.

3.2   Government Departments

The government has departments which provide a variety of services including statistics and government publications or forestry commissions which control the production and harvesting of timber.

3.3   Local Authorities

Local Authorities provide services for the benefit of the local community including schools, hospitals, police and fire services and recreational facilities such as parks, playing areas and libraries.

 Why do public corporations exist?

 Discussion Forum

    a. What future do small businesses have in the era of global markets?!

    b. Should a state-owned enterprise such as a railway operate on a commercial basis or should it be seen primarily as a social service to the community?

    c. How much democracy exists in plcs and what power and influence do shareholders really exert?

    d. Companies often walk themselves into difficulties. Discuss.

VOCABULARY

A	
to abide by	sich halten an
abuse	Missbrauch
access	Zugang
accountant	Buchhalter, Buchprüfer, Wirtschaftsprüfer
accounting	Buchführung, Rechnungslegung, Abrechnung
act	Gesetz
annual accounts	Jahresabschluss
annual general meeting (AGM)	Hauptversammlung
to appoint	ernennen, berufen
approval, to approve	Zustimmung, zustimmen
to approve	billigen, genehmigen
Articles of Association	Satzung (einer AG)
asset	Vermögen(swert)
to audit, auditor	prüfen, Wirtschaftsprüfer, Buchprüfer
authorized (registered) capital	zur Ausgabe genehmigtes Kapital
B	
balance sheet	Bilanz
bank statement	Bankauszug
board of directors	Vorstand
bookkeeping	Buchführung

to borrow	(aus)borgen, (ent)leihen
bulk discount	Mengenrabatt
C	
to call a meeting	eine Versammlung einberufen
called-up capital	eingefordertes Kapital
cash sale	Barverkauf, Kaufvertrag mit Leistung Zug um Zug
to cease	aufhören
Certificate of Corporation	Gründungsbescheinigung
certificate of trading	Gewerbeschein
chairperson	Vorstandsvorsitzende(r)
chief executive officer/CEO (US)	Generaldirektor, Hauptgeschäftsführer
clause	Klausel
to commence, commencement	beginnen, Beginn
common	gemeinsam; allgemein
Companies Act	Gesetz über die Kapitalgesellschaften
company limited by guarantee	Gesellschaft, deren Mitglieder für Verbindlichkeiten in bestimmter Höhe haften (GB)
company limited by shares	Aktiengesellschaft
company secretary	Verwaltungschef
to compete (with)	konkurrieren (mit)
competition	Konkurrenz(kampf)
compliance	Beachtung, Befolgung
compulsorily	zwangsweise
to comprise	umfassen, einschließen
consent	Einwilligung
constitution	Satzung, Verfassung
contract	Vertrag
to convene (a meeting)	(eine Versammlung) einberufen
convenient	günstig
co-operative	Genossenschaft, Kooperative
corporation tax	Körperschaftssteuer
court order	gerichtliche Verfügung
creamery	Molkerei, Milchgeschäft
credit union	Kreditgenossenschaft
creditor	Gläubiger
D	
debenture (holder)	(Inhaber einer) Schuldverschreibung/ Obligation
debt	Schulden
to declare dividends	Dividende festlegen
deed of partnership	Gesellschaftsvertrag

to default on	in Verzug geraten mit
delivery	Lieferung
deposit	Einzahlungen, (Bank)Einlagen
detriment	Nachteil, Schaden
dissolution	Auflösung
distinct	verschieden, getrennt
distribution, to distribute	Vertrieb, vertreiben
dividend	Dividende
E	
economies of scale	Größenvorteile, Kostendegression
egalitarian	egalitär, (Gleichheits-)
estate	Vermögen, Grundbesitz
examiner	Revisor, Prüfer
executive	hauptamtlich
extraordinary general meeting	außerordentliche Hauptversammlung
F	
fierce	scharf, heftig
to file	einreichen, anmelden
fraud	Betrug
fund	Fonds, Kapital, Mittel, Gelder
G	
general partner	unbeschränkt haftender Partner, Komplementär
to go bankrupt	Konkurs machen, bankrott gehen
to go bust	pleite machen
to go public	an die Börse gehen
goodwill	Goodwill, ideeller Geschäftswert, Firmenansehen
to grant	gewähren
H	
head, to head	Leiter, Chef; leiten, führen
I	
in turn	wiederum
to incorporate	als Kapitalgesellschaft/juristische Person eintragen
to incur (losses, debts)	eingehen, erleiden
insurance	Versicherung
interim report	Zwischenbericht
to issue (shares)	(Aktien) ausgeben
to issue	ausgeben, in Umlauf setzen, emittieren
issuing house	Emissionsbank

J	
joint stock company	Teilhabergesellschaft, Aktiengesellschaft
joint venture partnership	Gelegenheitsgesellschaft
jointly and severally liable	gesamtschuldnerisch haftbar
L	
latter	letzterer
legal entity	juristische Person
legal requirements	(Rechts)vorschriften, Anordnungen
legalities	gesetzliche Bestimmungen
liabilities	Verbindlichkeiten
liability	Haftung
liable (for)	haftbar (für)
limited (commercial) partnership	Kommanditgesellschaft
limited (unlimited) liability	(un)beschränkte Haftung
to liquidate	liquidieren, abwickeln, auflösen
liquidator	Liquidator, Abwickler, Konkursverwalter
loan	Darlehen, Kredit ; Leihen, Ausleihung
M	
managing director (BE)	Generaldirektor, Hauptgeschäftsführer
manner	Art und Weise
Memorandum of Association	Gesellschaftsvertrag, Gründungsurkunde
merger	Fusion
minutes	Protokoll
N	
nominal capital	Grundkapital, Nominalkapital (AG), Gesellschaftskapital, Stammkapital (GmbH)
notice	Ankündigung
O	
to obey	beachten
objective	Ziel, Zweck
ordinary partnership	(*meist*) offene Handelsgesellschaft
overstaffed	überbesetzt, mit zu hohem Personalbestand
P	
paid-up capital	eingezahltes Kapital
partnership	Personengesellschaft, Sozietät, Teilhaberschaft

to pass (a resolution)	(einen Beschluss) annehmen, fassen
pension fund	Pensionfonds
personnel department/human resources department	Personalabteilung
to pool	zusammenlegen
possession	Besitz, Eigentum
precedence	Vorrang
pre-emption	Bezugsrecht; Vorkaufsrecht
preferential creditor	bevorrechtigter Gläubiger
private limited company/Ltd	Gesellschaft mit beschränkter Haftung
profit and loss account	Gewinn und Verlust Rechnung
property	Eigentum
prospectus	Prospekt
public (sector) enterprise	staatliches Unternehmen
public corporation	wirtschaftliche Unternehmung der öffentlichen Hand (GB), öffentlich-rechtliche Körperschaft
public limited company/plc	Aktiengesellschaft
to purchase	(ein)kaufen
Q	
quasi partnership	Scheingesellschaft, Scheinsozietät
to quote	notieren
R	
ratio	Verhältnis
receiver	Konkursverwalter, Zwangsverwalter; Treuhänder
to record	aufzeichnen, festhalten
Register of Companies	Handelsregister, Gesellschaftsregister
Registrar of Companies	Registerführer für Aktiengesellschaften
to request	fordern, ersuchen, bitten
to resign	zurücktreten
resolution	Beschluss
retail shop	Einzelhandelsgeschäft
to retire	in den Ruhestand treten
return on investment	Ertrag aus Kapitalanlagen
rural	ländlich
S	
safety at work regulations	Arbeitsschutzbestimmungen
salary	Gehalt
to second	(Antrag) unterstützen

secured creditor	gesicherter/bevorrechtigter Gläubiger
senior executive	(obere) Führungskraft, leitender Angestellter
severally	gesondert, einzeln
to share, share	teilen, aufteilen, Anteil, Teil
shareholder	Aktionär
sleeping/dormant/silent partner	Stiller Teilhaber
sole proprietor, sole trader	Einzelunternehmer
Stamp Duty	Stempelsteuer (auch Übertragungsurkunden)
standing orders	Geschäftsordnung
stock exchange	Börse
to submit	einreichen
subscribed capital	gezeichnetes Kapital
subscriber	Unterzeichner (der Gründungsurkunde), Gründungsgesellschafter; auch: Zeichner (von Wertpapieren/ Aktien)
subsidiary (company)	Tochtergesellschaft
subsidy	Subvention
to sue	verklagen
supervisory board	Aufsichtsrat
supplier	Zulieferer
surplus	Überschuss
to suspect	vermuten
T	
takeover	Übernahme
trading account	Verkaufskonto (ohne Gemeinkosten)
Trading Certificate	Handelserlaubnis
trading company	Handelsgesellschaft
V	
venture	Unternehmen
voluntarily	freiwillig
to vote on	abstimmen über
voting right	Stimmrecht
W	
to wind up	auflösen, abwickeln
winding up	Abwicklung, Liquidation
wrongdoing	rechtswidrige Handlung

MERGERS; MARKETS AND MORE

> *A good plan executed right now is far better than a perfect plan
> executed next week.*
>
> *George S Patton*

FOCUS Reading through the business section of an newspaper or
magazine can be confusing, as business has become increasingly
complicated. This unit attempts to explain the various types of
large scale enterprises plus the various markets that exist in the
business world.

1.0 Introduction
2.0 Forms of Large Scale Enterprises
3.0 Mergers
    3.1 Forms of Mergers and Takeovers
    3.2 Merger Trends
    3.3 Merger Blues
    3.4 Demerger
4.0 Key Markets

1.0   INTRODUCTION

Every business passes through various stages of growth, each one
involving different problems and solutions. Some firms fail and
close down; others survive, expand and in some cases become very
big.

Reasons for Creating Large Scale Enterprises

The main reasons for creating large scale enterprises are:

- **Synergies**

  This is where companies produce greater overall effects by
  joining forces rather than acting separately. Synergy is usually
  expressed as the *2+2 = 5 effect* meaning that the sum is greater
  than the total of the parts. An example is the sharing of
  technological know-how as done by the car manufacturers
  Daimler and Chrysler.

- **Cost savings**

  As a firm expands, it can gain the advantage of operating on a large scale. Costs per unit fall as output increases because of the **economies of scale** which refer to the reductions in unit costs and higher profits when goods are produced in large quantities, which in turn allow firms to grow to their optimal, or best, size.

- **Increased market share**

- **Increased creditworthiness**

- **More opportunities for innovative Research and Development (R&D)**

- **More marketing expertise**

2.0   FORMS OF LARGE SCALE ENTERPRISES

Corporations (in UK limited companies) can be 'parents'; each 'child' is known as a **subsidiary company** - a company whose voting shares are completely or mostly owned by another corporation.

This owner can be either a **holding company** or a **parent company**, both of whom own most or all of the voting shares of their subsidiaries.

The holding company is normally an investment company that buys the shares for income returns, i.e. dividends and future equity growth, and takes no part in the actual management.

In contrast a **parent company** takes an active role in managing the subsidiary or subsidiaries.

Some organizations eventually go on to become monopolies. A **monopoly** can be public (state owned) or private.

It can be defined as a producer of products, which controls a particular market having eliminated all potential or existing competitors and thus is able to dictate supply and price. Examples in the past included Deutsche Bahn and Deutsche Post while current examples include Microsoft and De Beers.

An **oligopoly** is a term commonly used by economists to explain a form of competition in which a few firms, each large enough to influence price, sell similar or differentiated products. An example is the petroleum industry with a few key players such as Shell, BP and Esso.

A **conglomerate** is a company which has business interests diversified in many different industries. It is an organization that often consists of subsidiaries (at least 51% owned) and **associated companies** (at least 20% owned). An example is Siemens.

A **multinational** is often referred to as an international corporation and is a large organization with interests situated throughout the world, e.g. Pepsi. It usually has at least six subsidiaries abroad; those companies with less than six subsidiaries abroad are referred to as **transnational companies**.

Multinationals structure themselves on a global basis and although they may originate, have their headquarters, or be registered in a particular country, they are rarely committed to that state unless there are specific investment advantages, e.g. different wage levels, preferential tax rates or lax environmental regulations.

They are often controversial as they have increasing strength and have more power than national governments. Examples include Shell, Unilever, IBM, Esso and VW.

Other firms make different arrangements with one another for different reasons. A **cartel** is the term used to describe a number of organizations that come together with the objective of monopolizing a particular market and dividing it up into agreed areas.

An agreement is made to curtail the quantity of goods available for sale thus making prices high and profits big. Price competition is eliminated as prices are agreed by the members. One pertinent example is the Organization of Petroleum Exporting Countries (OPEC) which leaves oil companies with no option but to pay high prices or else face an oil shortage.

A **consortium** (i.e., a group) is formed when large project contracts are involved, which no single company can do by itself. For this reason a number of companies come together and form an association in order to take on and complete the project. It is generally a *once only* combination for the purpose of bringing together a number of quite different skills or areas of specialized knowledge. A classic example was the creation of the German ICE high speed train involving a consortium of ABB, AEG and Siemens.

A **joint venture** is an arrangement where domestic and foreign companies join together in a partnership in which ownership and risk is shared. Joint ventures have been quite common with companies operating in China, e.g. VW and the Chinese government.

A **syndicate** is a group of people who are not necessarily partners but who agree to work together on a *long term* basis towards a common objective, usually profit.

Each member of the syndicate is in business on his/her own account even though the cooperation of the other members is essential if the individual members aims are to be achieved. An example is Lloyd's of London (see Unit 8).

A very common way of creating large scale enterprises is through **mergers and acquisitions (M&A).**

     a. Why are large scale enterprises created?
      b. Summarize the main types of large scale enterprises.

3.0   MERGERS

A **merger (amalgamation, fusion, absorption)** is the combining of two or more organizations often, but not always, in the same industry in order to increase overall efficiency. A Japanese example is the merger of Mazda and Mitsubishi, both primarily car manufacturers. A merger is usually a voluntary, co-operative amalgamation.

Different is an **acquisition** or **takeover** where one company acquires at least 51% of another company's equity, thereby taking control. This can often be done in an aggressive or *hostile* style. A good example was Vodafone's attempt from the UK to take over Germany's Mannesmann in the telecoms sector.

However, some takeovers can actually be *friendly*. Take the example of the troubled British car manufacturer Rover which was more than glad to be taken over by Germany's BMW in 1994. BMW managed to spend $7 billion on the deal before selling it in 2000 for $15!

3.1   Forms of Mergers or Takeovers

Vertical integration involves business organizations coming together with each organization producing similar goods or providing similar services but concerned with a different stage in the production of those products.

An example is where a manufacturer merges with its supplier of raw materials, such as where a brewery buys a hop farm - this is known as a **backward merger**. A brewery that buys public houses is an example of a **forward merger**.

Horizontal integration is the joining up of organizations producing similar products or providing similar services at the same level in the production of products, e.g. a brewery buys another brewery. It is often referred to as lateral integration.

EXAMPLES OF MERGERS

The Daimler-Benz and Chrysler car manufacturing merger represented the first truly global merger. Analysts rated it initially as one of the better merger success stories although conflicts have occurred at the managerial and cultural levels.

The reasons for Daimler to enter into this arrangement were the strong competition where competitors were encroaching on their traditional territory plus lower profit margins and problems with their small cars which were tarnishing the company's image.

Chrysler was suffering from an over-proportional production of trucks, vans and sports utility vehicles. Car sales had fallen considerably and the company had been almost overtaken by competitors. In addition it had an underdeveloped international market.

Other noteworthy examples of mergers include:

• AOL and Time Warner (communications merger)
• Glaxo Wellcome and SmithKLine Beecham (drug company merger).

Strategic (Corporate) alliances occur when two or more separate businesses join together to offer a broader set of skills or services to joint clients, for the mutual benefit of the businesses involved. A merger can be compared to a marriage while an alliance is more like a cohabitation.

The past decade has seen a large increase in the number of corporate alliances, one of the biggest successes being the Renault-Nissan connection. An example in the world of air transport includes the strategic alliance of Lufthansa, United(USA) and Thai Airlines.

Alliances are easier to set up and present fewer problems such as suspicion and mistrust. Each party feels that it is gaining more or less the same. Alliances also offer an opportunity to form closer links or to end these links altogether.

    a. Differentiate between mergers and acquisitions.
    b. Explain the different forms of mergers.

3.2 Merger Trends

The early 21ˢᵗ century has seen:

- Fewer and bigger multinationals dominating the world economy
- An increasing trend towards conglomerates
- A trend towards oligopolies and monopolies
- More bankruptcies of small and medium-sized enterprises (SMEs)

3.3 Merger Blues

Business journals maintain that two out of three mergers have not been successful.

Typically, problems have arisen due to:

- Cultural differences in cross-border mergers
- Information technology incompatibility
- Management conflict (e.g. with DaimlerChrysler the German management had lower remuneration than their American counterparts)

Some companies have been forced to abandon merger plans or even to demerge when they have become the target of antitrust regulators/monopoly commissioners.

Many economists argue that major mergers should be more closely controlled by the authorities, even when they do not threaten to reduce competition directly.

3.4 Demerger

A **demerger** is the reorganization of a company, so that its existing assets and liabilities are divided into one or more additional companies; and the shares of the newly formed companies are received by the shareholders of the demerged (or original) company.

It is often stated that a demerger is simply the opposite of a merger. This is not strictly true because a demerger involves just one set of shareholders, but a merger involves two.

From a general perspective, there are two main methods of demerger that can be used by conglomerate companies that wish to refocus their business activities. These are known as 'spin-offs' and 'split-ups'.

In the case of a **spin-off**, the original company (the parent company) will continue to exist and the demerger is achieved by establishing one or more new companies and transferring business to them. The parent company issues shares in its subsidiary, or subsidiaries, and gives them to current shareholders on a *pro rata* basis.

In the case of a **split-up** the original company will cease to exist and all of its business and assets are transferred to the new companies (or existing subsidiaries). A split-up is legally different to a spin-off though in economic substance they are much the same – but not precisely so.

    a. Describe trends and problems connected with mergers.
    b. What is a demerger?
    c. Differentiate between a spin-off and a split-up.

4.0 KEY MARKETS

A **market** is defined as any situation where buyers and sellers are brought together. Many different types of markets exist in the business world.

Some of the more important markets include:

Wholesaling

Retailing

Commodities   **Insurance**

Financial (Money, Capital)

Institutional Investors

Shipping

Stock Exchange

Issuing Houses

Foreign Exchange

A.   Retailing and Wholesaling

Both retailing and wholesaling are part of the Distribution Mix or Channels of Distribution (see Unit 7, Section 6.4).

B.   Commodity Markets or Exchanges

These are markets where manufacturers throughout the world can purchase raw materials. London is the principal city for this type of activity.

Principal types of commodity markets are:

- The **Metal Exchange**, which sells minerals such as aluminium, tin, zinc, silver and lead.

- The **Baltic Exchange**, which sells agricultural products like grain, seeds, etc. The Baltic Exchange is also involved in air transport and shipping.

- The **Commodity Exchange**, which is involved in the sale of rubber, cocoa, coffee, sugar, jute, etc.

C.   Shipping and Insurance Markets

Lloyd's of London (see Unit 8 on Insurance) is the world's principal risk insurance market while the Baltic Exchange sells shipping freight services.

D.   Financial Markets

A financial market deals in money. The two main financial markets include the money market and the capital market.

- **The Money Market**

    The money market consists of institutions which borrow and lend money for *short periods* at a specific rate of interest. Institutions which deal in the money market include the commercial, merchant banks and specialist finance houses. The government also borrows money by issuing Treasury Bills (T-bills) which are short-term credits on behalf of the government to pay for immediate expenses in running a country

    Unique institutions in the world are the UK **discount houses**, which specialize in borrowing from banks in order to buy government Treasury Bills.

- **The Capital Market**

  The capital market deals with the provision of *longer-term* finance for the individual, the corporate customer and the government. This market includes institutional investors, the stock exchanges and issuing houses.

E.   Institutional investors

Institutional investors are organizations which use other people's money for investment or to provide credits. They consist of insurance companies, building societies, pension fund companies and trade unions among others. Popular organizations are unit trusts and investment funds.

Unit Trusts (mutual funds) are mutual organizations set up for the purpose of investing in the shares of different companies. The risk is spread over a large portfolio of investments which the general public are invited to buy in *units*. Profits are maximized by experts who manage the trust.

Investment Trusts are companies that are listed on the stock market. The general public buys *shares* in the investment trust company, whose sole purpose is to buy shares in other companies.

Because an investment trust is itself a listed company, its shares can be bought and sold in the usual way.

F.   The Stock Exchange

The Stock Exchange is a market for buying and selling securities (see Unit 5).

G.   Issuing Houses

Issuing Houses specialize in the issue of new shares (see Unit 5) to the general public.

H.   The Foreign Exchange Market

This market is involved in the buying and selling of foreign exchange. It is not in any fixed location, consisting instead of a global network of financial institutions and dealers. Deals are either spot or forward.

Spot deals involve buying currencies immediately, i.e. on the spot, at the current rates.

Forward deals occur when an individual or firm agrees to buy a given amount of currency or currencies at a future date and at an agreed upon rate.

Summarize the main types of markets.

 ## Discussion Forum

a. Choose one of the following statements to defend or refute.

- In the future the business world will be dominated by a handful of large multinationals which will increase innovation and contribute significantly to the world economy.
- The future of business depends on small and medium-sized enterprises (SMEs).

b. Large scale enterprises and financial markets have too much power and are not accountable to anyone. The result is that democracy is being endangered. Discuss.

VOCABULARY

A	
to abandon	aufgeben
(to be) accountable (to)	(jdm gegenüber) verantwortlich/ rechenschaftspflichtig (sein)
acquisition	Übernahme
amalgamation	Vereinigung
assets	Vermögenswerte
B	
break bulk	in kleinere Mengen umgruppieren
brewery	Brauerei
building society	Bausparkasse
bulk	große Menge, Masse
C	
to cease	aufhören
cohabitation	Lebensgemeinschaft
commodity	Ware
compelling	zwingend
conglomerate	Konglomerat, Mischkonzern
controversial	umstritten
creditworthiness	Kreditwürdigkeit
to curtail	beschränken, kürzen
D	
demerge	entfusionieren
discount house	Diskontbank
E	
economic entity	Wirtschaftseinheit

to encroach	eindringen
to entitle	berechtigen
exchange	Börse
F	
foreign exchange	Devisen
forward deals	Termingeschäfte
G	
to gain	erreichen, gewinnen, erwerben
H	
headquarter	Hauptsitz
holding company	Holding-Gesellschaft
hostile	feindlich
I	
income returns	Rendite, Gewinn
incompatible	nicht kompatibel, unvereinbar
institutional investors	institutionelle Anleger
investment trusts	Investment Trust, Kapitalanlegegesellschaft
issuing house	Emissionsbank
M	
merger	Fusion
multinationals	multinationale Unternehmen, Multis
mutual	gegenseitig
mutual funds	Investmentgesellschaft
O	
oligopoly	Oligopol
on the spot	auf der Stelle, sofort
to originate	entstehen, den Ursprung haben
P	
parent company	Muttergesellschaft
pertinent	passend, relevant
preferential	Vorzugs-
preferential tax rates	Steuervergünstigungen, günstige Steuersätze
pro rata	anteilig, dem Anteil entsprechend
profit margin	Gewinnspanne, Gewinnmarge
R	
remuneration	Bezahlung, Vergütung
replicate	replizieren, kopieren
retail	Einzelhandel
to retain	behalten
S	
shortage	Mangel, Knappheit
spin-off	Ausgliederung, Spin-off

split-up	Splitting, Aktiensplitt
spot deals	Kassageschäfte
stock exchange	Wertpapierbörse
subsidiary (company)	Tochtergesellschaft, Tochterunternehmen
suspicion	Verdacht, Argwohn, Misstrauen
T	
to tarnish	beflecken, beschädigen
tax relief	Steuerbefreiung, Steuervergünstigung
to threaten	drohen
treasury bills	Schatzwechsel
trust	Trust; Treuhand(verhältnis)
U	
unique	einzigartig
unit	Einheit, Stück
unit costs	Stückkosten
unit trust	Investmentfonds
V	
voting shares	stimmberechtigte Aktien
W	
wholesale	Großhandel

THE STOCK EXCHANGE

> *October is one of the peculiarly dangerous months to speculate in*
> *stocks. The others are July, January, September, April, Novem-*
> *ber, May, March, June, December, August and February.*
> *Mark Twain*

FOCUS This unit focuses on the history of the stock exchange, its
role nowadays, the different type of securities, and a look at LIFFE.

1.0   HISTORY OF THE STOCK EXCHANGE

1.1   The Early Years

The history of the commercial Stock Exchanges can be clearly
linked with the historical development of the London Stock
Exchange, which in turn is related to the rise of the British
Empire.

The reign of Elizabeth I (1558-1603), had seen the first rapid
expansion in overseas trade necessitating considerable capital.
Trading companies such as the East India Company (1600) and
the London (Virginia) Company (1606) were founded. The traders

and shipowners sought loans for their export and import businesses and for such risk ventures as the exploration of little known territories.

A system of joint venture between owners of ships and investors of capital gradually developed. Huge returns were made or all was lost depending on whether the winds were fair or foul or whether the sailors survived the dangers of uncharted regions. Investors in these ventures were given certificates or 'shares'. They had become **shareholders** but there were no quick returns as ships could be away months or years.

What could an investor do when, during the waiting interval, he wanted to sell his shares in order to invest in more lucrative ventures that had appeared or wanted to end his involvement in the venture for fear it would be unsuccessful? There were fortunately other people with money to invest who were more optimistic about profits and were prepared to purchase the shares from the original investors.

It was, however, difficult to estimate both the degree of risk and the expected profit and therefore not easy to determine a sale price for these shares. Over time persons who considered themselves more expert than the general public in such matters began to buy and sell these shares as a profession and became known as **jobbers**. They gathered for business in the coffee shops in a business area of London, today referred to as The City.

It was here in 1709 where England's central bank, the Bank of England, was founded primarily to properly manage the national debt. The Bank decided to borrow money from the general public by offering them a fixed amount of interest after a certain period of time. The jobbers now also started to buy large 'stocks' of this government paper for immediate or future sale via new types of specialists known as **stockbrokers.** These stockbrokers acted as intermediaries between the jobbers and the general public.

In 1802 an expanding British Empire, essentially a business rather than a military empire, resulted in the founding of the London Stock Exchange. Subsequently local stock exchanges were founded in the major cities of the UK.

Stock Exchanges were also founded in this period in many prominent European cities and also on a New York street in lower Manhattan called Wall Street, which quickly became the main financial centre, then and now, of the United States. This was 1792 and the first corporate stock to be traded was that of the Bank of New York. On May 15, 1878 the Tokyo Stock Exchange Co. Ltd was established.

a. Give a brief summary of the development of the Stock Exchange up to the early 1800s.

b. What is the difference between jobbers and stockbrokers?

1.2   Recent Developments

The outbreak of the Great War (1914-1918) threw Europe's markets into disarray, and it wasn't until the boom years of the 1920s that it recovered.

The American investor, being more speculative than his European counterpart, often invested with borrowed money. Prices on the New York Stock Exchange rose higher and higher as the money poured in. Finally, the inevitable happened and in October 1929 prices started to fall resulting in panic as speculators who had borrowed up to 90% of their investment from financial institutions sold their shares. On October 24 alone, 11 people jumped to their deaths from buildings on or near Wall Street.

The next obstacle was the Second World War (1939-1945). Social changes after the war created nationalization on a vast scale in Western Europe side by side with the emergence of new socialist states in Eastern Europe. The 1960s and 1970s, however, saw gradual growth.

Margaret Thatcher's 1979 government in the UK led to the beginning of the privatization of nationalized companies, resulting in more rapid growth in stock exchange dealings. This privatization process would have the same effect in Continental Europe over the following decades.

The 1986 liberalizing and modernizing process (known as Big Bang) at the London Stock Exchange resulted in the merger of the activities of both the jobbers and the stockbrokers into brokers/dealers who could buy and sell securities directly to clients. Some of these new brokers/dealers decided to become more specialized market-makers dealing only in particular classes of stocks and shares.

Traditional trading floor activities also ended with the introduction of a continuously-updated computer database containing price quotations and trade reports.

The collapse of socialism in 1989 saw the reopening of stock exchanges in Eastern Europe and gave another huge boost to the stock market.

What was the development of the stock exchange in the 20th century characterized by?

1.3   Important Stock Exchanges

The four principal exchanges in the world today, (with their respective indices), are:

Stock Exchanges	Indices
• New York Stock Exchange (NYSE)	• Dow Jones Industrial Average (DJIA)
• London Stock Exchange (LSE)	• Financial Times-/Stock Exchange Share Index (FTSE)
• Tokyo Stock Exchange (TSE)	• Nikkei 225
• Frankfurt Deutsche Börse (FBE)	• Deutsche Aktienindex (DAX)

New York's Stock Exchange **DJIA** contains 30 stocks chosen by Dow Jones & Co and the Wall Street Journal to represent a balanced selection of *old economy* blue-chips such as Coca-Cola and McDonald's. Dow Jones was the original editor of the Wall Street Journal.

The **National Association of Securities Dealers Automated Quotations (NASDAQ)** is a nationwide electronic trading network founded for trading in securities that are not listed on the New York Stock Exchange (NYSE). It concentrates on *new economy* or TMT (technology, media and telecom) shares.

The London Exchange is ideally placed in a 'Golden Triangle' time zone. Able to deal with Tokyo in the morning and New York in the afternoon this exchange links the world in a 24-hours-a-day global stock market.

The **London FTSE (Footsie)** indices include the FTSE 100 index, which is a list published by the Financial Times and the Institute and Faculty of Actuaries to illustrate the performance of 100 specially selected shares in various sectors of the UK and European markets. Examples include Vodafone and British Airways.

AIM is the London Stock Exchange's Alternative Investment Market, providing a further choice for young and growing companies.

The **Nikkei 225,** formerly known as the Nikkei Dow is the original Japanese share index published by Nihon Keizai Shimbum.

The **DAX** contains 30 stocks from the main German stock markets and is one of the few indices which include a measurement of the return provided by the dividends paid to shareholders as well as price appreciation. The **NEMAX** is an index of new economy shares. **XETRA** is an electronic trading system for shares.

 a. *What were the effects of Big Bang?*
 b. *Summarize the main market indices*

2.0 FUNCTIONS OF THE MODERN STOCK EXCHANGE

As we have seen a **stock exchange** can be defined as a central marketplace where the public buy and sell securities through intermediaries. The stock exchange reflects the needs of governments and companies to raise monies from members of the public who have surplus funds to invest in order to obtain an income or a capital gain, or both.

It is called a 'stock' exchange because the biggest area of activity in exchanges used to be the buying and selling of government stocks or bonds. Stocks used to be a term for shares that had been consolidated into one block or groups, whereas shares are purchased and sold in individual units. In America the word 'stock' is nowadays used in ordinary speech to refer to shares.

The functions of a Stock Exchange are to:

- provide a ready market for sound and saleable securities by bringing buyer and seller together.
- increase the safety of dealings in securities by preventing irregular or fraudulent methods of dealing and to prevent the issue of forged or fraudulent securities.
- aid in the promotion of new enterprises and to bring capital and projected business ventures together.
- furnish a business barometer since quoted prices have a direct relation to business conditions and the economic situation.
- allow the government to borrow funds through the sale of bonds and government stocks.

 a. *Explain the most important functions of a Stock Exchange*
 b. *What is the difference between stocks and shares?*

3.0 SECURITIES

Securities is the general name for stocks and shares of all types. They can be defined as written or printed documents, which acknowledge the investment of money. Securities traded on a stock exchange fall into two main divisions:

- the public sector consisting of government and public authorities' borrowings.
- capital and loans raised by joint stock companies.

The **bid price** refers to the buying price for securities in the market while the **offer price** is the asking or selling price. **Liquidity** refers to the ease with which a security can be traded on the market.

Why do people buy and hold securities? Because it is an investment with potential. The returns are fixed interest, dividends and appreciation of current value.

The **securities** that are bought and sold consist of:

1. **Fixed interest securities** such as government, municipal, local-government or company issues. They include:

   Bonds, which are debt securities that are usually issued by governments or local authorities and entitle the holder to a fixed-rate of interest during their life and repayment of the amount of the bond at maturity. **Gilts** or **gilt-edged securities (Treasury Bonds - AE)** are terms used to describe stocks or bonds, issued on behalf of a government which enjoy absolute security.

   Debentures, which are company bonds, (in reality loans to a company) may be secured by the company's assets. The investor receives the principal plus interest at maturity and is compensated before any dividends are paid to the shareholders of the company. Debentures and other corporate bonds are taxable and often only guaranteed by the creditworthiness of the company. However, they have the potential to generate higher returns than government bonds.

   Eurobonds, which are interest-bearing securities issued across national borders, often in a currency other than that of the issuer's home country.

2. **Equities** are the ordinary shares or stock issued by domestic and international companies such as Nokia, Intel, Pepsi, etc.

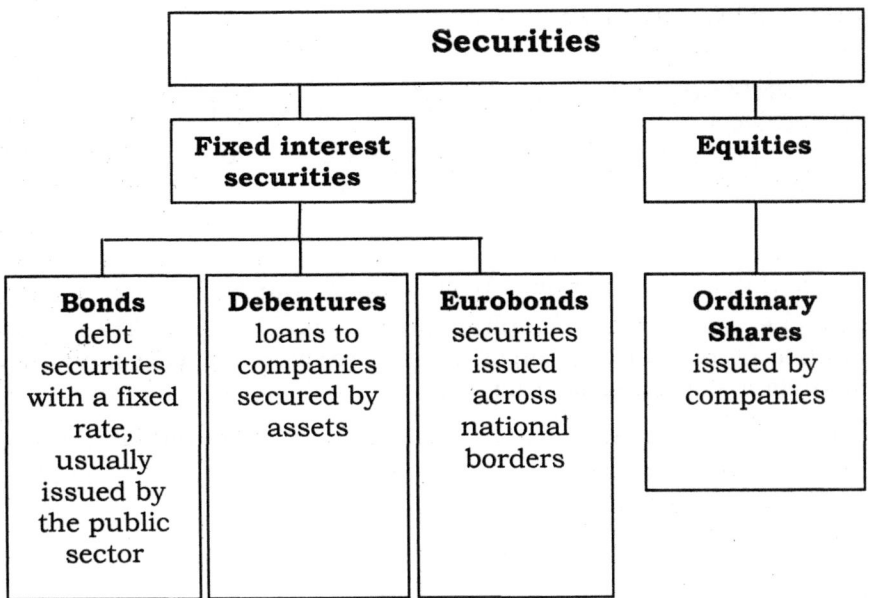

 Define what securities are and explain the different types.

4.0 DIVIDENDS

A **dividend** is that portion of a company's profit after tax which is marked for distribution to the shareholders. The amount is decided at the Annual General Meeting (A.G.M.) in line with the company's profitability level and recommendation of its directors for distribution to the shareholders and is usually expressed as a percentage of the nominal value of the shares.

The **rate of dividend** is the dividend divided by the issued capital.

An **interim dividend** is a partial payment of the dividend to the shareholders during the year.

Dividend Yield is the rate of dividend multiplied by the nominal value divided by the market price.

E.P.S (Earnings Per Share) is the net profit divided by the number of issued shares.

D.P.S (Dividend Per Share) consists of the profits paid to the shareholder divided by the number of issued shares.

P/E (Price Earning ratio) is the current market price of the share divided by the last published Earnings Per Share and is a measure of the level of confidence investors have in a company. The general rule is, the higher the figure, the higher the confidence.

Cum Dividend means that the person who purchases the share will receive the next declared dividend. **Ex Dividend (XD)** means that the person who purchases the share will not receive the next dividend. The next declared dividend will be sent to the seller of the share.

Yield refers to the true return to an investor on an investment taking into account the annual income and its present capital value, i.e. dividend income plus current value of share. There are a number of different types of yield, and in some cases different methods of calculating each type.

 What is a dividend and how is it paid out to the shareholders?

5.0   TYPES OF SHARES

The most common classes of shares that are traded are:

Ordinary Shares (Equity Share Capital), which are normally bearer shares whose shareholders receive a dividend only after preference shareholders receive their dividend. These shares are normally referred to as *equity* since every share receives an *equal* share of the profit. Ordinary share shareholders have the advantage of voting rights at the A.G.M.

Deferred Ordinary Shares are also known as Founders' Shares and are issued to the founder of a firm who, after selling his business to a company, agrees to accept shares as partial payment and to defer any dividend until the other shareholders have had their cut. The proportion of the dividend the deferred shareholder will then receive depends on the terms stated in the memorandum or articles of association.

Preference Shares have a prior right or first call on a fixed rate of dividend before any other dividend is distributed to other classes of shareholders but, unlike ordinary shares, they carry no voting rights.

If a company were to go into liquidation, preference shareholders would rank above ordinary shareholders for the repayment of their investment in the company.

Cumulative Preference Shares enable their holders to receive dividend arrears from the years when no profit or dividend was declared – perhaps all the profits were ploughed back or no profits were made. Once the company does declare a dividend they are entitled to the current dividend plus the dividends for the years when none was declared. The owners of **non-cumulative preference shares** are entitled to a dividend but only out of the profits of the current year.

Participating Preference Shares are shares which, to some extent, enjoy the increasing profits which ordinary shareholders can earn. Such shares entitle the owner to a preferential dividend at a fixed rate and also a share of any profits remaining after the ordinary shareholders have received a stated percentage (e.g. 9%).

Redeemable Preference Shares are shares, which the company intends buying back from the owners sometime in the future.

Convertible Preference Shares where the company has the right to convert them into ordinary shares at some future date at fixed specified prices.

    a. What are the main types of shares?
         b. What type of shares would you personally prefer to hold? Why?

6.0   SALE OF SHARES

The **nominal price** is the value of a share on its issuing day but the **actual** or **current market value** varies with supply and demand and the profitability of the company.

Obtaining a Stock Exchange Quotation or **Going Public** is the process a company must go through in order to have its shares quoted on the Stock Exchange.

A **flotation** is when a company's shares are admitted to trading on the Stock Exchange for an **initial public offering (IPO)** i.e., where the shares are advertised for sale to the general public.

A company may float (i.e. sell) shares and gain a quotation using the following methods:

- **Issue by Prospectus** – This is where the company itself sells the shares to the general public at a given price; the share offer is **underwritten** (see underwriting in Glossary) so that any shares unsold will be purchased by the underwriting institution, usually a Merchant Bank.

  A **prospectus** is an invitation to the general public to subscribe for shares in a company. It must be submitted to the Registrar of Companies and the Stock Exchange quotation department for inspection and registration.

The prospectus consists of an information booklet detailing information on the company, its accounts and directors, and the securities to be listed as required in an exchange's rules. Investors apply for shares by filling in the form at the end of the prospectus. The nominal or **par** value of a share is the price quoted on the prospectus, but companies often sell new shares at a **premium**, i.e. with an extra charge over the nominal price because they feel there is likely to be strong demand for them

- **Offer for Sale** – In this widely used method shares are sold by an **issuing house** (a banking house that specializes in the launching of new shares) to the general public. The public can apply for shares directly at a fixed price. Details of the sale must be printed in a national newspaper.

- **Placing** – The company sells shares to a broker who then places them with his clients, mainly institutions such as pension funds and insurance companies.

- **Issue by Tender** – Here the public names the price at which it is prepared to buy. This method is rarely used.

The following are methods of gaining a quotation *without* a share issue:

- **Stock Exchange Introduction** – This method is useful for well-known companies and involves no underwriting expenses. It is simply a way for a company with a large number of shareholders or a company which is already quoted on one stock exchange to gain a quotation on another exchange.

- **Reverse Takeover** – This is either a takeover of a larger company by a smaller one, or more usually of a public company by a private (unquoted) company. In the latter case the main purpose is to gain a back-door quotation on the Stock Exchange with a minimum of fuss.

The following are methods of raising share capital *without applying* for a quotation:

- **Rights Issue** - This is an invitation to existing shareholders to purchase additional shares in the company, normally below the market price.

- **Private Placing** – Here a large block of shares are put up for sale through one broker.

  a *Explain what a prospectus is.*
  b *What are the most common methods of gaining a quotation?*

7.0   THE SPECULATORS AT THE STOCK EXCHANGE ZOO - BULLS, BEARS AND STAGS

A **bull** is an optimistic speculator who buys shares hoping that they will appreciate and who will then sell them at a profit. A 'bullish' market is one in which dealers expect prices to rise.

A **bear** is a pessimistic speculator who sells shares expecting them to fall in price and then buys them back at the lower price.

Stags are speculators who are involved in the purchase of *new issues* of shares as they anticipate a quick rise in price when the shares are quoted on the Stock Exchange.

    a   Differentiate between a bull and a stag.
    b   How does a bear earn a profit?

8.0   LONDON INTERNATIONAL FINANCIAL FUTURES EXCHANGE (LIFFE)

LIFFE is a worldwide electronic market for trading in financial derivatives. Members are drawn from the principal banks, stockbrokers, fund managers (persons or companies that, for a fee, invest money on behalf of a number of individuals or companies) and treasury operations (the Treasury is the Finance Ministry in the UK and USA that controls public finance and spending).

Derivatives are financial products whose value is dependent on changes in response to movement in the prices of other securities, goods, etc. The main categories of derivatives are futures and options.

Futures and **options** are forward transactions, i.e. they are based on a transaction which will only be executed in the future.

A **futures contract** commits the buyer to buying **commodities**, i.e. raw materials or agricultural products such as cotton or sugar, at an agreed on price at a future date.

An **option** refers to the right (but not the obligation) to buy or sell securities at a fixed price within a specified period. Options are concerned with **securities**.

A **call option** gives an investor the right to *purchase* securities at a fixed price in the future if he/she wishes. The buyer hopes the share price will rise before the option expires. A **put option** is where the investor has the right to *sell* securities also at a specific price and up to a certain date. Options are not new. In the 17th century options were sold on tulip bulbs in Holland.

Warrants are nothing more than securitized options (i.e. negotiable instruments with physical certificates), which can be traded easily and in small quantities.

    a What is a fund manager?
    b Differentiate between futures contract and option.

9.0   GLOSSARY OF OTHER COMMON TERMS

Active Stocks are securities for which there have been the highest number of recorded bargains during the day.

Arbitrage involves buying securities in one country, currency or market, and selling in another to take advantage of price differences.

Bargain is a deal on the Stock Exchange.

A **blue chip** is an ordinary share of the highest calibre, e.g. Shell Oil, Deutsche Bank.

A **bonus** or **scrip issue** (**stock split** - AE) is a free issue of ordinary shares to existing shareholders depending on the number of shares they already hold. The issue is paid out of company reserves, i.e. ploughed back profits. The process whereby funds from a company's reserves are converted into shares through a bonus issue is referred to as **capitalization**. This does not, however, increase the value of the shareholder's holding – he or she has more shares, each of which are worth less.

Hedging is a step taken by a buyer or seller to protect him/herself against a change in prices. It involves the buying forward or selling forward of a commodity, share or other investment to protect against a possible loss through any changes in price that may occur.

Insider dealing refers to the purchase or sale of securities by someone who possesses 'inside' information affecting securities, which has not yet been made available to the market and which, if made available, would significantly affect the share price. Such deals are a criminal offence in most countries.

Market capitalization refers to the market value of a company's issued share capital.

A **portfolio** is a collection of securities belonging to one investor or institution. It is sometimes referred to as an investment portfolio.

POTAM is the Panel on Takeovers and Mergers, which regulates the conduct of takeovers and mergers in the UK.

Price sensitive information is information, which, if made public, is likely to have a significant effect on the price of a company's securities.

Primary market is the function of a stock exchange in bringing securities to the market for the first time.

A **private company (limited liability company - AE)** is a company which is not a public company and which is not allowed to offer its shares to the general public while a **public limited company (corporation -AE))** can have its shares purchased by the public and has a capital which is not less than a statutory minimum.

Settlement refers to the process of transferring stock from seller to buyer and arranging the corresponding movement of money between the two parties.

Stop (loss) order is an instruction given by a customer to a stockbroker to sell should prices fall below a certain level.

Underwriting is an arrangement by which a company is guaranteed that an issue of shares will raise a given amount of cash. Underwriters undertake to subscribe for any of the issue not taken up by the public or institutions. They charge commission for this service.

 Discussion Forum

     a. It makes more sense to back the favourite in a five-horse race than speculate on the Stock Exchange.
     b. What factors influence share prices?
     c. Discuss the role of the stock market in the global economy.

VOCABULARY

A	
access	Zugang, Zugriff
to acknowledge	bestätigen, anerkennen
active stocks	lebhaft gehandelte Aktien
actual	tatsächlich
actuary	Aktuar, Schätzer
to affect	sich auswirken auf
Annual General Meeting (A.G.M.)	Jahreshauptversammlung

to anticipate	erwarten
to appreciate	im Wert steigen
arbitrage	Arbitrage
articles of association	Satzung, Gesellschaftsvertrag
asset	Vermögen(swerte)
B	
to balance	im Gleichgewicht halten, ausgleichen
bargain	hier: Börsengeschäft, Abschluss
bear	auf Baissespekulant, Baissier
bearer shares	Inhaberaktien
bid price	Angebotspreis
Big Bang	Big Bang (Liberalisierung des britischen Wertpapiermarktes am 27.10.1986)
blue chips	Standardwerte, Spitzenwert/papier
bond (or debenture)	Schuldverschreibung
bonus issue	(Ausgabe von)Gratisaktien
boost	Auftrieb
broker/dealer	Makler/Händler
bull	Haussier, Haussespekulant
buying forward	Terminkauf
C	
call option	Kaufoption, Vorprämie
capitalization	Kapitalisierung, Aktivierung
to charge	berechnen
coffer	Truhe
to commence	beginnen
commission	Provision
to commit	verpflichten
conduct	Erledigung, Abwicklung; Führung
confidence	Vertrauen
consolidate	zusammenlegen/schließen; konsolidieren
convertible preference scares	wandelbare Vorzugsaktie
cum dividend	mit/einschließlich Dividende
cumulative preference shares	kumulative Vorzugsaktien
current value	Zeitwert, derzeitiger Wert
D	
D.P.S.(Dividend Per Share)	Dividende pro Aktie
to deal in	handeln mit
debenture	Schuldverschreibung, Obligation

debt securities	schuldrechtliche Wertpapiere
to declare	festsetzen
to defer	aufschieben
deferred ordinary shares	Nachzugsaktien
disarray	Unordnung
to disseminate	verbreiten
dividend arrears	Dividendenrückstände
dividend yield	Dividendenrendite, Effektivrendite
dividend	Dividende
E	
E.P.S. Earnings Per Share	Gewinn je Aktie
to entitle	berechtigen
equities	Aktien, Stammaktien, Eigenkapital
equity share capital	Stammaktienkapital
ex dividend	ex/ohne Dividende
expenditure	Ausgabe(n)
exploration	Erforschung
F	
favour	Gunst, Gefallen
fixed interest securities	festverzinsliche Wertpapiere
float	floaten, in Umlauf bringen, ausgeben
floatation	Gründung, Ausgabe
forged	gefälscht
forward transaction	Termingeschäft
founder shares	Gründeraktien
fraudulent	betrügerisch, arglistig
to furnish	liefern, geben
futures	Termingeschäft, Terminwaren
G	
gain	Gewinn, Vorteil
gilt-edged securities, gilts	mündelsichere Wertpapiere, Staatspapiere/anleihen
to go public	an die Börse gehen, in Publikumsgesellschaft umwandeln
H	
hedging	Hedging, Absicherung, Risikoeingrenzung
I	
initial public offering	Erstemission
insider dealings	Insidergeschäfte
interest	Zins
interest-bearing	verzinslich, zinstragend

interim dividend	Zwischen/Abschlagsdividende
intermediary	Mittler
investment portfolio	Effektenportefeuille, Wertpapierbestand
investment trust	Investmentgesellschaft
issue by prospectus	Emission durch Prospekt
issue by tender	Emission durch Zuteilung an den Meistbietenden
to issue	emittieren, ausgeben
issuer	Emitent, Aussteller
issuing house	Emissionsbank
J	
jobber	Jobber, Wertpapier(eigen)händler
joint stock company	Aktiengesellschaft
L	
latter	Letztere
to launch	auf den Markt bringen
liquidity	Liquidität
to list	zum Börsenhandel zulassen, an der Börse notieren
loan	Darlehen
M	
maturity	Fälligkeit; Verfall, Laufzeit
memorandum of association	Gründungsurkunde
mundane	profan; weltlich
municipal loan	städtische Anleihe, Kommunalanleihe
N	
national debt	Staatsverschuldung
nominal value	Nominalwert, Nennwert
O	
offer for sale	Zeichnungsangebot
option	Option
ordinary shares	Stammaktien (ohne Vorrechte)
P	
panel	Gremium, Ausschuss
par value	Nennwert, Nominalwert, Pariwert
participating preference shares	Vorzugsaktien mit Gewinnbeteiligung
pension fund	Pensionsfonds, Rentenfonds
placing	Platzierung
to plough back	einbehalten (und reinvestieren)
portfolio	Bestand an Wertpapieren, Portefeuille

portion	Anteil
preference shares	Vorzugsaktien
premium	über dem Nennwert, über pari, Agio, Aufgeld
to prevent	verhindern
price earnings ratio	Kurs-Gewinn-Verhältnis
price sensitive information	kursempfindliche Informationen
price	Kurs
primary market	Primärmarkt, Emissionsmarkt
principal	Darlehenssumme
private placing	private Effektenplacierung, Direktverkauf
projected	geplante
prospectus	(Emissions)Prospekt, Börsenprospekt
put option	Verkaufoption
Q	
quotation	Notierung
quotation	(Kurs)Notierung, Kurs
R	
to raise (a loan)	(ein Darlehen) aufnehmen
to rank above	(auf der Rangliste) über jdm liegen/stehen
rate of dividend	Dividendensatz
to reap(returns)	(Gewinn) ernten
to redeem	einlösen, tilgen, zurückzahlen/-kaufen
redeemable preference shares	rückzahlbare Vorzugsaktie
to refer to as	bezeichnen als
Registrar of Companies	Führer des Gesellschaftsregisters
return	Ertrag, Rückerstattung
reverse takeover	gegenläufige Übernahme
rights issue	Bezugsrechtsemission
S	
scrip issue	(Ausgabe von)Gratisaktien
scrip	Scrip, Zwischenschein, Bezugsschein
SEAQ(Stock Exchange Automated Quotation System)	automatisches Kurs(informations)system
securities	Wertpapiere, Effekten; auch: Sicherheiten (Gläubiger)
securitized option	verbriefte Option
selling forward	Terminverkauf
to set a price	einen Preis festlegen

settlement	Liquidation, Abrechnung
share premium	Aktienagio, Emissionsagio
share	Aktie
shareholder	Aktionär
sound	solide, gesund
spoils	Beute
stag	Spekulant bei Neuemissionen
state/government paper	Staatspapiere, Staatsanleihe
statutory	gesetzlich
stock exchange introduction	Einführung von Effekten an der Börse
stock exchange quotation	Börsennotierung
stock exchange	Wertpapierbörse
stock	Bestand; Aktie, Wertpapier, Anleiheschuld
stockbroker	Wertpapiermakler
subsciber	Zeichner; Abonnent
to subscribe	zeichnen
subsequently	von da an, später
T	
tax-deductable	Steuerlich absetzbar
terms	Bestimmungen
trading floor	Börsensaal
trust	Trust, Treuhandgesellschaft
tulip bulb	Tulpenzwiebel
turnover	Umsatz
U	
uncharted	unerforscht, unergründet
to underwrite	garantieren (der Übernahme von nicht realisierten Verpflichtungen), fest übernehmen
underwriter	Garant
underwriting	Garantie (o. Übernahme) einer Effektenemission
unit trust	Investmentfonds
unit	Anteil, Fondsanteil; Stück
V	
venture	risikoreiches Unternehmen
voting right	Stimmrecht
yield	Rendite
W	
warrant	Optionsschein, Bezugsrecht (s-schein)

PEANUTS! - BANKING

> *A bank is a place that will lend you money if you can prove you don't need it.*
>
> *Bob Hope*

FOCUS This unit examines the main functions of commercial, merchant and central banks. Services of commercial banks are examined in detail.

1.0   HISTORY OF THE BANKING SYSTEM

Birth of Banking Activities

Traces of banking functions may be found far back in history. The temples of early Greece served as safe deposit vaults; there were private bankers in Athens and Alexandria who made loans; and banking offices beside the Forum in Rome were familiar with deposits, loans and mortgages. But during the Dark Ages in Europe most of this banking technique was lost, and the history of banking began anew in the Italian cities of the 10th century, with their wide commercial connections, their wealth and their enterprise.

In spite of clerical opposition to usury, monasteries with large incomes often made loans. Jews and Lombards gradually developed the business of money lending and money changing.

The UK - The Pioneer of Modern Banking

It is true to say that modern banking, as we know it, descends from the activities of London goldsmiths who used to store customers gold in their safes and issued the depositor with a note stating how much was being stored. These notes or 'banknotes' became the forerunner of today's notes and cheques. The goldsmiths gradually started to use these stored funds as loans, charging interest and maintaining a certain percentage of these funds in case of unexpected demand.

By the 17th century private banking was developing through merchant banks (see 2.2), which helped develop foreign trade.

The success of the Bank of England (1694) in bringing financial stability led over the following two centuries to a rapid development in the commercial banking network and the founding of several joint-stock banks, which eventually superseded the merchant banks in importance.

These commercial banks engaged in the classic bank functions of taking surplus money from customers on deposit and making this money work by granting credits. The third function was taking care of the day-to-day transactions in and out of customers' accounts. A bank clearing system was developed, enabling the banks to exchange cheques and bills of exchange via a clearing house.

The US System

The United States' modern commercial banking industry began in 1782, the first financial institution being the Bank of North America. The banking system was a decentralized one with different states having different regulations. That is why the structure in the USA is quite different from other industrialized countries consisting of almost 12,000 commercial banks, about 2000 savings and loan associations, about 500 mutual savings banks (co-operative banks owned by the depositors) and 13,000 credit unions (mainly consisting of members of a particular group, e.g. employees of a firm or a trade union.) American banks have a strong international presence in South America, the Caribbean, the Far East and London.

The German System

Banking in Germany began a rapid development from about the middle of the 19th century, with the establishment of several joint-stock banks. German banks are more closely in touch with industry and foreign trade than most other countries, and, in fact, German banks are often shareholders in companies. They were also one of the first to develop the concept of a universal banking system offering all financial services under one roof, a kind of one-stop shopping point.

Very important in Germany are the *public savings banks* which have a large network and were originally set up to cater for the collection of savings and lending on real estate. They have developed nowadays to offer more or less the same services as commercial banks although foreign operations and stockbroking still lag behind. With a few exceptions these credit institutions are incorporated under public law and have guarantors who are mostly local authorities such as town, district or city municipalities. These localities constitute the area of operation although a lot of cooperation occurs between the various public savings banks.

Recent Changes

In the mid-1980s the financial markets of the world were subjected to massive reform, which eliminated barriers and enhanced competition. London was the first European financial centre to experience the globalization of the world financial markets.

Nowadays, several types of financial institutions exist including commercial banks, merchant banks, post offices, hire-purchase companies, finance companies, building societies and credit unions (see Co-operatives in Unit 3).

The last few years have seen many changes in the world of banking. There have been huge investments in technology and a resulting decline in the number of staff required. Internet and online banking are prime examples of this trend.

Opening hours have become more flexible as one can see from Saturday and Sunday opening times. Banks now offer a wider range of services and there is a stronger focus on marketing and the development of new product variations. It is increasingly common to see a complete range of services under one roof - universal banking - throughout the world.

There is now more international competition and banks have engaged in rapid foreign expansion through a process of takeovers and mergers.

Another unique development is the common EU currency or euro and the establishment of the European Central Bank (ECB), which supersedes the role of the national central banks of the participating states.

a. *Explain the historic development of the banking system in the UK, USA and Germany.*
b. *Describe recent changes in banking.*

2.0 TYPES OF BANKS

2.1 Commercial Banks (Associated Banks)

These are banks that provide a vast range of services to the general public and are usually the best-known banks in the country. Examples include Barclay's in the UK, Citibank in the USA and Commerzbank in Germany.

Services include payments, savings, deposits, investments, foreign exchange transactions and credit facilities, which are discussed in more detail in the following part.

2.1.1 Payments

Payment related services of a commercial bank are:

- offering customers **current (BE)** or **checking (AE) accounts** with **credit transfer/bank giro facilities** for transferring funds from one a/c to another.

- engaging in **standing order** (where a bank customer instructs his/her bank to make payments to a payee for fixed amounts such as hire purchase instalments or rent) and **direct debit** (where a bank customer authorizes a payee to withdraw money from the customer's a/c, normally used for transactions such as a telephone bill where the amount paid varies from month to month).

- issuing traveller's **cheques** and **foreign exchange.**

- distributing **notes and coins** for the Central Bank.

- providing **night safe** (for lodging cash, cheques, etc outside banking hours) and **strongroom facilities** for storing valuables.

- providing **Automated Teller Machine (ATM)** or **cash machines** and **bank statement** (statement of account) **dispensers** for plastic cards. **PIN** stands for personal identification number code, **PAC** for personal access code - both are required when using the above facilities.

- offering a range of **credit cards** (which give customers free credit for a period on purchases, but unless the a/c is cleared by the due date, high interest charges must be paid on the outstanding balance). Examples include Visa or Mastercard.

- offering other plastic **cards** with a variety of functions.

Examples of cards and their functions include:

a) *cheque card* (guaranteeing payment of a cheque to a prearranged limit)

b) *cash card* (ATM withdrawals and bank statement printouts)

c) *debit card* (used for purchases, e.g. in a store, where the amount is automatically taken from the holder's a/c)

d) *smart card* (computer chip facility allowing holder, for example, to 'load' card with units of money similar to a telephone card)

Usually all these functions are performed by one card which is often referred to as a **bank card**.

- providing **cheques**, which are unconditional orders in writing, drawn by a person on a **drawee** (bank or financial institution), signed by the **drawer** (person who writes or issues the cheque), requiring the bank or financial institution to pay on demand a certain sum in money to a **payee** (specified person or bearer).

A bank will **honour**, i.e. pay a cheque if the a/c has sufficient funds and if the cheque is drawn correctly.

An **open** cheque can be cashed, but a **crossed** cheque, which has two parallel lines (a crossing) drawn across its face, must be lodged onto the payee's a/c.

2.1.2 Savings, deposits, investments, etc

Services include:

- providing **savings** and **deposit** account facilities for customers
- offering **insurance** and **stockbroking facilities** for the buying and selling of securities
- engaging in **leasing**, e.g. with large car dealers.
- advising customers on **income tax**. This is, however, not currently permitted in Germany
- providing **advice** for retail (private) and corporate customers relating to investment, financial planning, etc.
- offering **trustee services** for the execution of wills, trustee administration of pension funds, charitable funds, trusts, etc.

2.1.3 Foreign Trade Transactions

Commercial banks fulfil the following needs for customers conducting foreign trade:

- engaging in foreign exchange transactions for customers including electronic money transmission payments, **letters of credit** (see Unit 12 on Foreign Trade), etc.

- providing **bill of exchange** (which is a written promise to pay the bearer a sum of money in the future) services, **foreign exchange forward contracts** (buying or selling currency at a fixed rate on a specified date in the future), **hedging contracts** (normally for the buying of commodities such as cotton, copper, etc at a fixed price for delivery in the future - used as a protection against losses caused by possible changes in price)

- granting **export credit finance** allowing customers to deal with ease on foreign markets

2.1.4 Credit Facilities

An important function of a bank is granting credits in the form of bank overdrafts, loans and mortgages (also known as home and property loans).

Types of Credits

- **Overdraft facilities** are designed to provide temporary working capital to firms and households with current accounts. The current account can be overdrawn to the credit limit set by the financial institution.

- **Term loans** are medium term with standard monthly repayments. Interest can be fixed or variable.

- **Mortgages** were originally given by building societies for the purchase of property or land but are also now granted by banks and other financial institutions.

Standard Procedure for Granting a Loan

When applying for a loan personal and financial details must be disclosed.

- **Business Plan**

  A business seeking a loan must normally prepare a **business plan** showing:
  - financial projections for coming year
  - projected profit and loss a/c plus balance sheets
  - projected cash flow
  - existing finance, i.e. funds or grants available
  - business projections, e.g. future production plans

- **Security**

  The borrower will usually be asked to provide **security (collateral AE)** which must be normally more valuable than the loan, stable in value, liquid and easily realisable, (easy for the bank to establish title to, i.e. possess or take control of).

  It can be a:

  Fixed charge security – where a *specific* asset is used to back the loan, e.g. premises

  Floating charge security – where *all* assets are used to support the loan, e.g. premises, machinery, land, stock, etc and the lender has priority on which assets should be sold to secure repayment if difficulties arise.

  Life Assurance policy

  Guarantee from shareholders – in the case of a company where its shareholders act as guarantor for the credit.

- **Other criteria**

  When granting a loan a financial institution will consider:
  - character of applicant(s)
  - capacity to repay
  - security
  - risk involved
  - time period
  - purpose of the loan

Customers are usually divided into three specific risk categories for lending purposes depending on creditworthiness, collateral and on the ability to pay

- **A.A.A.** – this is the 'best class' and includes government, incorporated companies, schools, local authorities, and charities. These pay the lowest rate of interest.
- **A.A.** – this includes manufacturing, construction and primary (agricultural) firms as well as direct services (distribution, tourism, etc.)
- **A.** – this is the 'worst class' and is for all other borrowers, e.g. personal loans (excluding house loans).

The rate of interest charged will depend on which category the applicant is in, the duration of the loan, the reason for the loan and the risk involved.

If there are difficulties after a loan has been granted the financial institution can terminate the loan and recall the money, revise the customer's credit rating or renegotiate the terms of the loan

APR is the annual percentage rate (of charge) and represents the annual amount of interest and administration charges or true cost of borrowing as charged on a loan

    a. Explain the services of the commercial banks.
    b. Differentiate between the different types of credits
    c. Explain the procedure for granting a loan.

2.2   Merchant Banks (Investment Banks - AE)

These are financial institutions which provide banking and financial services for the corporate customer with a very limited branch network. Examples include Internationale Handelsbank AG in Germany and Deutsche Morgan Grenfall and Rothschild's in London.

Main functions

The main functions of merchant banks are:

- to provide bridging finance and international loans
- involvement in mergers, takeover bids and rationalization of companies
- to manage investment portfolios on behalf of large investors

- to engage in leasing and Factoring i.e. the sale of a company's debts (accounts receivable) to a factoring firm (factor) which accepts the responsibility of debt collection and credit risk. A fee is charged by the factor.
- to provide advice and underwriting facilities (see glossary in Stock Exchange) for companies wishing to go public
- to offer expert service in transactions in foreign exchange
- to discount bills of exchange, i.e. pay the value of a bill of exchange less interest and administration charges.

2.3   Central Bank

The aim of a Central Bank is to safeguard the integrity of the national currency. Famous examples are the Federal Reserve (Fed) in the USA and the Bank of England in Europe.

Member states of the EU are involved in the European System of Central Banks (ESCB), which is composed of the European Central Bank (ECB) based in Frankfurt and the national central banks (NCBs) of all the member states. The Eurosystem is the term used to describe those states which have agreed to adopt the euro - those that have not adopted the euro have a special status, being allowed to conduct their respective national monetary policies, but are not allowed to participate in the decision-making process regarding single monetary policy for the euro zone.

A major difference to the USA is that the Federal Reserve deals with only one government, while the ECB is faced with a variety of national governments that all have their own fiscal policies, not to mention different cultures, languages and traditions. EU participation countries have agreed on a stability and growth pact that aims to keep fiscal policies in line.

The hopes of the ECB are that the euro will become one of the world's leading currencies, cut transaction costs and encourage cross-border mergers that will enable Europe to compete in the race for globalization. For the consumer it should mean that prices will be more transparent and end the necessity of changing money and paying transaction fees in the participating member states.

Functions of a central bank

The standard functions of central banks are the following:

1.   Lender of last resort

This means that the Central Bank is ready to lend to banks and other financial institutions in serious financial difficulties, especially when they are so big that their failure would have a devastating effect on the economy.

2.   **Banker to the government**

In many countries the Central Bank is responsible for implementing the government's monetary policy and keeping inflation under control through:

- open market operations (activities such as the buying and selling of government securities undertaken to influence the money supply; e.g. by selling securities the Central Bank takes in money, thereby reducing the money supply).

- adjusting the quantity of new notes being put into circulation

- imposing reserve requirements (where financial institutions have to keep a certain percentage of their liquid assets and also hold cash balances with the Central Bank).

- setting the **discount rate** (the percentage rate originally used to discount bills of exchange but nowadays used more to decrease or increase interest rates) as appropriate.

- issuing **treasury bills (T-bills)** which are bills of exchange issued on behalf of the government to pay for immediate expenses.

- administering the national debt.

3.   **Sole right to issue notes and mint coins**

4.   **Responsible for exchange controls,** i.e. restricting the availability of certain foreign currencies to importers.

5.   **Issuing trading licences** to financial institutions.

6.   **Supervision** of the financial institutions.

?
    a. What are merchant banks?
    b. What is the ECB?
    c. Explain the functions of a central bank.

3.0   INTERNATIONAL FINANCIAL INSTITUTIONS

International Monetary Funds (IMF)

This was founded in 1944 at the Bretton Woods Conference, which actually created two institutions - the International Monetary Funds (IMF) and the International Bank for Reconstruction and Development (World Bank).

This Washington based super-bank made up of 182 countries was set up to bring stability to international exchange rates and help countries experiencing balance of payments problems.

The functions of the IMF are as follows:

- To provide funds to enable countries to cope with their balance of payments deficits.
- To promote international monetary cooperation.
- To eliminate foreign exchange restrictions which hamper the growth of world trade.
- To achieve stable exchange rates.

International Bank for Reconstruction and Development (World Bank)

The International Bank for Reconstruction and Development (World Bank) was set up to encourage international investment in developing countries. Its main tasks are:

- To lend for productive purposes so that countries can expand their infrastructure and improve their capital base.
- To advise governments on financial matters in general, for example, on appraising possible investment opportunities.
- To raise standards of living in developing countries.

International Finance Corporation (IFC)
This is a subsidiary body of the World Bank to promote private enterprise and joint ventures in developing countries.

European Bank for Reconstruction and Development

This bank has been set up to provide loans for countries in Eastern Europe to help them achieve economic progress.

European Investment Bank (EIB)

The EU also has a European Investment Bank, a sort of merchant bank.

Its main functions are to:

- lend to backward regions in the EU.
- assist in infrastructural developments which are of common interest to EU members.

  a. *Differentiate between the IMF and the World Bank.*
   b. *What is the European Investment Bank?*

  ### Discussion Forum

   a. *Is the fact that German banks are shareholders in companies a positive or negative aspect?*
   b. *Bank profits should be taxed more. Discuss.*
   c. *The euro is the share price of the EU. Discuss.*
   d. *Debts from developing countries should be written off.*
   e. *Do banks have an overdue influence in the global economy?*

VOCABULARY

A	
(bank) account; a/c	Konto
account holder	Kontoinhaber
accounts receivable	Forderungen, Außenstände, Debitoren
to accrue	anlaufen, anfallen
accrued expenses	antizipative Passiva
acid test ratio	Verhältnis von flüssigen Mitteln zu kurzfristigen Verbindlichkeiten
administration	Verwaltung
administration charges	Kontoführungsgebühr, Verwaltungs-/ Bearbeitungsgebühr
APR (Annual Percentage Rate)	Effektivzins
asset	Vermögen; Aktiva
Automated Teller Machine (ATM),	Geldautomat
B	
bad debts	uneinbringliche Forderungen
balance	Kontostand; auch Bilanz, Saldo, (Rest)Betrag
bank giro	Bankgiro, Überweisungsauftrag (bargeldloser Zahlungsverkehr)
bankrupt	Bankrott

bearer	Inhaber
bill of exchange	Tratte, Wechsel
to borrow (money)	(Geld) leihen, borgen
bridging loan	Überbrückungskredit, Zwischenfinanzierung
building society (BE)	Bausparkasse
bulk-buying	Mengeneinkauf

C

capital goods	Investitionsgüter
to cater for	ausgerichtet sein auf, sich kümmern um,
to cash a cheque	einen Scheck einlösen
cash balances	Barguthaben
cash card	Geld(automaten)karte
charge card	Kunden(kredit)karte
charge, to charge	Gebühren, Gebühren erheben
charitable	Wohltätigkeits-, karitativ
checking account (AE)	Girokonto
cheque (BE), check (AE)	Scheck
circulation	Umlauf
to clear an account	Rechnung bezahlen, Konto ausgleichen
to clear, to pay off	tilgen
clearing house	Clearinghaus, Abrechnungsstelle
clearing system	Verrechnungssystem
clerical	klerikal, geistlich
commercial bank	Universalbank, Geschäftsbank
commercial paper	Handelspapier
compound interest	Zinseszins
credit facilities	Kreditmodalitäten
credit limit, credit line	Kreditrahmen, Kreditlinie
credit note	Gutschrift
credit rating	Kreditwürdigkeit, Bonität
to credit	gutschreiben
credit	Kredit; Haben
credit union	Kreditgenossenschaft
creditor	Gläubiger; Kreditor
crossed cheque (BE), for deposit only (AE)	Verrechnungsscheck
current account (BE),	Girokonto
current assets	Umlaufvermögen
current liabilities	laufende/kurzfristige Verbindlichkeiten
current ratio	Liquiditätskennzahl

D

debentures	Obligationen, Schuldverschreibung; Pfandbrief, Schuldschein (Br)
debit card	Kundenkarte (z.B. Euroscheckkarte)
debit note	Lastschrift
debit	Soll(saldo)
to debit	belasten
debt equity ratio	Verhältnis von Fremd- zu Eigenkapital
debt	Schulden
debtor	Schuldner
default interest, interest on arrears	Verzugszinsen
default	Verzug, Versäumnis, Nichtzahlung
deposit (account)	Einlagen(konto)
deposit	Anzahlung
depositor	Hinterleger, Deponent, Einleger
to descend from	abstammen von
development capital	Startkapital
direct debit	Bankeinzug
discount bill	Diskontwechsel
to discount	diskontieren
to draw	ausstellen
drawee	Bezogener
drawer	Aussteller
due	fällig

E

to engage	(sich) beteiligen (an)
to enhance	verstärken
equity	Eigenkapital, Anteils/ Aktienkapital
exceed	übersteigen
to exchange	austauschen
execution	Vollstreckung, Ausführung

F

factoring	Factoring
fee	Gebühr
finance company	Finanzierungsgesellschaft
fixed assets	Anlagevermögen
fixed charge	feststehend
fixed rate	fester Zinssatz, Festzins
floating charge	schwebend(es Sicherungsrecht)
floating rate, variable rate	variabler Zinssatz

foreign exchange transactions	Devisenhandel
forward contract	Terminkontrakt
G	
government securities	Staatspapiere, Staatsanleihen
to grant	gewähren
grant	Zuschuss, Subvention
H	
to hedge	sichern, Risiko eingrenzen
hedging	Hedging, Abschluss eines Sicherungsgeschäftes, Risikoeingrenzung
hire purchase	Ratenkauf, Teil-/ Abzahlungskauf
hire-purchase company	Kundenkreditbank, Teilzahlungsinstitut
to honour	einlösen, bezahlen (weil anerkannt)
I	
to implement	durchführen, realisieren, umsetzen
to impose	auferlegen
incorporated company	Aktiengesellschaft, rechtsfähige(Handels) Gesellschaft
instalment	Rate, Teilzahlung
insufficient funds (i.f.)	mangelnde Deckung
interest (no pl.)	Zins
interest free	zinslos
low/high interest loan	niedrig-/hochverzinsliches Darlehen
interest rate	Zinssatz
inventory	Inventar, Lager-/ Warenbestand
investment portfolio	Wertpapierbestand
to issue (with)	ausgeben, versehen (mit)
J	
joint stock bank	Aktienbank (Br)
L	
to lend (money)	(Geld) verleihen
lender of last resort	letzte Refinanzierungsinstanz
lender	Kreditgeber
lessee	Leasingnehmer, Mieter
lessor	Leasinggeber, Vermieter
life assurance	Lebensversicherung
loan	Darlehen

to lodge (money)	(Geld) deponieren, hinterlegen, einzahlen
M	
merchant bank	Merchant Bank
merge	Fusion
to mint	prägen
monastery	Kloster
mortgage	Hypothek
mutual savings bank	(genossenschaftsähnliche) Sparkasse
N	
national debt	Staatsschuld
(re)negotiate	(neu-/wieder-) verhandeln
O	
open cheque	Barscheck
open market operations	Offenmarktgeschäfte
outstanding	ausstehend, offenstehend
overdraft (facility)	Überziehung(skredit)
to overdraw	überziehen
overtrading	Liquiditätsklemme trotz hoher Rendite
to owe	schulden
P	
payee	Zahlungsempfänger
pension fund	Pensionsfonds
plough back	reinvestieren
possess	Besitz
premises	(Geschäfts)Grundstück, Gebäude
principal	Darlehens-/Kapitalsumme
to project	planen, prognostizieren
promissory note	Schuldschein, Schuldanerkenntnis; Eigenwechsel
property	Grundstück, Grundbesitz; Eigentum, Vermögen
R	
realisable	realisierbar, veräußerbar, flüssig zu machen
to remit a cheque	einen Scheck überweisen
to remit (money)	überweisen
remittance	Überweisung
to rent	mieten, pachten
to reschedule (debt)	neu terminieren; umschulden
retained profits/earnings	einbehaltene Gewinne/ Gewinnrücklagen

return on investment	Ertrag aus Kapitalanlagen, Kapitalrendite
to revise	ändern, revidieren
to run/get into debt	sich verschulden, Schulden machen
S	
to save (money)	(Geld) sparen
savings account	Sparkonto
savings bank	Sparkasse
savings	Spareinlagen
securities	Wertpapiere
security (BE), collateral (security) (AE)	Sicherheit, (zusätzliche)Sicherheit
seed	Saat
setting-up charges	(Konto)Einrichtungsgebühr
standing order (BE),	Dauerauftrag
statement of account, bank statement (dispenser)	Kontoauszug (Drucker)
statement	Nachweis, Aufstellung
stockbroking	Makler/Effektengeschäft
stopp (loss) order	Stopp-(Loss) Verfügung/Auftrag
strongroom	Tresorraum, Stahlkammer
subject to	unterworfen
sufficient funds	ausreichendes Guthaben, genügende Deckung
to supersede	ablösen, überholen
surplus	Überschuss, überschüssig
T	
to take out a loan/mortgage	ein Darlehen/eine Hypothek aufnehmen
takeover bid	Übernahmeangebot
tax	Steuer
term deposit (BE),	Termineinlage, Festgeld
term loan	mittelfristiger Kredit
to terminate	beenden, kündigen
title	Eigentumsrecht
trade credit	Warenkredit
trading license	Gewerbeerlaubnis
to transfer	überweisen
treasury bills	Schatzwechsel
trust	Treuhandvermögen
trustee	Treuhänder, Vermögensverwalter
U	
underwriting facilities	agieren als Garant einer Effektenemission

unique	einzigartig
unless	wenn nicht
usury	Wucher(zinsen)
V	
vault	Tresor
venture capital	Risikokapital
W	
will	Testament
to withdraw (money)	(Geld) abheben; einziehen, zurückziehen
withdrawal	Abhebung, Entzug, Rückzug
working capital	Betriebskapital

HAPPINESS IS JUST ROUND THE CORNER - MARKETING & ADVERTISING

> *The definition of 'waste': A busload of marketing experts plunging over a cliff with seven of the seats unoccupied.*
>
> Con Cullen

FOCUS This unit looks at standard marketing activities and includes an extended section on advertising.

> *Marketing is trying to figure out what people want so you can give it to them.*
>
> Shelley Lazarus

1.0 INTRODUCTION TO MARKETING

A **market** is a group of persons that is willing to purchase products and has the ability to pay for them.

Marketing can be defined as the process by which the demand for goods and services is anticipated and satisfied, through the conception, production, distribution and sale of goods and services.

This definition covers all aspects of business from the initial idea stage of a new product or service to its final sale to the public. That is why we say that marketing is concerned with the *whole* business of selling goods or services.

2.0 HISTORY OF MARKETING

Every business or organization has its market, which can be anything from a limited market to a mass market. In the past, different approaches were formulated regarding existing and potential customers. Developments in the last hundred years have, however, changed the world dramatically leading to mass consumerism and huge surpluses in the quantities of products available. The different orientations explained below still exist, although the sales and marketing approaches are now dominant.

2.1 Production Orientation

Here the organization concentrates on production efficiency, distribution and costs. Sellers in earlier times realized that consumers would buy almost any goods produced. This situation is referred to as a seller's market, which of course, is fine when demand exceeds supply and where the cheap price encourages people to buy. A classic example was Henry Ford's mass-produced Model T car.

2.2 Product Orientation – A Good Product will Sell Itself

In this case the organization stands or falls by the quality, performance and innovative features of its products. The influence of other factors such as packaging and pricing are often not sufficiently considered, nor are the activities of competitors or the desires of customers. The reasoning behind this approach is that the supplier of the products knows best what the consumer needs and believes the products they produce are the best on the market. It follows that each improvement will generate more sales. This orientation was prevalent up to the 1920s when products seemed to sell themselves. The Great Depression changed all that and suppliers were forced to adopt a sales or selling approach.

2.3 Selling Orientation

The starting point here is an existing product which people, due to overcapacity in the market, will not buy unless they are persuaded to purchase through the use of energetic and creative advertising and sales approaches.

The belief is that the right advertising message will encourage consumers to buy so the focus is more on the skills of selling than on the needs of the buyer. Profit is ultimately achieved through sales volume. Examples include the selling of encyclopedias.

2.4 Marketing Orientation - The Customer is King

A marketing-oriented organization is one which focuses on the needs of its customers. Its primary concern is to find out what its customers' needs and wants are in order to meet them with the highest level of customer satisfaction.

In the marketing orientation scenario production responds to the demands of marketing rather than the other way around, i.e. profit is achieved through customer satisfaction.

The marketing concept is actually a way of thinking as much as anything else. It is a philosophy that puts customers at the centre of the organization's activities – *the customer is king*. The marketer needs to be aware of products in terms of the market and the position of the product in relation to other products.

The marketing orientation concept emerged in the 1950s. The most outstanding example was McDonald's, followed by Disney and Wal-Mart.

2.5   Societal Marketing Orientation

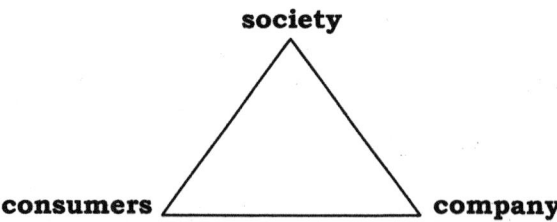

A new concept is the societal marketing or relationship orientation, first discussed in the 1990s. In addition to focusing on consumer satisfaction and company profits, it considers the long term effects on society and consumers' welfare. This is particularly important in an age of worldwide environmental and economic problems, population growth and shortage of resources.

Examples here are the avoidance of excessive packaging, the use of environmentally friendly materials (even when higher prices are charged) and the emphasis on business ethics. This orientation is also a result of the growing conviction of businesses, consumers and authorities that suppliers should take responsibility for the effects of their products on society. Good examples are Johnson & Johnson (an American health care products company) and Anita Roddick (The Body Shop) admired for their community and environmental responsibility.

 Explain and differentiate between the various orientations.

3.0   MARKET RESEARCH

Market Research (MR) is the collecting, recording, detailed examination and analysis of all the data dealing with what the customer requires and his/her behavior. It is widely used by firms with marketing and societal marketing orientation. It involves finding out what the consumer requires through research and is necessary in the following situations:

- If a new product is being launched.
- If an old product's sales are declining.
- To examine a competitor's product range and market share.
- If price changes are being contemplated.
- If a new advertising campaign has just started.

- To examine a firm's brand share, which tells a firm how well its products are selling compared to competitors.

Large firms will often have their own research departments to undertake the necessary activities. Those firms with no specialized marketing department will employ the services of a market research agency (bureau) to research and advise their clients.

Through the market research process we learn how big the market is and where it is. MR indicates the present market situation, the competitive forces and future trends.

Consumer Behaviour (Motivational) Research sets out to discover the motives behind consumers' purchasing of particular goods or services.

There are many **costs** involved in undertaking market research: preparation costs, general administrative costs, fieldwork costs such as labour and monitoring plus the costs of analyzing the data.

The **data** collected from market research can be:

- **Quantitative**, i.e. in the form of facts and figures.
- **Qualitative**, i.e. in the form of opinions and buying motives.

The **steps in MR** are to:

- collect data or information
- collate, i.e. check it
- analyze the results and make decisions on the basis of the data

The **response rate** refers to the number of people who agree to answer the questions. Normally a **questionnaire** is used.

3.1   Tools of Market Research

The main tools of market research are the following:

Desk Research

This involves investigating without ever moving from the office desk. It means looking through the firm's sales figures, sales reports, reading the trade press (i.e. magazines and journals concerned with the particular area of business).

Field Research

Field research involves:

- **Postal Interviews** - This is the sending of questionnaires by post (*mail* in American English).
- **Telephone Interviews**
- **Observation** - Firms often test new food products, for instance, by asking people to taste them and comment. This small-scale testing of a new product is often referred to as **Test Marketing**.
- **Personal Interviews** - Face-to-face interviews using a questionnaire.
- **Consumer Panels** - This involves selecting a group of consumers who list all their purchases within a certain time period. This information is then sold by MR agencies to companies who use it to change things such as their product range or selling techniques.

3.2 Types of Data

There are two types of data:

- **Primary data** is data collected for *specific* research purposes such as the possible launch of a new product. It is collected using questionnaires and interviews.

- **Secondary data** refers to all other information available to researchers engaged in a specific project which they have *not collected directly themselves*. It is quick and inexpensive to collect and includes information from government statistics, syndicated data agencies (agencies that collect statistics and sell it on, e.g. A.C. Nielsen), consumer panels, retail audits (information from retailers), the Internet and desk research. It is often referred to as **off-the-peg research** because of its immediate availability.

3.3 Sampling

This is where a certain section of the market is picked as a representative of the entire market (referred to as the **universe** in MR terms). The following represent the main sampling methods:

- **Random Sampling**

Each member of the population has an equal chance of being chosen to answer the questions. The accuracy and reliability of this method will depend on the size of the sample in relation to the size of the market share under consideration.

- **Stratified Random Sampling**

This is probability sampling in which the total population is divided into sub groups depending on income groups, age levels, etc and a random sample is chosen from each subgroup.

- **Judgement Sampling**

The researcher uses his/her judgement to select respondents who believe in their own judgement and represent good prospects for accurate information.

- **Quota Sampling**

A sampling technique where interviewers look for respondents who are chosen according to their age, sex, class, etc. in the same proportion as that which exists in the population as a whole.

- **Cluster Sampling**

This is the random selection of a cluster or group of respondents rather than individuals. An example is area sampling where an area is selected and then a random selection is initiated.

   a. Why is MR necessary?
   b.   What is desk research?
   c.   Differentiate between primary and secondary data.
   d. Explain how MR works.

4.0   MARKET SEGMENTATION

This involves identifying the potential buyers of a firm's products and the reasons for their desire to purchase. The objective is to make homogenous groups, which are made up of consumers who are alike. There are different *methods of segmentation:*

- **Demographic Factors**

These refer to the age, sex, family size, marital status, race, religion, income, occupation and education of a population. The family life cycle is especially used to predict spending power and consumption. Ever changing social mores make demographic factors increasingly complex.

Socio-economic classifications are often used as they help to classify people according to the occupation of the household.

Group	Social Status and Occupations
A	Upper Middle Class - higher managerial, administrative or professional
B	Middle Class - intermediate managerial, administrative or professional
C1	Lower Middle Class - supervisory or clerical, junior managerial, administrative or professional
C2	Skilled Working Class - skilled manual workers
D	Working Class - semi-skilled or unskilled manual workers
E	Pensioners, Students, Unemployed - lowest level of subsistence including state pensioners or widows, casual or low grade workers.

- **Geography**

This is connected with the world region or country the consumers come from, whether they live in an urban, suburban or rural environment, and, of course, the climate, e.g. people living in Barbados don't need Siberian-style winter clothing.

- **Behaviour**

This refers to consumer behaviour for products for occasions such as Christmas, birthdays, etc.

Other important factors are the benefits derived for the consumer, the usage rate, loyalty status and the consumer's attitude towards the product.

Lifestyles (Psychographics) are also important because people have different attitudes, habits and possessions. Some individuals might prefer to spend their money on travel while others might buy cars or antiques.

- **Culture**

Some companies operate more and more internationally - the influence of culture must be kept firmly in mind. **International (global) marketing** focuses on the needs of buyers around the globe, including consumers, producers, governments, etc knowing that each market type has special characteristics that require careful study on the part of the seller.

5.0   TARGETING

This step involves finding the appropriate target for an organization's products.

A **target market** can be defined as a group of people who have in common a need or desire for a particular product.

Target marketing is the process in which a firm evaluates a number of market segments, decides which one or ones to serve and develops and implements an appropriate marketing mix for the targeted segments.

After a segment has been defined and targeted the next step is **positioning.** This involves using the marketing mix (see below) to present the products so as to make them unique and attractive to consumers.

Product features, brand names, packaging, price and place are crucial in positioning the product in the appropriate segment or niche within the competitive market.

 Why and how are markets divided into segments?

6.0 THE MARKETING MIX - THE 5 Ps OF MARKETING

A clear **marketing strategy** will consider five key elements. Together they are referred to as the **marketing mix**. These are:

- Product
- Price
- Promotion
- Place
- Packaging (sometimes put together with Product)

Let us examine the *Five Ps.*

6.1 Product

The word **product** refers to goods and services.

Goods

Goods can be either consumer goods or industrial goods (raw materials, factory equipment, etc).

Goods can be further classified into:

- ***convenience goods*** – everyday simple, low cost goods, e.g. toothpaste

- ***shopping goods*** - more expensive goods where it pays to shop around, e.g. computers

- *speciality goods* – special goods with unique characteristics, e.g. crystal, hand-made watches and other luxury goods.

They can be considered on **three levels**.

- The first is the *core function* a product provides, e.g. a refrigerator provides the means to keep food and drink cold.

- The second level is *tangible product* which refers to the features a product may have, e.g. a TV can have superb digital sound quality or high definition colour.

- *Augmented product* or the third level refers to additional services and benefits that are connected with the product, e.g. guarantees and after-sales service.

Services

A service is an *intangible product* that satisfies the needs of consumers or business users. In *service marketing* the organization must demonstrate a commitment to making a happy customer by paying attention to every detail, such as excellent service in a restaurant.

Product mix

The product mix consists of all the product lines and items sold by the firm. A **product line** could be, for example, cosmetics – the **sublines** could be lipstick, face powder, etc.

6.1.1 The Product Life Cycle

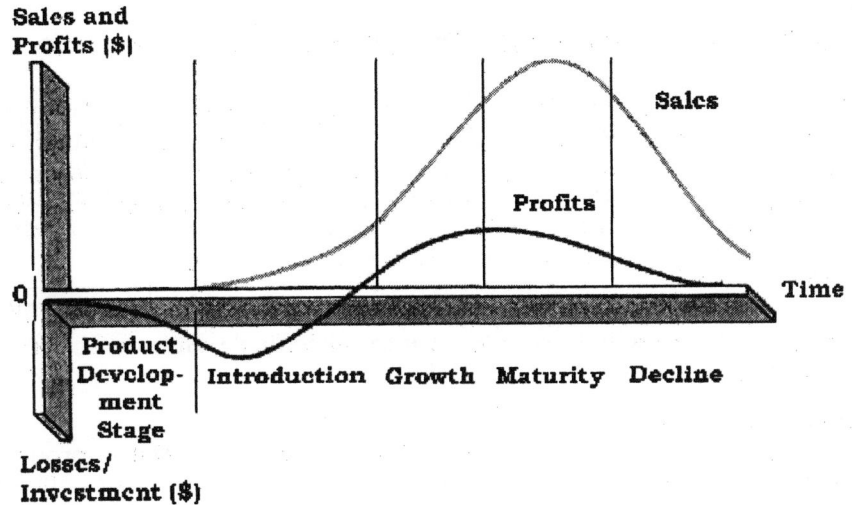

Diagram Source: *Peter Doyle, "The Realities of the Product Life Cycle.(Quarterly Review of Marketing).*

A **product life cycle (PLC)** refers to the various steps products go through including their market share and profits. It can be represented by curves illustrating the various phases. (see above)

The **introduction** is the first main phase after the **product development stage**. A newly launched product is unlikely to be profitable and will require support from other profitable products in the firm.

This is followed by **growth** when more consumers begin to buy the product. Higher production volume results in **economies of scale** (the reduction of unit cost and increase in profit obtained when goods are produced in large quantities) but profits may still be small. More marketing is needed to increase consumption and to defend the product from rival products, which may be already entering or about to enter the market.

Maturity is where competitors are beginning to make their presence felt. Some experts refer to the end part of this stage, where everyone has the product and price may have to fall, as **saturation**.

Next is the **decline** phase where sales are falling back. The product may be able to survive and generate some profit - without or with a minimum of marketing. This is referred to as **product harvesting**.

It should be noted that branded products such as Coca Cola have a very long, sometimes even unending life cycle.

6.1.2 The Boston Consulting Group (BCG) Matrix

The **BCG Matrix** is a marketing tool normally used to evaluate the profitability of businesses as well as of products. It consists of a square divided into four quadrants, which describe markets and the firm's share of these markets. Terms associated with this matrix include:

Stars
These are products with high growth and high market share. They are often on the way to becoming market leaders. Stars will become cash cows.

Question Marks
These represent low share with high growth potential – products situated here will become stars or dogs.

Cash Cows
This quadrant segment stands for low growth with high market share. This is a very profitable quadrant and brings in a steady income to finance the question mark or star quadrants of the market.

Dogs
These mean low share with low growth. They need to be got rid of.

Strategic Business Unit (SBU)

A product or product line is often referred to as a **Strategic Business Unit (SBU)**. A SBU is simply a unit of the business. It can be, as mentioned above, a product or product line within a division, or a brand; it can even be a company division, and the activities of each can be planned independently from the rest of the company activities.

Each SBU is indicated by a dot on the BCG Matrix. Note that the size of the dot corresponds to how much money the unit of business brings in for the organization. As time passes SBUs change their position in the BCG Matrix according to the stage in their life cycle.

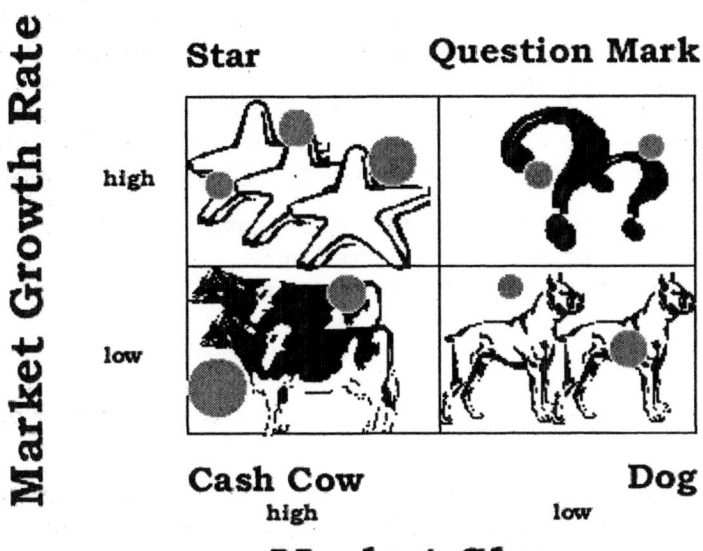

Market Growth Rate (vertical axis, with **high** and **low**)

Star   **Question Mark**

Cash Cow   **Dog**
high   low

Market Share

The 9 dots in the matrix above represent the 9 current SBUs in Company X. It has 3 stars, 2 question marks, 2 cash cows and 2 dogs. The company is performing well.

6.1.3 Brands

> *If anyone can build a brand it is the customer. The marketer can only create favourable conditions for a brand image to develop in the customer's mind.*
>
> *Christian Grönross*

A **brand** can be defined as a name, term, symbol, design or some combination of these that identifies a firm's products and sets them apart from the competitors' products.

Brand names support advertising, convey an image, help sales and stimulate loyalty. Examples of brand names are Mercedes-Benz and Microsoft.

A **brand mark** refers to a symbol or design, e.g. the Mercedes Star logo.

Branded goods bear a copyright registered name which is legally protected for exclusive use by its owner and is referred to as a **trademark.**

A **USP** refers to **Unique Selling Proposition** and must normally be developed if a brand is to sell. This involves picking one or more unique attributes such as 'lowest price' or 'most advanced model' which have the maximum impact on the potential buyer. If the product is similar or the same as those of the competitors, a **Unique Advertising Proposition** can be employed. This attempts to compensate for the absence of any unique attributes by using psychological effects (see Persuasive Advertising, Section 6.3.1 B).

   a. *Explain how the product life cycle works.*
   b. *What are brands characterized by?*
   c. *What is the BCG Matrix and how does it work?*

6.2   Price

The importance of the **price** will depend on the competition and also the market the product is aimed at.

Pricing policy is crucial. Prices of course must cover costs, match those of the competitors(s), be acceptable to consumers and take account of taxes. Prices fall into three broad groups:

A.   Competition Oriented Pricing

This involves:

- *discount pricing.*
- *loss-leaders* - e.g. supermarkets sell certain products below the normal price in order to entice people into the store.
- follow-*my-leader pricing* - i.e. pricing based on what competitors are charging.

B.   Demand Oriented Pricing

This includes:

- *skim pricing* or *creaming* - charging a high price when a new product enters the market.
- *penetration pricing* - charging low prices on entry to the market in order to *achieve* high market share and prohibit other entrants.
- *price-quality pricing* - charging prices as in relation to the quality, e.g. high prices for luxury goods such as perfume.
- *psychological pricing* - selling products at uneven amounts, e.g. $1.99 instead of $2.00.

C.   Cost Oriented Pricing

This is where all costs associated with offering a product on the market, such as production, transport, marketing, etc, are added to the **mark-up**, i.e. that amount which is added onto the cost price to give the seller a profit. The cost-oriented pricing approach covers any unexpected or overlooked expense and helps guarantee a profit.

   a. How can prices be fixed?
b. Explain mark-up.

6.3   Promotion

Promotion creates consumer *awareness*, provides *information* to arouse interest, produces *desire* and leads to consumer *action*, i.e. the purchase. Therefore, this consumer decision process is referred to as AIDA.

Promotion involves communicating with customers using

- **Advertising**

- **Sales Promotion**

- **Public Relations**

- **Direct Marketing** (see section on Place)

- **Personal Selling**

Corporate identity, **sponsorship** and **product placement** are also increasingly important forms of promotion.

Corporate identity is the way in which a company projects itself to the world and is formed by everything including the company name and logo, advertising, corporate literature, business cards, presentations and website(s).

Sponsorship can be defined as monetary assistance provided for sports, education, research, arts, or other cultural events by an individual or organization with the object of advertising or gaining public approval.

Product Placement, which involves, for example, placing products in movies like well-known sports cars in James Bond movies is a special category of advertising.

6.3.1 Advertising

> In our factory, we make lipstick. In our advertising we sell hope.
> Charles Revson

Advertising can be defined as paid media exposure involving the communication of information about a good or service to its market, usually in a persuasive manner, using various media formats.

It consistently tries to appeal to certain motives including the desire for an easier life, ambition, success, romance and hero worship.

A. The Functions of Advertising

The main functions of advertising are to:

- increase sales of new and existing products in order to keep or increase market share
- differentiate a company's product from the competitors' products
- inform
- sell a brand name
- improve the public image of an organization and its products

B. Types of Advertising

There are six main types of advertising. They are:

- **Informative Advertising** – which is merely a statement of fact, informing the general public that a particular product is available, its uses, advantages, price and quality. It is also used to educate and inform people, e.g. a government Department of Health *Don't Drink and Drive Campaign.*

- **Persuasive Advertising** – does not necessarily inform people about the product, it often only uses psychological or manipulative techniques to persuade people to buy – by appealing to peoples' emotions, attempting to portray a certain image, etc. This is the most common type of advertising and is used in its purest form for products such as perfume, alcohol and tobacco.

- **Competitive (Comparative) Advertising** – where one organization compares its brand or company to another, citing its superior features and/or the negative features of the competitor or its products. It is often very subjective and can be misleading and distasteful. This type is common in the USA, less so in Europe. A classic example is Visa bashing American Express - *Bring your Visa card. Because they don't take American Express.*

- **Generic Advertising** – means that all the producers of a single industry come together to promote their products in general and not a particular brand or company, e.g. the beef industry in the UK with *Eat British Beef!*

- **Reminder Advertising** – which is used to inform consumers that a product is still available on the market or to keep it in customers' minds during off-seasons, as in the case of Mon Chéri.

- **Reinforcement Advertising** – is used to assure existing customers that they have chosen wisely – often used when new competitors are appearing.

Two other types of advertising worth mentioning are:

- **Global Advertising** – involves advertising world brands using the same advertising materials and commercials worldwide, e.g. Pepsi.

- **Subliminal Advertising** – an advertising approach where, for example, a message is flashed on the screen so quickly that the audience does not consciously see it – but consciously responds. An example used in the United States involved flashing phrases like *Eat ice-cream* on a cinema screen.

C.   The Choice of Advertising Media

The medium used by the advertising manager of the advertising department or the advertising agency will depend on the cost, budget available, product involved, target group and income level of the consumer.

Many firms employ an advertisement agency which will appoint an account executive to take charge of a particular firm's account and get the copywriters and visualizers to create the ad or advertising campaign. This also involves drawing up a media plan to ensure maximum exposure and monitoring results. These agencies also undertake market research.

A wide choice of advertising media is available. These include:

- Internet
- TV and radio (international, national and local)

- newspapers (international, national and local)
- cinema
- exhibitions and trade fairs
- street hoardings (AE billboards), neon signs, posters
- magazines and trade journals
- catalogues and brochures
- window display
- wrapping paper

D. Advantages and Disadvantages of Advertising

Advertising is regarded very critically by some people. The following provides an overview of the benefits and problems connected with advertising.

Advantages and Disadvantages of Advertising for the General Public

• Informs the public about the availability of products	• Can be misleading and wasteful
• Increases employment directly (in the advertising industry) and indirectly (through increasing demand in the economy)	• Can stimulate habits and motives which can be questionable from a social viewpoint, e.g. tobacco, alcohol, greed, etc.
• Keeps the costs of printed media, such as newspapers and magazines, down	• Presents overly positive messages while neglecting potential dangers or side-effects of products
• Promotes innovation	
• Encourages competition	• Can be environmentally negative through the waste of scarce resources
• Makes the environment a more colourful place.	
• Makes free private TV channels possible	• Consumers carry the cost of advertising in most cases
• Allows the free use of Internet services	• Encourages consumers to buy products that are often unnecessary
	• Increasingly the use of violence, crude images, etc is employed
	• Evidence in the UK that it increases the crime rate in order for poorer sections of the community to afford advertised products

Advantages and Disadvantages of Advertising for Firms

- Effective advertising increases sales and profits
- Provides revenue for newspapers, magazines, radio and TV
- Provides relevant information about products and product changes or developments
- Necessary for launching new products

- Difficult to rate effectiveness accurately
- Difficult to attract consumers attention due to resistance caused by over-saturation of advertising and an increasingly advertising-literate consumer who is sophisticated in what s(he) sees, reads, and listens to.
- Firms are very often forced to allocate a substantial part of the budget to advertising due to market competitive-ness

a. *What are the most common types of advertising?*
b. *Explain the pros and cons of advertising for a firm and for the general public.*
c. *Describe the work of an advertising agency.*

Discussion Forum

Describe one of your favorite TV commercials/spots/ads. Why is it so effective?

6.3.2 Other Types of Promotion

A.   Sales Promotion

Sales promotion is a form of indirect advertising (known as *below-the-line)* compared to normal or direct advertising (known as *above-the-line)* using short term incentives to encourage the purchase of products or to initiate a product relaunch.

It emphazises a 'buy now' approach. The seller attempts to attract and reward - the focus being to build a long term market share or to increase short term sales. Sales promotion consists of *consumer promotion* and *trade sales promotion.*

Examples of **Consumer Promotion** (for *consumers*) are:

-    free samples, e.g. free shampoo samples in your mailbox

- price reductions marked directly by the producer on the label or package
- competitions
- free gifts, e.g. free calculator if you take out a subscription to a magazine.
- trading stamps
- coupons

Trade Sales Promotion (for *store owners*, etc) includes:

- trade discounts offered by producer/wholesalers to retailers
- rack jobbing i.e. where a wholesaler assumes responsibility for a particular section of a retail store (delivers goods, installs display and maintains inventory).

In sales promotion, as in other types of promotion, the producer can use a ***push strategy*** which involves pushing the products through the channel members (producer, wholesaler, retailer) to the final consumers.

Alternatively a ***pull strategy*** is directed at generating consumer demand which pulls or forces the channel members to stock the products.

     a. How is sales promotion different from advertising?
            b. Differentiate between consumer and trade sales promotion.

B.   Public Relations

Public Relations (PR) involves building good relations and presenting an acceptable company image to the general public including (potential) customers, investors, suppliers, politicians, etc. It has a strong impact on public awareness at a much lower cost (unpaid media exposure!) than advertising.

Some organizations have their own public relations department, headed by a **public relations officer (PRO)** while others employ the services of outside specialist agencies.

Methods used to secure favourable comment include:

- press releases for journalists concerning the organization's activities and developments
- press conferences to announce forthcoming events or products
- stands and displays at trade fairs and conferences
- lobbying, i.e. building and maintaining good relationships with government and local community officials
- taking part in public events

C.   Direct Marketing

Direct Marketing is promotion in the form of in-home retailing mainly through telephone selling (telemarketing), direct mail and mail-order catalogues. The catalyst for it is computer technology, which can gather and manipulate vast amounts of personal data. Cruder earlier forms involved only junk mail and **cold calls**, i.e. telephoning someone you have never met in order to sell a product. (see also E-commerce in Section 6.4)

D.   Personal Selling

Personal Selling is face-to-face selling by salespeople, sales representatives, agents, etc. and is undertaken mainly in industrial markets for products such as machines or aircraft rather than in consumer or mass markets. It is the most expensive form of promotion.

a. Why is PR so important?.
b. Differentiate between direct marketing and personal selling.

6.4   Place

This refers to the ways to be used to distribute and sell the product. Place is broken into two distinct parts. These are:

A.   Distribution Mix (Channels of Distribution)

A firm may sell its goods in a variety of ways:

- **Wholesaling**: This represents the traditional producer to wholesaler to retailer to consumer channel of distribution.
- **Producer (Direct) to Consumer**: This is selling from the producer to the consumer via the producer's <u>factory</u> or from the producer's <u>outlets</u>. *(cf Direct Marketing)*
- **Retailing**: This chain is from the producer to the retailer to the consumer
- **Mail Order**: This is from the producer to the Post Office or a forwarding agent to the consumer

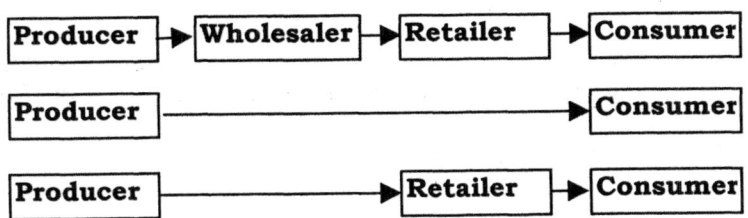

More modern channels of distribution include:

- **Direct Selling/Marketing**: This is from the producer to the consumer using direct communication with targeted customers consisting of <u>direct mail</u>, <u>catalogues</u> and <u>telemarketing</u>. Note that direct marketing (often referred to as Direct Selling) is a method of <u>promotion</u> (see Section 6.3.4.) as well as a channel of distribution.

- **E-commerce**: This is from the producer via the Internet to the consumer or from the retailer to the consumer via the Internet. Today the **Internet** is helping to create vast new possibilities in expanding marketing's traditional boundaries. It is being used to link the employees of the organization, send sales information and other data more quickly, build closer relationships with customers and the general public and sell and distribute products more efficiently and effectively.

- **Franchising**: A **franchise** is a concession given by the owner of patented products, the **franchisor**, for their use to the **franchisee** in return for a fee. Examples include McDonald's, Benetton and Body Shop International.

- **Licensing**: An easy way for a producer to enter a foreign market is by contracting with the **licensee** who gets the right to use a manufacturing process, trademark, patent, etc. for a fee or royalty. Examples include the right to manufacture Coca-Cola, Budweiser and Marlboro products.

Point of Sale

The final **point of sale** is very important. Most sales occur through large retailers, e.g. supermarkets, hypermarkets, department stores and discount stores. Some marketing strategies for luxury products dictate, however, the logic of selling in restricted outlets, such as exclusive boutiques.

B.   Physical Distribution (Marketing Logistics)

Physical Distribution or **Marketing Logistics**, as it is sometimes referred to, is concerned with planning, order processing, warehousing, transport, packaging of products, stock/inventory levels and customer service.

    a. Differentiate between the traditional Producer (Direct) to Consumer and the more modern Direct Marketing channels of distribution.

    b. Explain what franchising is.

6.5. Packaging

This refers to the presentation of goods and includes those activities connected with designing and producing a product's cover or wrapper to ensure product safety and to make it look attractive. It is sometimes included under the *product* element of the marketing mix.

Packaging not only protects products but it also advertises them by identifying brands. It actually takes over the function of the salesperson – in that it provides the information the customer seeks. Of course, packaging is also controversial because environmental activists claim that it has become excessive.

   Why is packaging so important?

7.0. THE MARKETING PLAN

This is a blueprint of the marketing strategy or strategies that help the business achieve its overall strategic objectives. It contains the following:

- **Corporate Mission Statement** - which is a statement of where the organization is heading and what it aims to achieve - it should be idealistic but also realistic. The following example is from Czech Oil Refineries whose mission is to:

  Refine crude oil into valuable products and sell them on a profitable basis creating benefits for customers, shareholders, employees and the community.

- **Corporate Objectives** – these are developed from the company's mission and could focus on the range of products to be produced including new products or the organization's productivity, profitability, cost reduction measures, social responsibilities, human resources, management/leadership structure, etc.

- **Marketing Objectives and Strategies** – seek to identify and develop a strategy on *how* the organization can achieve the objectives decided upon, e.g. to produce new sports cars for the luxury car market, or to become market leader, or to concentrate on the low-price market for washing machines. It is important to have developed a set of alternative plans in case things go wrong.

- **Current Marketing Situation** – which describes the market the business is in, its products, the competition, predictions about the future, etc. The process in collecting this information is referred to as a *marketing audit*.

- **SWOT Analysis** – which shows the position of the business and its products in the market. It focuses on:

    1. the *internal factors*, i.e. <u>strengths</u> (e.g. new product range, good management) and <u>weaknesses</u> (e.g. personnel shortages, high Research & Development costs)

    2. the external *factors*, i.e. the <u>opportunities</u> (e.g. new markets in China, little competition) and <u>threats</u> (e.g. higher oil prices, new government taxes, recession)

- **Controls** - the progress or non-progress of the marketing plan needs to be monitored carefully. Normally a new plan needs to be developed every twelve months.

? *Explain the most important components of a marketing plan.*

Discussion Forum

  a. *What does the marketing strategy of an enterprise depend on?*
  b. *Marketing and ethics are irreconcilable. Discuss.*
  c. *Marketing - A creative art or a science? Discuss.*
  d. *If you wanted to determine the feasibility of starting a coffee and snack shop at your college, what sources of information and approach would you use?*
  e. *How would you address the criticism that marketing and advertising make people buy products which they don't really need?*

VOCABULARY

A	
account executive	Sachbearbeiter eines Werbeetats; Kundenbetreuer
to acquire	erwerben
advertisement	(Werbe)Anzeige; Werbung
advertising	Werbebranche, Werbung
advertising expenditure/costs	Werbeausgaben
to afford	sich leisten
affordability	Erschwinglichkeit
after-sales service	Kundendienst
alike	gleich, sehr ähnlich
to allocate	zuweisen, zuteilen

to anticipate	vorhersehen, voraussagen
to appeal (to sb)	(jemanden) ansprechen, anziehen
approach	Verfahren, Methode, Herangehen
appropriate	passend, geeignet
approval	Zustimmung
assumption	Annahme, Voraussetzung
to augment	vergrößern, erweitern
to avoid	vermeiden
B	
bargain	Sonderangebot, 'Schnäppchen'
to bash	hauen, schlagen, prügeln
behaviour	Verhalten
benefit, to benefit (from)	Nutzen, Nutzen ziehen aus
blend	Mischung
brand	Marke
branding	(Marken)Kennzeichnung
C	
casual worker	Gelegenheitsarbeiter
cluster sampling	Clusterauswahl, Stichprobenverfahren mit Klumpenauswahl
to collate	vergleichen, kollationieren
commercial	Werbespot
commercial break	Werbeunterbrechung
common	gemeinsam
comparative advertising	vergleichende Werbung
to compete against/with	konkurrieren
competition	Wettbewerb, Konkurrenz; Preisausschreiben
competitive/-ness	konkurrenzfähig, Konkurrenzfähigkeit
conception	Idee; Plan(ung), Konzipierung
consciously	bewusst
consultancy	Beratungsfirma
consumer panel	Verbraucherpanel, -runde, -gremium
to contemplate	in Erwägung ziehen, betrachten
convenience goods	Waren des täglichen Bedarfs
to convey (a message)	(eine Botschaft) vermitteln
conviction	Überzeugung
copywriter	Werbetexter
'creaming'	Elitepreisbildung
crucial	entscheidend, äußerst wichtig
crude	roh, grob

current	aktuell
D	
decline, to decline	Rückgang, zurückgehen, sinken
desire	Wunsch
desk research	Schreibtischforschung
distribution	Vertrieb
E	
to encourage	fördern, anregen, ermutigen
endorsement	Unterstützung, Billigung
to entice	locken, verleiten
to evolve	sich entwickeln
excessive	übermäßig
F	
field work	Außendienst
to flash	aufblinken
forthcoming	bevorstehend
G	
(free) gift	(Werbe) Geschenk
generic advertising	Gemeinschaftswerbung
give-away price	Schleuderpreis
goal	Ziel
H	
habit	Gewohnheit
hoarding (BE), billboard (AE)	Reklametafel, Plakatwand
I	
in terms of	in Bezug auf, hinsichtlich
incentive	Anreiz
informative advertising	Informative Werbung, Social Spot
J	
judgement sample	subjektiv ausgewählte Stichprob
L	
to launch (a product, a campaign	herausbringen, auf den Markt bringen, starten
leaflet	Werbezettel
loss leader	Lockangebot
M	
mail shot	Briefwerbeaktion
market research/survey	Marktforschung
marketing audit	Marketinganalyse
mark-up pricing	Vollkostenkalkulation
to match	entsprechen
maturity	Reife
merchandise	Ware
more	Sittenkodex

N	
niche	Nische
O	
objective	Ziel
off-the-peg	Konfektions-, konfektioniert
opinion poll	Meinungsumfrage
opportunity	Gelegenheit, Möglichkeit
P	
packaging; to package	Verpackung, verpacken
to penetrate a market	sich auf einem Markt durchsetze
penetration pricing	Penetrationspreispolitik
personal selling	Direktverkauf
to persuade	überzeugen
persuasive advertising	Suggestiv-, Überzeugungswerbung
to plunge	stürzen
point-of-sale	Verkaufspunkt, Verkaufsort, POS
possession	Besitz, Eigentum
precipice	Abgrund
press release	Presseverlautbarung. Pressemitteilung
price plateau	Preisniveau
pricing	Preisgestaltung
product harvesting	Produkt'ernte'
to prohibit	verhindern, verbieten
promotion	Verkaufsförderung, Werbung
prospective	potentiell
Q	
quota sampling	Quotenauswahl
R	
rack jobber	Regalgroßhändler, Service Merchandiser
random sampling	Stichprobenauswahl
random	zufällig, zufallsbedingt
range (of products)	Sortiment, Angebot, Auswahl
reasoning	Argumentation
reinforce	verstärken
reinforcement	Bekräftigung, Unterstützung
reminder, to remind (of)	Erinnerung, erinnern an
to respond to	reagieren auf
response rate	Rücklaufquote, Antwortquote
retail audit	Handelspanel, Handelsprüfung
retail, retailer	Einzelhandel, Einzelhändler
revenue	Einnahme

S

sales pitch	Verkaufsargument
sample	(Waren-, Stich-)probe; Muster, Sample
saturation, to saturate	Sättigung, sättigen
share	Anteil
shopping goods	Shopping Goods, Waren des nich täglichen Bedarfs
skim price	Elitepreis
societal marketing	Soziomarketing, Ganzheitliches Marketing
special offer	Sonderangebot
spending power	Kaufkraft
stratified sample	geschichtete/stratifizierte Stichprobe
subliminal advertising	unterschwellige Werbung
subscription, to subscribe	Abonnement, abonnieren
subsistence level	Existenzminimum
sufficient	ausreichend, genügend
surplus	Überschuss
SWOT analysis (analysis of the strengths, weaknesses, opportunities and threats)	SWOT-Analyse
syndicated	gemeinsam, Gemeinschafts-

T

tangible	materiell, greifbar, Sach-
target	Ziel
tenet	Lehre, Grundsatz
threat	Bedrohung
trade press	Fachpresse
trademark	Warenzeichen
trading stamps	Rabattmarke

U

unique advertising proposition	einmaliges Werbeargument
unique selling proposition	einmaliges Verkaufsargument
unique	einzigartig

V

violence	Gewalt
visualizer	Werbegraphiker, Gestalter
voucher	Gutschein

W

wholesale, wholesaler	Großhandel, Großhändler
window display	Schaufensterreklame
wrapping	Verpackung

THE RISK ELEMENT - INSURANCE

A North Carolina man having purchased a box of very rare, very expensive cigars insured them against fire among other things.

Within a month of having smoked his entire stockpile of cigars and without having made even his first premium payment on the policy, the man filed a claim against the insurance company.

In his claim, the man stated the cigars were lost "in a series of small fires." The insurance company refused to pay, citing the obvious reason: The man had consumed the cigars in the normal fashion and hadn't paid a premium.

The man sued ... and won! In delivering the ruling, the judge agreed that the claim was frivolous. He stated nevertheless that the man held a policy from the company in which it had warranted that the cigars were insurable and also guaranteed that it would insure against fire, without defining what is considered to be "unacceptable fire," and was obligated to pay the claim.

Rather than endure a lengthy and costly appeal process, the insurance company accepted the ruling and paid the man $15,000 for the rare cigars he had lost in the "fires."

After the man cashed the check, the insurance company had him arrested on 24 counts of arson. With his insurance claim and testimony from the previous case being used against him, the man was convicted of intentionally burning his insured property and sentenced to 24 months in jail and a $24,000 fine.

(This is a true story and it won the US Criminal Darwin Award.)
Submitted by Siobhan Dalrymple

FOCUS Life is full of risks. This unit looks at the need for insurance and the principles and classes of insurance available to individuals and businesses.

1.0 History of Insurance
    1.1 Lloyd's of London Today
2.0 Elements of Insurance
3.0 Principles of Insurance
4.0 Types of Insurance
    4.1 Accident
    4.2 Fire
    4.3 Marine
    4.4 Aviation
    4.5 Life Assurance (Life Insurance in AE)
5.0 Glossary

1.0   HISTORY OF INSURANCE

 The word **insurance** is derived from the Latin word for *security*. There is evidence that this practice began among traders as far back as 2100 BC in the Arabian Peninsula and this concept was well known among the Phoenicians, Greeks, Hindus and Romans. Insurance on a 'premium' basis probably began in the cities of Northern Italy at the end of the 12th century and was exclusively concerned with shipping, i.e. marine insurance. Italian merchants, trading with the UK in the 13th and 14th centuries, brought with them their trading customs as well as insurance. London merchants entered into marine insurance contracts as part of their general trading activities but some centuries elapsed before insurance became a full-time specialist activity.

In the late 17th and early 18th centuries coffee houses played an important role in the social and commercial life of The City (name of business district in the centre of London) businessmen, and, in contrast to inns and taverns, were suitable places for finding out the latest news (in the absence of newspapers) and in engaging in serious and clear-headed conversation. One such establishment was opened by Edward Lloyd around 1688 and frequented by ship owners, merchants and sea captains. It was his customers who would develop the modern system of insurance as we know it. Gradually Lloyd's grew in strength and moved into proper office accommodation.

The Great Fire of London in 1666 had been a complete disaster but it was the Tooley Street Fire of 1861 which drew attention to the absence of any co-ordinated method of fighting fires and the need for more specialized types of insurance in addition to marine insurance.

The Industrial Revolution in the UK in the 18th century with the huge expansion in material wealth, i.e. factories, machinery, warehouses and stocks of goods resulted in new classes of insurance such as accident and life assurance. Later theft cover, motor insurance, war risks and aviation became standard in a market where there were now several competing companies leaving Lloyd's to specialize in marine insurance, aviation insurance and reinsurance.

1.1   Lloyd's of London Today

Lloyd's is not an insurer but an insurance market, which is controlled by syndicates (groups of members, who vary greatly in size). The syndicates consist of **investors** or **names** who have a managing agent who looks after the investor's affairs at Lloyd's and is responsible for running the syndicate. Each syndicate has an active **underwriter**, (or number of underwriters), with the task of accepting and writing insurance policies on behalf of the names of the syndicate.

Prospective clients requiring insurance must work through the intermediary of a Lloyd's broker. In the past Lloyd's names had unlimited liability; however, since 1992 new names have limited liability. This was due to the billions in losses suffered by the names as a result of everything from natural disasters such as hurricanes and earthquakes to terrorist bombings.

Lloyd's today is the world's leading insurance market, transacting business worth billions of pounds in premiums each year. It provides insurance coverage for risks across the complete range of domestic and commercial insurance which other insurance companies often refuse to take on, e.g. such as the World Trade Center in New York. Lloyd's has also shown a willingness to introduce new types of insurance cover, which demonstrates their interest in innovation.

      a. Give an overview of the development of insurance.
      b. Explain the importance of Lloyd's.

2.0   ELEMENTS OF INSURANCE

Insurance works on the belief that accidents can happen. So, if a large number of individuals pay a small sum into a central pool there will be enough in the pool to compensate the very few people to whom accidents occur. The insurance companies, who run the pool, calculate from statistics how many accidents are likely to occur and how much they will cost to compensate. This work is done by **actuaries** who are specialists in their field.

Technically insurance refers to the payment of a sum of money by one person (the person requiring insurance or **insured**) to another (the insurance company or **insurer**), in return for which the second person will make good a particular loss suffered by the first person.

Assurance is the term used where the event insured against is bound to occur some time (e.g. death), whereas insurance covers the insured person against an event that may or may not occur (e.g. fire).

A **contract of insurance** is where the insurer undertakes, in return for a certain payment (premium) to cover any loss of or damage to an exposure unit (item insured) as laid down in the contract of insurance (insurance policy).

Taking out an insurance policy is no big deal. The prospective client should approach an insurance agent, broker or company in order to get the most favourable terms and premium. An application form known as the **proposal form** is then filled in and when the client has been accepted by the insurer a premium is paid.

A temporary policy, known as a **cover note**, may be issued pending the drawing up of the completed policy. A policy is then issued; in the case of motor insurance a certificate of insurance is also issued to enable the insured to carry proof of the contract.

A **renewal notice** is a reminder of when the next premium payment is due; such a notice is usually sent annually. If the premium is not paid on time some days of grace or extra days are allowed by the insurer to the insured to renew the policy by paying the premium due. This is, however, never allowed in the case of motor insurance.

Objects or events can be **over** or **under insured**.

 Explain the process of taking out insurance.

3.0   PRINCIPLES OF INSURANCE

Like other agreements between parties, insurance is covered by the law of contract. Contracts of insurance have the following features:

1. They are contracts of **utmost good faith** (uberrimae fidei). This means that the person seeking insurance must disclose all material facts to the object insured against, otherwise the contract is null and void. For example, taking out a policy on a car while withholding the information that the potential insured driver was involved in an accident would invalidate the policy.

2. The person seeking insurance must have an **insurable interest** in the object insured against - this means the person seeking insurance must bear some relationship, recognized by law, to the subject matter insured. For example, a person may take out insurance on his/her car, but not on the neighbour's car.

Insurable interest also means that the insured must own something of *value* that will result in a financial loss as a result of a particular event happening, e.g. goods stolen from a factory in a burglary.

3. All insurance policies, with the exception of life and personal accident policies, are contracts of **indemnity**. This means that the insured cannot profit from the loss or damage that is insured against in the event of a claim. The insurer will replace only up to the current value of what has been lost, regardless of the amount of insurance taken out.

4. **Subrogation** refers to the right of the insurer to take over what is left of the property that has been claimed for by the insured and the right to sue a third party for damages. If, for example, an insurance company had paid out on stock damaged in a fire, then the insurer would be entitled to take over any undamaged stock and sell it to recover some of the compensation paid. If the fire was started deliberately the insurance company can take action against the offender in order to recover the indemnity they have paid out.

5. **Contribution** is where an insurer that has paid full compensation under a policy can call upon or ask other insurers, which are equally or otherwise liable under the terms of the same policy, to contribute to the compensation payment. This simply means that if the same risk happens to be covered by two insurers each insurer pays half, e.g. a camera stolen during your holidays could be covered under both holiday and household insurance resulting in both companies paying 50% of the loss each.

6. **Proximate cause** is where the loss or damage must result from some event directly insured against. In other words, if you have a policy insuring your premises against fire only, then you cannot claim for theft.

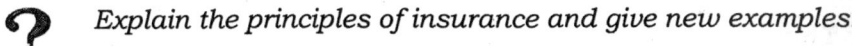 *Explain the principles of insurance and give new examples.*

4.0   TYPES OF INSURANCE

The main types are:

- Accident
- Fire
- Marine
- Aviation
- Life Assurance

4.1 Accident

This type of insurance covers either the insured or a **third party** (i.e. another party apart from the insured and the insurer) against loss resulting from an accident.

Personal accident contracts are not indemnity contracts, which means that the insured may benefit financially from the settlement of the claim.

Employers must cover themselves against claims by employees, e.g. loss of a hand from using a cutting machine **(employer's liability insurance)** and members of the general public, e.g. a customer slips and falls on a wet floor resulting in a hip injury **(public liability insurance).**

Accident policies cover a wide brief, not just events that you would usually refer to as accidents. Examples include:

*   personal accident and sickness
*   burglary
*   machinery breakdown
*   glass breakage
*   money lost in transit
*   legal costs
*   dishonesty or fraud by employees **(fidelity guarantee insurance)**
*   loss of computer records
*   defective products **(product liability insurance)**
*   health insurance, which is compulsory in most countries

Motor insurance

This is also a form of accident insurance and is focused on private and commercial customers.

There are three basic types of motor insurance available:

*   **Third party**, which is compulsory and which covers injury to the other person (the third party) but not the insured in the event of an accident. Damage to the other person's vehicle is also covered.
*   **Third party, fire and theft (TPFT).**
*   **Comprehensive** or **full cover** insurance, which covers the damage to all persons and all vehicles, including the insured's vehicle, involved in an accident.

When an accident occurs and a claim is made on the insured's motor policy, the insured then loses what is referred to as the **no-**

claims bonus, which is a discount on the premium awarded for having no claims.

4.2   Fire

The main types of fire insurance policies are the following:

- **Household**, one of the most common types of policy, covering fire, burglary and other damage to the home.
- **Reinstatement**, which covers the cost of replacement of buildings and contents on the same or another site.
- **Stock declaration**, which covers stock. The insured is required to declare the value of the stock at intervals and the premium is adjusted accordingly.
- **Blanket cover** where all the buildings comprising the risk are insured for a single sum.
- **Building in course of construction**, i.e. where a building is being built.
- **Loss of rent due to fire**.
- **Additional perils** cover damage arising from an explosion, from civil disturbances, storm, flood, thunderbolt, earthquake, subsidence and impact by animals, etc.
- **Sprinkler leakage** cover against leakage from sprinkler systems designed to activate only in case of fire.
- **Consequential loss** insurance against loss of revenue arising out of a fire during the time needed to repair or reconstruct the building(s).

4.3   Marine

- **Hull** insurance where the machinery and hull of the ship are insured against maritime perils.
- **Cargo** insurance can be taken out by either buyer or seller, as either may have insurable interest at different times.
- **Freight** insurance covers the money paid for the transportation of goods or the hire of a ship.
- **Time** policy insures the subject matter for a period of time, which does not normally exceed (but may) a period of one year.
- **Voyage** policy insures the cargo and ship for one voyage from the port of shipment to the port of destination irrespective of the length of time taken.
- **Mixed** policy insures the ship for both a voyage and a period of time, i.e. a voyage and a period of time in the port of destination after arrival needed in order to unload the freight.

- **Building risk** policy insures a vessel during the construction period.
- **Floating** policy covers a number of voyages. A lump sum payment is made up front and when this is exhausted the policy must be renewed or let lapse. This spares regular shippers the inconvenience of constantly renewing insurance policies.

Losses in marine insurance can be total or partial.

Actual total loss is where the ship is completely or effectively destroyed, i.e. the Titanic. A ship that is missing for a long period of time can be presumed to be an actual total loss.

Constructive total loss arises when a ship is not completely lost, but has been abandoned because the cost of saving it would exceed its value.

Partial loss or **general average** affords indemnity for losses *voluntarily* incurred, such as when cargo is **jettisoned**, i.e. thrown overboard in order to save the ship from the **perils of the sea**, e.g. dangers such as a storm or hurricane.

Barratry is the term used to describe dishonesty or general wrongdoing on the part of the captain or crew.

4.4   Aviation

This consists of:

- **Comprehensive aircraft** policy covering
    a) accidental damage to the aircraft
    b) legal liability of the insured for the death or bodily injuries to the passengers
    c) legal liability of the insured for death or bodily injuries to third parties (excluding passengers).

- **Airport liability** policy covers damage to property, including aircraft at the airport, caused by the fault or negligence of the insured.
- **Product liability** policy protects a manufacturer from claims arising from a fault in the design or manufacture of an aircraft. Aviation policies can be effected either with an insurance company or more usually with Lloyd's.

4.5 Life Assurance (Life Insurance in AE)

> *Nancy Astor, MP: If you were my husband, I'd poison your coffee.*
>
> *Winston Churchill: If you were my wife, I'd drink it.*

There are numerous types of policies available; the following are among the most common:

- **Term (or temporary)** where a sum is only paid if the person assured dies within a specified period. This type of policy is often used to cover a debt, e.g. to cover the amount due on a mortgage to a bank, building society or other financial institution in the event of the death of the mortgagee (borrower).
- **Whole life** where the sum assured is payable only on the death of the assured to the assured's dependants.
- **Endowment policy** is where the sum assured or a regular payment is made on the assured reaching a certain age, or on death, if death occurs before that date.

Life policies can be either non-profit or with-profit dependent on various investment performance criteria.

    a. Summarize the main classes of insurance.
    b. Differentiate between employer's liability and public liability.
    c. Explain third party and full cover motor insurance.
    d. What do additional perils (Fire Insurance) refer to?
    e. Differentiate between a whole life and an endowment policy.

5.0 GLOSSARY

Surrender value is where a certain percentage of the premiums paid is returned to the insured in the event of the policy being terminated before death or maturity.

Reinsurance is common where a large risk is insured; here it is usual for the insurer to reinsure all or part of the risk with other insurers. Underwriters in Lloyd's specialize in this field. The insurer spreading the risk to other insurers is referred to as the ceding insurer. The reinsurer or underwriter accepts the cessions of business.

An **ex gratia payment** is a payment made by the insurer to compensate the insured for a loss suffered, even though they are not legally obliged to do so.

The **adjustor** or **assessor** is a person who visits the place where the loss or damage has occurred. The assessor will examine the cause of the damage and the extent of the claim and will then decide on the level of the pay-out to be made to the insured person.

 Explain reinsurance in your own words.

 ### Discussion Forum

    a. What would the insurance requirements be of a medium-sized furniture manufacturer?
    b. Should health insurance be voluntary or compulsory?
    c. Germans are often said to be overinsured. Do you agree?

VOCABULARY

A	
accident insurance	Unfallversicherung
actual total loss	tatsächlicher Totalschaden
actuary	Versicherungsmathematiker, Aktuar
to adjust	anpassen
adjustor, assessor	Schätzer
annually	jährlich
apart from	abgesehen von, außer
appraisal	Schätzung, Bewertung
arson	Brandstiftung
to arise	sich ergeben
aviation insurance	Luftfahrtversicherung
B	
barratry	Barratrie, Betrug (durch Schiffskapitän)
to be bound to	verpflichtet/gebunden sein, müssen
to be due to	zurückzuführen sein
to be entitled to	berechtigt sein
to be involved in an accident	in einen Unfall verwickelt sein
to be legally obliged to	gesetzlich verpflichtet sein
to be likely to	wahrscheinlich sein
to benefit from	Nutzen ziehen aus

beneficiary	Begünstigter
blanket cover	umfassende Deckung, Vollversicherung
brief	hier: Bereich
broker	Makler
building society	Bausparkasse
burglary	Einbruch
C	
cargo (policy)	Güter (police)
ceding insurer	Primärversicherer, Direkt/Hauptversicherer
certificate of insurance	Versicherungsschein
cession	Zession, Abtretung
civil disturbances	öffentliche Störung
claim	(Versicherungs)Anspruch, Schadensfall
to claim for	einen Anspruch erheben auf
to compensate	entschädigen
comprehensive/full cover motor/vehicle insurance	Vollkaskoversicherung
compulsory insurance	Pflichtversicherung
consequential loss	Folgeschadenversicherung
constructive total loss	fingierter Totalschaden
to contribute	beitragen
to convict	verurteilen, überführen
cover	Versicherungsschutz, Deckung
cover note	Deckungsschein, vorläufige Deckungszusage
to cover a risk	ein Risiko abdecken
to cover oneself against risk	sich gegen ein Risiko absichern
current value	Zeitwert
D	
(un)damaged	(un)beschädigt
days of grace	Respekttage, (Aufschub)
debt	Schulden
to declare	erklären
deliberately	absichtlich, vorsätzlich
dependent	unterhaltsberechtigter Angehöriger
destination	Reiseziel
to disclose (information)	offen legen, bekannt geben
discount	Rabatt
dishonesty	Unehrlichkeit
disturbance	Unruhe, (Ruhe)Störung
due	fällig

E

to effect insurance	Versicherung abschließen
employer's liability insurance	Betriebshaftpflichtversicherung
endowment policy	Gemischte Lebensversicherung, Kapitallebensversicherung
to elapse	vergehen, verstreichen
to endure	erleiden
entire stockpile	gesamter Vorrat
ex gratia payment	Sonderzahlung
to exceed	übersteigen
excluding	außer
to exhaust	ausschöpfen, erschöpfen
exposure unit, item insured	Versicherungsobjekt, Versicherungsgegenstand
extent	Ausmaß

F

fault	Fehler, Defekt
favourable	günstig
fidelity guarantee insurance	Vertrauensschadenversicherung
fine	Geldstrafe, Ordnungsstrafe
floating policy	gleitende Pauschalpolice, Abschreibepolice, Generalpolice
fraud	Betrug,
freight insurance	Frachtversicherung

G

general average	Havarie-Grosse

H

health insurance	Krankenversicherung
hull insurance	Schiffskörperversicherung

I

impact	(Aus)Wirkung, Aufprall
incidental	Nebensächlich(keit)
to incur a loss	einen Verlust erleiden
indemnity, to indemnify	Schadenersatz, entschädigen
to injure, injury	verletzen, Verletzung
irrespective	ungeachtet, unabhängig von
insurable interest	versicherbares Interesse
insurance certificate	Einzelpolice
insurance policy	Generalpolice
to insure (against)	versichern
insurer	Versicherer, Versicherungsträger

the insured	Versicherter, Versicherungsnehmer
intermediary	Vermittler, Makler
to invalidate	ungültig machen
to involve	einbeziehen, verwickeln
to issue	herausgeben, ausstellen
J	
to jettison, jettison	Fracht über Bord werfen, Überbordwerfen
L	
lapse, to lapse	Verfall, verfallen, ablaufen, erlöschen
law of contract	Vertragsrecht
to lay down in a contract	vertraglich vereinbaren
life assurance/insurance (AE)	Lebensversicherung
(un)limited liability	(un)beschränkte Haftung
lump sum	Pauschalbetrag, einmalige Zahlung
M	
marine insurance	Seeversicherung
maturity	Fälligkeit
merchant	Händler
mortgage	Hypothek
mortgagee	Hypotheknehmer
motor insurance	Fahrzeugversicherung
N	
Names	Mitglieder von Lloyd's of London, Investoren, Versicherungsträger
negligence	Fahrlässigkeit
no claim(s) bonus	Schadenfreiheitsrabatt
notice	Nachricht
null and void	Null und nichtig
O	
overinsured/underinsured	überversichert, unterversichert
P	
partial loss	Teilschaden, Teilverlust
to pay out	Auszahlung
to be pending	noch anstehend, unerledigt
pending the drawing up of	bis zum Aufsetzen von
performance	Leistung
perils	Gefahr, Risiko
policy	(General) Police
to pool	(Ressourcen) zusammenlegen
premium	(Versicherungs)Prämie, Beitrag
product liability insurance	Produkthaftpflichtversicherung

proof	Nachweis, Beweis
proper	richtig, eigentlich
property	Eigentum
proposal (form)	Angebot
proposer	Antragsteller
prospective	zukünftig, voraussichtlich, potentiell
to protect from	schützen vor
proximate cause	unmittelbare Ursache
public liability insurance	allgemeine Haftpflichtversicherung
R	
to recover (money)	(Geld)zurückbekommen, einholen,
to refer to as	bezeichnen als
regardless (of)	unabhängig (von)
reinstatement	Wiederherstellung, Wiedereinstellung
reinsurance, to reinsure	Rückversicherung, rückversichern
reminder	Erinnerung; Mahnung
renewal notice	Fälligkeitsbescheid, Beitragsrechnung, Verlängerungsbescheid
rent	Miete, Pacht
revenue	Einnahmen
to run	verwalten
S	
settlement of a claim	Schadensregulierung
site	Stelle, Platz
to spare smb the inconvenience of	jemandem die Unannehmlichkeit(en) ersparen
sprinkler leakage	Leck, Defekt der Berieselungsanlage/des Sprinklers
stock	(Lager/Waren)Bestand
subject matter	Gegenstand
subrogation	Subrogation, Eintritt in Rechte
subsidence	Bodensenkung
to sue	(ver)klagen
to suffer losses	Verluste erleiden
surrender value	Rückkaufwert
T	
to take out insurance	Versicherung abschließen
to take over	übernehmen
temporary	temporär, vorläufig

term	Bestimmung, Bedingung, Klausel
term/temporary life assurance	Risikolebensversicherung
third party	Haftpflicht
third party, fire and theft	Teilkaskoversicherung
thunderbolt	Blitzschlag
U	
underwriter	(Einzel)Versicherer (der meist einen Teil des Risikos übernimmt)
utmost good faith (uberrimae fidei)	höchster guter Glaube
V	
vessel	Schiff
voluntarily	freiwillig
voyage policy	Reisepolice
W	
warehouse	Lagerhaus
whole life assurance	Lebensversicherung auf den Todesfall

FOLLOWING IN THE STEPS OF MOSES - MANAGEMENT AND LEADERSHIP

> Mother: *(calling upstairs in the morning): 'It's time to get up for school.*
> Chris: *'I'm not going to school'*
> Mother: *'Why not?'*
> Chris: *'Because everybody at school hates me – the teachers, the kids, the janitor – they all hate me!'*
> Mother: *'You have to go. You're the principal'*
>
> M.G. Fullan

FOCUS The first section focuses on the Anglo-American view of management, the second explores the world of leadership - an extension of the wider management role.

SECTION I: MANAGEMENT

1.0 Introduction to Management and Leadership
2.0 Management
    2.1 Functions and Qualities of Managers
    2.2 Management Theory
    2.3 Authority and Responsibility of Management
    2.4 Recent Developments in the Field of Management

SECTION II: LEADERSHIP

1.0 Leadership - A Part of the Wider Management Role.
    1.1 Charisma and Leadership
2.0 Leadership and Power
3.0 Theories of Leadership
    3.1 Leadership Traits (Trait Theory)
    3.2 Behavioural or Style Theories
    3.3 Contingency Theories or Situational Approaches
4.0 Conclusion

SECTION I: MANAGEMENT

1.0   INTRODUCTION TO MANAGEMENT AND
LEADERSHIP

Our human society is based on a system of organizations which helps its members to undertake activities related to their needs for survival. All organizations share the same requirement - appropriate management and leadership – if they are to achieve the goals of their inception.

Despite years of research and commentary by both academics and practitioners alike, the only truism that can be related to the management/leadership function is that there is no *right* answer- no-one has been able to provide the *perfect* blueprint of how an organization should be run in order to ensure its success. This applies not only to the social organization – family, country, etc - but also to business organizations.

This lack of a right answer has not deterred either academics or practicing managers/leaders from trying to develop generic and specific management and organizational theories that can be transferred from one successful organization to another, less successful, one.

A key question concerning management and leadership is whether they are the same or different.

Some academics have argued that there is no difference between the two, others that there are significant differences or that managers know what they ought to do but leaders know how to do it from instinct.

A generally accepted view is that the role of the **manager** is essentially one as an ***implementer*** - overseeing the operational concerns of a firm.

The role of the **leader**, on the other hand, is that of ***pathfinder*** or ***visionary*** - more an element of the *wider management role*. Leadership can be considered more strategical, concerned with setting the future direction of the organization as a whole.

     Differentiate between management and leadership.

2.0 MANAGEMENT

Management is concerned with designing and carrying out plans and objectives, getting things done and working effectively with people; i.e. it is people-oriented and task-oriented.

It involves having technical, human and conceptual skills. The latter refers to the ability to understand a complex situation and decide on a course of action.

Good management is very often the application of common sense, but sometimes common sense needs pointing out so that all can recognize it!

Important aspects of management are:

- managing yourself before you manage others
- knowing your strengths and weaknesses
- evaluating your own performance
- managing of time and paper
- recognizing the importance of feedback
- having clear goals
- being able to motivate and direct people.

2.1 Functions and Qualities of Managers

The four main **functions** of management are the following:

- **Planning**:- This involves defining goals and finding strategies for reaching them.
- **Organizing:** - This is concerned with arranging resources and employees in order to carry out plans.
- **Leading:** - This focuses on motivating and directing employees.
- **Controlling:** - The monitoring of activities to ensure that objectives are achieved plus the evaluation of the performance.

Qualities of Managers
Basic knowledge and information
1. Command of basic facts
2. Relevant professional (rather than academic) understanding
Skills and attributes
3. Continuing sensitivity to events
4. Analytical, problem solving and decision-making skills
5. Social skills and abilities
6. Emotional resilience

7. Proactive rather than reactive – ability to cause things to happen rather than waiting to react to outside events

Meta-qualities

8. Creativity
9. Mental agility
10. Balancing learning habits and skills
11. Self-knowledge

a. *What is management characterized by and what does it comprise?*

b. *Explain the qualities of a manager.*

2.2 Management Theory

> *It's easy to get good players. Gettin' em' to play together, that's the hard part.*
>
> *Casey Stengel*

There are three main groupings of management theorists:

1. Classical or Scientific Managers

These are associated with writers in the first half of the twentieth century. The dominant management approach of the time was that of Scientific Management, the guru of which was Taylor. He viewed man in terms of a *machine* capable of being adapted to work more efficiently and motivated solely by the size of his/her pay packet.

2. The Human Relations School

This school (not to be mixed up with Human Resource Management) is based on the theories of **motivation**, was developed between the two world wars and drew on the work of Max Weber. One of its most important commentators was Douglas McGregor.

In *The Human Side of Enterprise* (1960) Mc Gregor expounded his now famous **Theory X and Theory Y Model**. He sought to prove that every person has certain assumptions about other people's attitudes towards work and organization.

Theory X is strongly in the negative direction in that it believes that people basically dislike work, are lazy and will, if possible, avoid work altogether. As a result of this it is necessary to coerce, threaten and supervise to guarantee a minimum result. It also assumes that most people are passive low risk takers and rate job security very highly. They often do not object to and even like being managed and controlled.

Theory Y offers an opposing view. Here people like work and can be very creative in the right environment. When the objectives of the organization coincide with personal goals people will seek responsibility and work under limited supervision.

An alternative **Theory Z** was formulated by William Ouchi. This model, using a blend of American and Japanese approaches, suggests that both assumptions can in fact be correct at different times.

Frederick Herzberg's **Motivation-Hygiene Theory** concentrates on satisfaction at work. He conducted studies focusing on factors leading to satisfaction called *motivators* and those leading to prevent dissatisfaction called *hygiene* factors.

- *Motivators:* Achievement, recognition, the work itself, responsibility, job advancement.

- *Hygiene Factors:* Company policy and administrators, supervision and relationship with supervisors, salary, working conditions.

Another major influence was Abraham Maslow's work on motivation based on a **hierarchy of needs**, ranging from basic physiological needs (food, sleep, etc) to safety, love and esteem to higher psychological needs such as self-actualization, i.e. self-fulfilment.

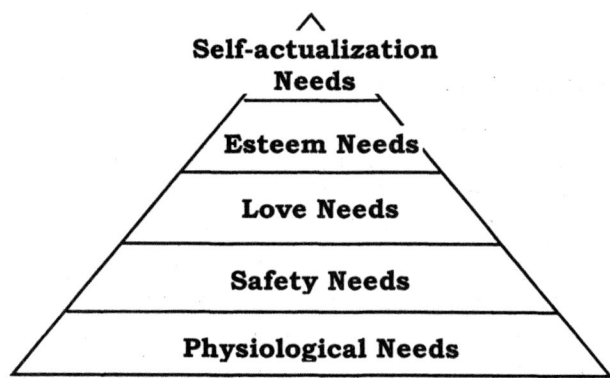

Other researchers have noted that employees also distinguish between **extrinsic** motivation (pay, promotion, pension, company car) and **intrinsic** motivation (job interest, personal achievement, responsibility, etc).

Employees are motivated through **job enlargement**, which involves expanding an employee's responsibilities by increasing the number and variety of tasks they entail. **Job enrichment** involves giving **empowerment** to employees, i.e. authority and responsibility to make decisions without traditional managerial approval and control.

A common term used in management and first coined *by Peter Drucker* is **Management by Objectives (MBO)** where the manager helps employees set the objectives and then develop action plans. The employees are motivated through their participation in the goal setting process. Finally the actual performance is evaluated against the plans.

Equity Theory examines how people make comparisons between themselves and others in regard to what they invest in their work, i.e. inputs and what outcomes they receive, i.e. outputs. This is their own perception, which can often be subjective rather than objective.

Goal Theory focuses on the fact that motivation is driven by goals and objectives set by individuals for themselves.

3.   **The Systems and Contingency Approach**

This school of thought was founded by the biologist *Ludwig von Bertalanffy* in the 1950s and continued by *John Adair, Frederick Fiedler* and *Paul Hersey* together with *Kenneth Blanchard*.

The essential point here is because there is no single theory which guarantees the effectiveness of an organization, management has to select a mix of theories which are appropriate for different situations.

 Summarize the main theories of management.

2.3   Authority and Responsibility of Management

Organizational Structures

Management consists of **first line managers** who are situated at the lowest level coordinating non-managerial employees and resources such as machinery and materials. Then there are **middle managers** who supervize the activities of the first line managers and implement the plans and policies of the organization. Finally, **top** or **upper managers** are responsible for the overall performance of the firm and for directing the major activities of the organization's various divisions or units.

Decision-making may be **centralized** with a concentration of decision making in one primary location or **decentralized** with empowerment spread throughout the organization.

The Chain of Command

An important part of the organizational hierarchy relates to the chain of command and the span of control. The **chain of command** is the line of authority that travels from the top of the management hierarchy down to the employees at the very bottom.

A company has an informal and formal organizational structure. An **informal** one describes personal relationships and interaction among employees.

A company's **formal** organizational structures consists of three basic types:

- **Line organization**, which involves a direct flow of authority from top to bottom. A line authority system has each person receiving instructions and being answerable to the person above them. This represents a narrow span of control and a long chain of command.

- **Line and staff organization** is a variation of the line system, which allows planners, advisors and specialists to cut across the departments of a linear structure to help the CEO and other line managers with their tasks.

- **Matrix organization is** where line and staff employees work together on a team on specific projects but retain their positions in the line and staff organization.

The Span of Control

The **span of control** (span of management or manager-employee ratio) relates to the number of subordinates any one manager is responsible for.

A *narrow* span is limited, i.e. tighter while a *wide* span means one person has a larger number of people and activities to control.

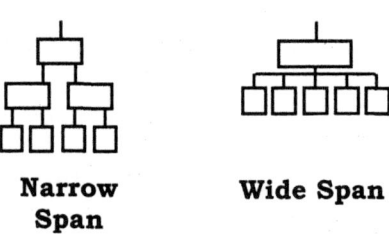

Narrow Span   **Wide Span**

Horizontal and Vertical Hierarchical Structures

Current management theory is in favour of **flatter** or **horizontal** (fewer levels within the hierarchy and a wider span of control) organizations because the **taller** or **vertical** (a long command chain and a narrow span of control) organizations can be very inefficient in times of change.

Typical management structure in a large company

The typical management structure in a large company is still predominately a vertical one, which may consist of a **board of directors**, often presided over by a **chairperson** or **president**. The Board usually appoints a **managing director** or **chief executive officer (CEO)** who is responsible for looking after the day to day running of the business and ensuring that policies formulated by the board are carried out.

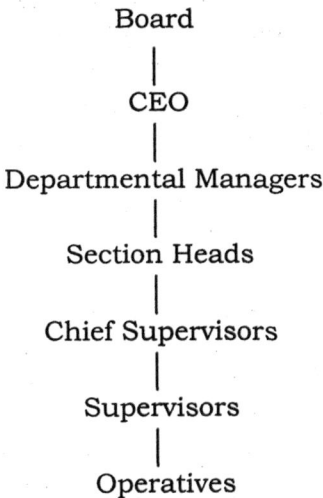

Board
|
CEO
|
Departmental Managers
|
Section Heads
|
Chief Supervisors
|
Supervisors
|
Operatives

The **departmental managers** or **heads of department** report to the CEO. Authority is passed by them, in turn, all the way down to the section heads, supervisors and operatives.

One of the most important managers is the **chief accountant** or **finance manager** who is the head of the **finance department**. This department is concerned with the financial affairs of the firm including incoming and outgoing invoices, credit control, payment of wages and the preparation of the company accounts. It also provides information which future planning can be based on, by drawing up budgets, forecasts and statistics.

The **company secretary** is in charge of the **administration department** and the **legal department**. Administration deals with coordinating the activities of and providing services to the other departments including general office facilities such as secretarial and computing services, centralized filing, handling of incoming and outgoing mail, etc. The legal department ensures that the company acts within the law and deals with legal matters such as contracts, guaranties, insurance, compensation, etc.

The overall function of the **marketing department** is to enable a business to sell its goods and services and includes market research, advertising and distribution and sales.

The **personnel department** is nowadays often referred to as **human resources** and is dealt with in more detail in Unit 10.

The **production manager** is concerned with producing the company's products. This involves the planning and organization of work on the factory floor to ensure that the goods are manufactured on time and that quality standards are maintained. The **production department** also investigates complaints from customers and deals with faulty goods, etc.

The **purchasing manager** is responsible for all supplies bought by the firm including the purchase of all raw materials, equipment and supplies for the company. The purchasing department deals with quotations from suppliers, issues orders and checks deliveries and may also be responsible for maintaining an efficient stock control system.

Other departments include the **transport department,** which has to arrange for delivery of goods to customers, and **R&D – research and development**, which deals with the development of new products and processes.

All departments are interrelated; all have to run smoothly and efficiently in order to meet the goals and objectives of the business.

Mission

Modern organisations often formulate a mission for their organisation.

The **mission** (usually contained in a mission statement) should state the:

- purpose of the organization
- strategy it is following
- level of service and quality aimed at
- values of the organization, i.e. ideology, shared values and beliefs

---

EXAMPLE

Mission Statement of IBM (UK):

We shall increase the pace of change. Market-driven quality is our aim. It means listening to our customers. It means eliminating defects and errors, speeding up all our processes, measuring everything we do against a common standard and it means involving employees totally in our aims.

The **strategic plans** are developed from the organization's mission and provide a greater definition of how the mission is to be accomplished by defining broad objectives and general methods for achieving them.

The **objectives** are the targets or standards by which the goals and ultimately the mission statement can be realized. (see also Marketing Plan, Section 7.0, in Unit 7).

      a. *Differentiate between chain of command and span of control.*
      b. *Explain the three formal types of organizational structure.*
      c. *Differentiate between taller and flatter hierarchial structures.*
      d. *Explain the main departments in an organization.*
      e. *What is a mission statement?*

2.4 Recent Developments in the Field of Management

Total Quality Management (TQM)

TQM is a 1980s American philosophy that affects all parts of an organization's operations, its employees, its suppliers, etc. It focuses on having an organizational culture in which all employees strive to satisfy the customer and encourages continuous improvement. Its goal is to practice business excellence, and it represents a move away from just product quality control.

Business Process (Re)engineering (BPR)

This is not just an American 1990s cost-cutting tool but a large-scale systematic application of Information Technology to management. It is the process of mapping out processes in detail to identify potential reductions in time and costs by applying technology. It involves modifying management systems, job designs and work flows.

E-Business and the e-Manager

The Internet in the 21st century has revolutionized business forever, so in order that a good manager also becomes a good e-manager certain considerations should be kept in mind.

- **Good staff**

  E-businesses need fewer but better people. New types of jobs have emerged such as the chief e-business officer, content manager, chief knowledge officer or chief information officer (CIO). Nowadays IT staff serve as strategists, bridge builders, implementers and communicators.

- **Speed**

  The decision-making process should be fast - bureaucracy is a killer. Being quick is often the decisive factor.

- **Good communication and openness**

  This refers to internal and external/global communication. Given the pace and complexity of change, communicating the business strategy to staff members has become more important than ever. Another important aspect is communication with the public. Nowadays many e-businesses allow their suppliers and customers a lot of access to their databases and inner workings. This requires a degree of trust plus a willingness to expose mistakes and other negative sides to the outside world.

- **Collaboration skills**

  This involves good teamwork (even when the team is separated by geographic distance) and the ability to work with customers, suppliers and partners.

- **Content-management skills**

  The firm's web site shouldn't contain too much information – what ends up there should be pertinent and expressed clearly to avoid confusing customers.

- **Customer focus**

  The Internet allows firms to shift from a mass market strategy to treating customers more as individuals as witnessed by the growth in customization.

- **Knowledge management**

  With the sheer mass of information available pooling and sharing of relevant knowledge is assuming increasing importance.

- **Leadership by example**

  Leaders at all levels should try to keep themselves up-to-date although this may not be easy

    a. Differentiate between TQM and BPR.
    b. How has IT changed the way of managing a modern business?

 Discussion Forum

    a. How do you manage yourself?
    b. Discuss cultural differences in management styles.
    c. Is a flat hierarchy always better?
    d. What can be done to increase the commitment of employees?
    e. How would you describe the modern (international) manager?

SECTION II: LEADERSHIP

> *For many, the word leadership implies that one person is the dictator; he makes all the decisions and does all the work of leadership. This is wrong.*
>
> *John Adair*

1.0 LEADERSHIP – A PART OF THE WIDER MANAGEMENT ROLE

Leadership is concerned with the ability to motivate and inspire, to have an impact on employees' attitudes and beliefs and to move individuals to a level of performance in excess of conventional expectations. Leadership relates to mission, direction and inspiration.

During the last three decades the topic of leadership has enjoyed something of a boom with hundreds of populist, as well as scholarly, studies and papers every year.

One of the most important comments on leadership was made by Peter Drucker who refutes the idea of leadership quality and personality and believes that its essence is:

♦ **Performance** - A leader must think through the organization's mission, and define and establish it clearly and visibly. A leader must be seen to work hard.
♦ **Flexibility** - Being prepared to make compromises, as an effective leader is clearly aware that he or she is not in control of the universe.
♦ **Accepting responsibility rather than rank or privilege** - A leader is not afraid of strong associates and subordinates even though there is a risk in that they are or may be competitors. A good leader is not afraid of empowering - giving power to others.
♦ **Earning trust and having integrity**
♦ **Managing change successfully** – Dealing with crisis and renewal, dealing with ambiguity and being able to act even when the future is unclear. An effective leader must be alert at all times to the reaction of members in his organization, to changing conditions and to his/her abilities and reactions.

Everyone is aware of one or more leaders from the past or from the present, be it in the political, military, scientific, academic or business fields. These leaders have employed many different methods and styles, have been good or evil, have come in many shapes and sizes and have had varying degrees of success.

Leaders from history go in and out of fashion. Two of the most well-known feminine leaders seem to be Joan of Arc and Elizabeth I.

The main problem for many in the field of leadership today is that if they turn to literature for advice on sound practices they are likely to be confounded by the conflicting advice and numerous prescriptions for success.

An incredibly successful leader in the world of business was Jack Welch of General Electric (GE) who became Time Magazine's CEO of the 20th century. He was a leader who had no experience of working in another organization, joining GE in 1960 and retiring in 2001.

Welch demanded that each GE business become first or second in its market. The Harvard Business School Management Newsletter noted that Welch continued to launch a new internal revolution every few years and that today each GE unit has a full-time *destroyyourbusiness.com* charged with reinventing the group's way of managing, operating and even thinking.

Explain Peter Drucker's thoughts on leadership.

1.1 Charisma and Leadership

Charisma is usually ascribed to great world leaders with outstanding personalities be they political like Ghandi, Kennedy, Mandela or Martin Luther King or religious like Moses, Jesus or Mohammed.

Some theorists believe charismatic leaders have a high level of self-confidence and a strong need for power. They engage in behaviours to enhance their reputation for wisdom and competence. They generate an attractive vision of the future in which all can share through the attainment of organizational goals. Charismatic leaders set high but realisable goals for followers and influence followers by using referent and expert power (see Section 2.0). They arouse in followers motives relevant to the accomplishment of the group's goals.

Peter Drucker, while accepting that effective leadership matters, believes that it doesn't depend on charisma. In fact, he says charisma has been the undoing of many leaders because it makes them inflexible, convinced of their own infallibility and unable to change. Stalin, Hitler and Mao were misleaders who had great charismatic qualities; Kennedy was perhaps one of the most charismatic presidents of the USA but he is also one who got very little done.

Unquestionably charismatic leaders have had a profound effect on followers inspiring loyalty and trust and achieving major change. When one seeks to assess the possibilities of charismatic leadership at an organizational level it is necessary to examine whether charisma is a property of the leader or is a quality accorded by subordinates.

 How do charismatic leaders behave?

2.0 LEADERSHIP AND POWER

> *I'm not interested in money - only in power.*
>
>   George Lachmann

President Kennedy once remarked that the essence of leadership is whether one enjoys power or feels burdened by it. His successor Lyndon B. Johnson is reported to have believed that the minds and the hearts of subordinates go unreservedly to the leader who uses his power to affect their vital interests.

While it is admitted that power is an essential ingredient of leadership modern theorists are careful to remark that *while all leaders are actual or potential power holders, not all power holders are leaders.* The distinction arises from the leader's purpose when exercising power.

One can discriminate between the power wielder who uses his power to manipulate his or her subordinates so that the leader's goals take precedence over the followers needs and the leader who uses his or her power to help followers grow and develop instead of keeping them weak and dependent. Power is an emotive term possibly because we instinctively accept the truth of the old maxim that power corrupts all those who hold it.

John French and *Bertram Raven* discuss five sources of power that leaders use to influence those under him/her. These are:

* **coercive** (this is the leader's ability to create discipline)
* **legitimate** (which refers to the leader's official position in an organization)
* **reward** (which focuses on the ability of the leader to grant benefits)
* **expert** (this concerns the superior skill, knowledge and expertise of the leader)
* **referent** (where the leader is held in high esteem, admired and sometimes imitated).

The first three are organizational elements while the last two can contribute or take away from the strength of a leader.

  How does a leader exercise power?

3.0   THEORIES OF LEADERSHIP

The first two parts focus on what a leader is characterized by, the last one on how leadership is exercised in an organization.

3.1   Leadership Traits (Trait Theory)

> *Some are born great, some achieve greatness, and some hire public relations writers.*
>
> *Daniel Boorstin.*

Initial research into the phenomenon of leadership investigated the personal traits or characteristics of leaders. The underlying hypothesis was that leaders *were born not made.* The researchers believed that if they could identify the **traits**, or core features, which were consistently and exclusively associated with effective leaders, then the selection of future leaders based on their possessing such characteristics would be a guarantee of leadership effectiveness.

This theory is depressing for the individual as it relegates the possibility of aspiring to a leadership position to all but the chosen few. Trait theory was developed in the early years of the 20th century. Some general conclusions arrived at concerning **core features** have been that leaders:

- have above average intelligence but that if they are too intelligent there can be problems in co-operation and a higher possibility of conflict.
- appear to have a personality that is characterized by self-confidence, honesty, integrity plus creativity and initiative.
- have more education
- a higher socio-economic status can be an advantage.
- possess a *helicopter trait,* which is used to describe the ability of a successful leader to rise above a particular situation and see it in its broader context, and then to descend to attend to detail.

Other studies mentioned enthusiasm, sociability, courage, imagination, decisiveness, determination, energy and faith. This research seems to suggest that a leader is academic, intelligent, dependable and from the upper or middle classes.

Other researchers have considered **non-core factors**, which might be important. *John Hunt* of the London Business School conducted

research on the common characteristics of senior management in
the private and public sector. The effective leaders were in general:

- first child or first son
- high achievers
- had high energy levels
- tended to take the long-term view
- politically active
- goal-directed
- loners

None of these characteristics is necessarily related to socio-
economic background but it is a fact that the managerial and
professional classes do instil achievement goals in their children
who normally model their behaviour on their parents' level of
achievement (or can react with varying degrees against same).

Hunt also asked the people in top managerial/leadership positions
what they thought was important. They believed in certain
indicators or potential:

- ability to work with a wide variety of people
- early overall responsibility for important tasks
- strong achievement goals
- experience of leading a group early in career
- wide experience of several business functions before mid-career

It may be said that while the trait approach offers some insights it
is an inadequate basis on which to build a theory of leadership.
These traits which have been identified are widely distributed
throughout the population in non-leaders as well as leaders. One
can say that certain traits, provided that they are consistent with
the demands of the task and the expectations of the group increase
the likelihood that a leader will be effective but they do not
guarantee effectiveness.

   *Summarize the core and non-core characteristics of
leaders.*

3.2   Behavioural or Style Theories

The three **main categories** of leadership styles are

- **authoritarian**
- **democratic**
- **laissez-faire**

Authoritarian – This is where the leader has all the power, makes all the decisions (centralization of decision making), controls all rewards and punishments. No group input is allowed. Examples include *McGregor's* Theory X and *Rensis Likert's* authoritative Systems 1 and 2 (see below).

Rensis Likert Management Systems:

System 1	System 2	System 3	System 4
Exploitive-Authoritative	Benevolent-Authoritative	Consultative-Democratic	Participative-Democratic

◄────── Job centred ─────────── Employee centred ──►

Democratic – This is based on empowerment (decentralization of decision making) and employee participation where the group as a whole has more power, more input to decision making and the leader is more part of the team itself. Examples are McGregor's Theory Y and Likert's System 3 (consultative) and System 4 (participative-group) elements.

Laissez-faire – This is where the leader decides that the group can manage themselves. All power is passed to the group and the leader stays in the background ready to help if the group asks for it. Sometimes the leader gives general directions on the tasks to be tackled but the employees are then left to achieve them in the way they think is best.

 Differentiate between the three behavioural leadership styles.

3.3 Contingency Theories or Situational Approaches

The idea that one particular leadership style is appropriate in all organizational settings has been challenged by many researchers.

The contingency theorists advocate the view that the success of a leader depends on the relationship between the organizational situation and the leader's style. The organizational situation takes into consideration such things as the climate in the working environment, the values, attitude and experience of the manager and staff and the type of work. The leader has to ascertain which particular leadership style is most effective in a given situation.

Peter Fiedler used a **Leadership Contingency Approach Model,** which involves combining an analysis of the leadership style together with the pertinent working environment. Three situational variables are used from within the organization and how these interact with the leader.

These are:

- **leader-member relations** (which involve the acceptance of the leader by the group members)
- **task structure** (whether tasks are clearly stated or not)
- **leader position power** (using leader's sources of power to influence promotion and monetary payments).

Fiedler shows through this model that when the situation is neither particularly favourable nor unfavourable, a people orientated leader is more effective. He believes that leadership performance depends then as much on the organization as it depends upon the leader's own attributes.

A **Situational Approach Model** developed by *Paul Hersey* and *Kenneth Blanchard* identifies both the directive and supportive behaviour in a leader, which varies with the maturity level of the subordinate.

With experienced and committed staff the leadership style would be one of delegation with little direction or support. A young and motivated subordinate would receive a lot of direction and little support.

Then again an experienced employee with low commitment would receive high levels of direction and support, i.e. a coaching style. The experienced middle-manager who possesses varying levels of commitment and motivation would receive high levels of support coupled with little direction.

The problem with this theory is that it relies on the leadership being aware of the development of their employees and knowing how to react to different situations.

The contingency models can be regarded as an improvement on the one best style model but it neglects variables which do not fit neatly into its framework.

   a. *What is the Leadership Contingency Model characterized by?*
         b. *How does the Situational Approach Model reflect reality?*

4.0 CONCLUSION

The study of management/leadership is a complex issue influenced by internal (personality) traits and external factors alike.

Depending on their personality and the circumstances managers/ leaders adopt different styles and approaches to ensure optimal results for their organization.

However, one thing is certain; efforts to reach a complete understanding of the dynamics of management/leadership still remain unfulfilled.

 Discussion Forum

a. An education which encourages personal responsibility, initiative and self-reliance is all you need to produce future leaders. Discuss.

b. Which present day international leader do you admire and why?

c. Which kind of leadership do you prefer and why?

d. Do you think that leadership and management are the same or different?

Using the material studied in this unit attempt to analyze Roberto Guizueta and J.F. Kennedy.

OBITUARY

Roberto Guizueta

After the Cross, the Coca-Cola people like to say, the odd-shaped bottle is the world's most famous symbol. In reality, Coke's fame has spread far beyond the Christian world, into the domains of other religious beliefs and into the godless ones as well.

Roberto Goizueta, the head of Coca-Cola for 16 years, was never bothered by sneers of 'Coca-colonization'. Rather the opposite. When the Soviet Union broke up, Mr Goizueta's team marched in like liberators. The disunited workers of the world were offered the more enduring slogan of 'Always Coca-Cola'. Like many western industrialists, he dreamt of his product on every table in China. Supposing, he would say, every Chinese drank the same number of Cokes as the average Australian, that would push up global sales by, let's see, well, a lot. But unlike many western products, Coke has started to do it.

He was, it was said at the time, an odd choice. Roberto Goizueta was a Cuban who had worked for Coca-Cola in Havanna as a chemist. After Fidel Castro's revolution he moved with his family to the United States and slowly rose in the Coca-Cola hierarchy. The executive management at that time were all southern gentlemen. But Robert Woodruff decided that Roberto had drive, something that Coca-Cola, for all its reputation, lacked. The company's profits were falling and it was being seriously challenged by PepsiCo. Roberto was from a good family and had been educated at Yale.

When Mr Goizueta took over, the share value of Coke was $4.3 billion, but he soon increased it to $152 billion. When he was asked for his strategy for growth, he replied: 'This is a very simple business, when we complicate it we really mess things up'. Diversification, the idea that 'two lousy businesses' were better than one good one was 'crazy'. The lousy businesses he got rid of included a shrimp farm and a Hollywood studio. 'Coke is it' was the slogan and the philosophy.

Advertising was important, but even more important was distribution, the need to place Coke throughout the world. The body was seen as an undeveloped market: of the average 64 ounces of fluid drunk each day, less than two ounces was Coke. Diet Coke rode to success on the rich world's desire to slim. But New Coke, a sweeter version of Coke, was a flop. Coke drinkers were upset, sales fell and the firm quickly switched back to ist old recipe. Mr Goizueta said he had blundered.

Roberto Guizueta was a neat man, never seen in public without his jacket. He once reprimanded an employee for wearing odd socks. Financial analysts grumbled that he admonished them if they wrote anything less than favourable about Coke. Reporters found him a disappointing person to interview. He had no foibles. They tended instead to write about his wealth. In salary, bonuses and shares he was reckoned to have received about $1.33 billion during his term as chief of Coca-Cola. That was one obvious thing you could say about Mr Goizueta. He did like to reward success.

P.S. The board of directors, keen to honour Roberto Goizueta's wishes, chose his number two, Doug Ivesto, to succeed him after Roberto died of cancer. He lasted less than 18 months in the job.

Curriculum Vitae of:
John Fitzgerald Kennedy
(29 May 1917 – 22 November 1963)

1936   After attending a series of private schools enrols for the University of Harvard. His father was a multi-millionaire and a close friend of President Roosevelt. Family life was very competitive. Only serious topics were discussed around the dinner table.

1937   At Harvard University he becomes interested in politics and takes a trip to Europe. His father becomes US Ambassador to Great Britain.

1940   Graduates with highest honours.

1941   Enlists in the US Navy. Earns medal for outstanding bravery. Emerges from the war a hero.

1946   Elected to Congress for first time: re-elected 1948 and 1950.

1952   Becomes Senator for Massachusetts, his brother Bobby: runs his campaign; is re-elected in 1958.

1953   Marries Jacqueline Lee Bouvier.

1954   Undergoes two major back operations and writes a book on American politics, which becomes a bestseller.

1955   Fails to gain the Democratic nomination as Vice-Presidential candidate.

1960   Chosen as Presidential candidate by his party: narrowly wins the Presidency over Richard Nixon. Winning TV debate was crucial.

1961   Inaugurated as the youngest and first Irish-American Catholic President. Takes responsibility for failed invasion of Cuba by Cuban rebels against Fidel Castro although plan had been devised by the previous President.

1962   Sends Federal Troops to protect blacks and keep law and order in Mississippi. Wins more prestige with successful outcome of forcing Soviets to withdraw nuclear weapons from Cuba (Cuban Missile Crisis)

1963   Agrees Nuclear Ban Treaty with the USSR: A hotline is set up between Moscow and Washington. Announces new Civil Rights Bill. Visits Berlin and addresses crowd at the Berlin Wall. Assassinated in Dallas, Texas at the age of 46.

VOCABULARY

A	
to accord	verleihen erteilen
to affect	beeinflussen, berühren
accomplish	ausführen, bewältigen
accomplishment	Bewältigung
achievement	Leistung; Errungenschaft
achiever	Leistungstyp
to advocate	befürworten
to amaze	erstaunen, in Erstaunen versetzen
approach	Herangehen, Ansatz, Methode
to arouse	erwecken
array	Ansammlung, (stattliche)Reihe
to ascertain	ermitteln, feststellen
to ascribe	zuschreiben
to aspire to	streben nach, erstreben
to assume	annehmen, von etwas ausgehen
assumption	Annahme
to attain	erreichen
attempt	Versuch
B	
behaviour	Verhalten
to bewilder	verwirren; verblüffen
blueprint	Plan, Entwurf
buzzword	Modewort
C	
chain	Kette
to challenge	in Frage stellen, anfechten; herausfordern
clout	Schlagkraft
to coerce	zwingen
coercive	Zwangs-
to coincide	sich decken, übereinstimmen
common sense	gesunder Menschenverstand
comprehensive	umfassend
concern	Angelegenheit, Belang
to confound	verwirren. verblüffen
consistent, to be~with	übereinstimmend, etw. entsprechen
consistently	ständig, durchweg, einheitlich
to constrain	beschränken, eingrenzen
to contend	behaupten
contingency	Kontingenz, Eventualität, Fall

D

decisive	entschlossen, bestimmt
dependable	zuverlässig
to descend	hinuntergehen, herunterkommen
to deter (from)	abhalten(von), hindern (an)
determination	Entschlossenheit
to dispirit	entmutigen
to distinguish	unterscheiden
to draw on	sich stützen auf

E

elusive	schwer definierbar, schwer fassbar
emotive	emotional, emotionsgeladen
to empower	ermächtigen
to empower	ermächtigen
end	Ziel, Zweck
to enhance	verstärken, vergrößern
equity theory	Gleichheitstheorie
esteem	Wertschätzung, Ansehen
evil	böse
exhortation	Ermahnung
expertise	Sachkenntnis, Fachwissen
to expound	darlegen, erläutern

F

to facilitate	erleichtern, ermöglichen, unterstützen
faith	Vertauen
follower	Anhänger

G

generic	hier: allgemein

I

to implement	ausführen, umsetzen
implementer	Vollstrecker
to imply	implizieren, bedeuten
to impose	auferlegen
inception	Beginn, Anfang
infallibility	Unfehlbarkeit
ingredient	Bestandteil
to inspire	inspirieren
to instil	beibringen, einprägen

J

janitor	Hausmeister
judgement	Urteil

L

laissez- faire	laissez-faire

legitimate	legitim, rechtmäßig
likelihood	Wahrscheinlichkeit
line organisation	Linienorganisation
loner	Einzelgänger
M	
maintenance	Erhaltung, Aufrechterhaltung
means	Mittel
mental agility	geistige Wendigkeit
mission	Aufgabe, Auftrag, Mission
N	
notion	Idee, Vorstellung
O	
to object to	Einwände haben gegen, dagegen sein
objective	Ziel, Zielvorstellung
P	
pace	Tempo
patter	Fachjargon
pattern	Muster
performance	Leistung
pertinent	relevant
power holder	Machtinhaber
praise	Lob
precedence	Vorrang
to predict	voraussagen
predispose	veranlagen, für etwas geeignet machen
prescription	Rezept
principal	Direktor (einer Schule), Rektor
promotion	Beförderung
proposition	Aussage
to prove	beweisen, sich erweisen
provided (that)	vorausgesetzt (dass)
punishment	Bestrafung
to purport to be	vorgeben etwas zu sein
R	
rank	Rang
to rate	(ein)schätzen
recognition	Anerkennung, Erkennung
reengineer	überarbeiten, neu gestalten
to refer to	bezeichnen als
referent power	'Vorbild - Macht'
to refute	widerlegen
reputation	Ruf
resilience	Widerstandskraft, Widerstands-fähigkeit

review	Überprüfung
to reward	belohnen
reward	Belohnung, Anerkennung
S	
scholar	Gelehrter, Akademiker
sensitivity	Sensibilität,
	Einfühlungsvermögen
share	teilhaben, teilen, beteiligen
single-handed	allein, ohne fremde Hilfe
sociability	Geselligkeit
solely	nur, allein
span	Spanne
stratum	Schicht
subordinate	Unterstellter
to supervise	überwachen, beaufsichtigen
T	
to tackle (a task)	(eine Aufgabe) in Angriff
	nehmen , bewältigen
to threaten	drohen
trait	Eigenschaft, Wesenszug
truism	(Binsen)Wahrheit
trust	Vertrauen
U	
ultimately	letztlich, schließlich
undoing	Ruin, Verderben
W	
wield	ausüben

HUMAN RESOURCE MANAGEMENT (HRM)

One day while walking down the street a highly successful executive was tragically hit by a bus and died. Her soul arrived up in Heaven where she was met at the Pearly Gates by St. Peter. "Welcome to Heaven," said St. Peter. "Before you get settled in though, it seems we have a problem. You see, strangely enough, we've never had an executive make it this far and we're not really sure what to do with you."

"No problem, just let me in," said the executive. "Well, I'd like to," replied Peter, "but I have higher orders. What we're going to do is let you have a day in Hell and a day in Heaven and then you can choose whichever one you want to spend an eternity in". "Actually, I think I've made up my mind ... I prefer to stay in Heaven," said the woman. "Sorry, we have rules ...," answered Peter.

And with that St. Peter put the executive in an elevator and went down to Hell. The doors opened and she found herself stepping out onto the putting green of a beautiful golf course. In the distance was a country club and standing in front of her were all of her friends and they were all dressed in designer clothes and cheering for her. They ran up and kissed her on both cheeks and they talked about old times and the wonderful share options and other fringe benefits being offered by the Devil. They played an excellent round of golf and at night went to the country club where she enjoyed an excellent steak and lobster dinner plus unlimited cocktails - all free of charge.

She even met the Devil who was actually a really nice guy and she had a great time telling jokes and dancing. She was having such a good time that before she knew it, it was time to leave. Everybody shook her hand and waved good-bye as she got on the elevator. The elevator went back up to the Pearly Gates and she found St. Peter. "Now it's time to spend a day in Heaven," he said.

So she spent the next 24 hours lounging around on clouds and playing the harp and singing. She had a great time and before she knew it her 24 hours were up and St. Peter came and got her. "So, you've spent a day in Hell and you've spent a day in Heaven. Now you must choose your place in eternity," he said. The woman paused for a second and then replied: "Well, I never thought I'd say this, I mean, Heaven has been really great and all, but I think I had a better time in Hell." So St. Peter escorted her to the elevator and she went back to Hell.

> *When the doors of the elevator opened she found herself standing in a desolate wasteland covered in garbage and filth. She saw her friends were dressed in rags and were picking up the garbage and putting it in sacks.*
>
> *The Devil came up to her and put his arm around her. "I don't understand," stammered the woman, "yesterday I was here and there was a golf course and a country club and we ate lobster and we danced and had a great time. Now all there is a wasteland of garbage and all my friends look miserable."*
>
> *The Devil looked at her and smiled: "Yesterday we were recruiting you. Today you're staff."*
>
> *(Many thanks to Robert Kunde)*

FOCUS This unit offers an insight into the main areas of HRM policy.

1.0 Introduction to HRM
2.0 Recruitment
    2.1 The Recruitment Process
    2.2 Types of Employment
3.0 Termination of Employment
4.0 Remuneration (Compensation) Policy
5.0 Training and Development
6.0 Industrial Relations

1.0 INTRODUCTION TO HRM

Everyone knows that a successful organization depends on its employees as efficient staff are vital for the smooth running and progress of every firm. HRM or personnel management involves attracting (hiring or taking on), compensating, developing, retaining, terminating (firing or sacking) and motivating staff to ensure that an organization's mission statement can be carried out. And, as we know, very often a broad gap exists between the expectations of managers and that of employees.

The Human Resource Manager sets the appropriate policies concerning personnel or human capital. This involves all management decisions and actions that concern the relationship between the organization and employees or human resources. Increasing global competition has ensured that today there is more focus on strategy and long term objectives.

The main **HRM policy areas** are:

- Recruitment
- Remuneration (Compensation) Policy
- Training and Development
- Industrial Relations

2.0 RECRUITMENT

2.1 The Recruitment Process

The first step in recruitment is a clear job description, which then results in first contacts with applicants needed to fill the company vacancies. Jobs can be filled internally or externally. Often companies place job advertisements in newspapers, magazines, the Internet, etc to find new staff. Sometimes a current employee can recommend friends or acquaintances. This is known as **employee referral**, and is often used in the IT industry where the demand for employees is great.

Potential recruits can be initially screened by being asked to submit written applications in the form of a **curriculum vitae (CV)** or, in American English, a **resumé**, together with a letter of application, or through the use of standardized application forms. Applications by telephone and the Internet are increasingly being used.

After the initial screening, the applicants are usually divided into **suitable, not suitable** and **marginal**. Appropriate responses should be given to these three groups. Laws are in force to ensure that applicants may not be discriminated against based on their race, religion, colour, sex or national origin. **Affirmative action** programs also exist to increase job opportunities for women, minorities, disabled people and other protected groups.

Applicants are then often tested. These can be **intelligence tests,** which are designed to measure thinking abilities or **aptitude tests**, which focus on innate skills such as mechanical ability, clerical and numerical ability and manual dexterity. **Attainment tests** focus on the knowledge or skills learned at school or college, e.g. typing, spelling and mental arithmetic abilities. **Personality tests** try to identify an individual's personality traits or dimensions.

Another step is the job interview. An interview is very much a two-way process, with the candidate assessing the company just as much as the company assesses the applicant.

The company checks the backgrounds of the potential employees and sometimes arranges that the successful applicant undergoes a medical check before starting employment.

Some organizations choose to allow **employment agencies** to carry out the recruitment process. Others engage in **outsourcing** in the form of employee leasing from specialist companies. This is often referred to as **alternative staffing**.

    Describe the recruitment process.

2.2   Types of Employment

These last decades have seen huge growth in **part time, temporary or contingency workers** who are employed on a part time basis or on certain projects. They normally are less well-paid than **full-time employees** or 9-5 regular employees who have limited or unlimited (permanent) contracts. Part-timers miss out on employee benefits as well.

Most employees sign standard employment contracts. Some do not sign anything. **Employment at will** or a **'gentlemen's agreement'** is an employer-employee relationship where both parties may end their arrangement at any time.

New staff in an organization are normally put on a **probation period**, or trial period, usually lasting six months to check out the new employee's job performance and suitability.

When people work is an important issue. Some organizations permit **flexitime**, which involves allowing employees to partially set their own work hours. A *band time* consists of the total time the company operates, e.g. 8am to 7pm, the *core time* is when all employees must be at work, e.g. 10am to 4pm.

Other companies that are open 24 hours a day operate on a **shift** system where employees work, for example, on a three shift system of 8 hours.

Work-at-home programs allow employees to do all or some of their work at home while **telecommuting** is a variation of this where employees are connected by technology to the workplace.

Job sharing is another way to vary how much people work. It involves two employees sharing a full-time job, each working on a part-time basis.

    Summarise the main types of employment.

3.0   TERMINATION OF EMPLOYMENT

Employees leave an organization for different reasons. **Dismissal** is where an employee is removed or discharged from the place of work as a result of incompetence, stealing, etc. **Natural wastage** is the reduction in the size of a workforce through retirement.

Attrition is the process of reducing staff through normal turnover and voluntary terminations. **Layoffs** or **redundancies** are situations where employees lose their jobs because the organization or position no longer exist, as occurs when a business ceases trading or is downsizing. **Downsizing** involves reducing the number of employees by eliminating jobs. The reasons may be to cut costs and streamline the organizational structure.

The employee then looks for another position elsewhere while receiving **unemployment benefit (BE)/compensation** or **'collecting unemployment'** (AE) which they had paid in the form of unemployment insurance while they had employment. If the unemployed person fails to find a job they will need to go on the more long-term **welfare (AE) or income support (BE)** when the insurance benefits run out.

A **period of notice** is a written communication stating the length of time required for notification of ceasing employment. It means that someone is to leave a job at a specified time. **Notice** can be given by the employee or employer.

Turnover in a company can be high or low. High turnover can result from poor remuneration, bad morale, etc.

Absenteeism relates to absence from work due to illness or other reasons. Voluntary absence is where there is no acceptable reason for the   absence; involuntary absence is when someone is legitimately absent.

    How and why can employment be terminated?

4.0   REMUNERATION (COMPENSATION) POLICY

An employee's salary or wage can depend on:

- national wage agreements or settlements which are agreed on a national level between organizations representing employers and employees.
- remuneration offered by competitors in the industry sector.
- the current unemployment situation

Employee (fixed) benefits are extra rewards such as health insurance, retirement plans or child-care, received in addition to salaries and wages. **Salaries** are normally paid monthly to white collar workers, while **wages** are traditionally paid weekly to blue collar or manual employees. **Fringe benefits** or **perks** can include free or subsidized meals, a company car, low interest credits, etc.

Some employees, typically salespersons, are paid on a **commission** basis rather than on a salary.

Employee performance related payments include:

A **bonus**, which is a cash payment in addition to their normal compensation for achieving an organizational goal.

Profit sharing, which is an incentive used to give employees a chance to share in the profits earned by the organization.

Employee stock options, which allow the employees to purchase company shares at discounted prices.

Staff welfare

Employee welfare, health and safety is an important aspect of working conditions and standards are often set by statutory requirements.

 Summarise the main types of remuneration/compensation.

5.0   TRAINING AND DEVELOPMENT

The usual approach to training and development has been to organize traditional programs to react, for example, to changes in procedures or equipment. This reactive rather than proactive approach is increasingly difficult in a fast changing world, where employees need to keep up to date with advances and developments in technological changes, the growth of IT systems, a growing dependence on science and the constant redesigning of occupations which require a "knowledge worker" who would be able to cope with a changing work environment.

No longer can a person acquire all the formal education he needs in the first twenty years of his life; the fact is that the clock starts running down the moment a young man or woman steps from the commencement platform.

Continuous Development (CD) is an approach that seeks to transform learning into a habit, into lifelong learning and holds the view that employees should seek out learning opportunities themselves.

In the past training was often sporadic and lacked a conceptual structure. The onus in training was on the organization rather than on the employee. A lot of us are familiar with the one-day training course, a kind of day off work with a nice lunch in the middle. While these were very often fragmented and imposed, this is not to say that they were not effective for that time or even now, for that matter, in certain sectors.

One must remember that it is also an option for an employer to forgo both CD or training and adopt a revolving hire and fire strategy to maintain skills by recruiting new employees who have been trained elsewhere or have acquired up-to-date knowledge.

On-the-job training usually involves receiving formal one-to-one instruction from another employee. **Mentoring** is an informal variation. **Off-the-job** training is normally undertaken by larger firms which can afford training centres away from the place of normal work with specialist instructors.

A **career path** is the career development path through a profession or occupation moving upwards through the organization. **Job rotation** means that each employee learns a variety of jobs for set periods of time so that he/she has a greater understanding of the organization and is more flexible.

Performance appraisal (staff assessment) is an evaluation of an employee's performance compared with specific goals, which are normally part of a performance plan. This can result in **promotion**, which is the receiving of a higher position or a more important job in the organization usually in conjunction with an improved remuneration package. The opposite is **demotion**, while a **transfer** involves changing your job sideways within the organization. This can be initiated by the employee or the employer.

Finally **succession planning** involves planning to replace employees who will be leaving the company.

Explain the different types of training and development.

6.0   INDUSTRIAL RELATIONS

Industrial Relations represent another crucial area in HRM. This refers to the way in which employees and management co-operate and work together on a daily basis for the good of the business. Many companies have some employees who are members of **trade unions**, which is an organization representing the workers in a particular trade, industry or profession concerning pay and working conditions. To achieve its aims trade unions negotiate with employers by a process known as **collective bargaining**. Each side tries to get the best deal and reach a collective agreement which they both find acceptable. Sometimes a settlement may also include a productivity agreement focusing on conditions or hours of work. A **productivity agreement** is a wage increase in return for employees producing more. This enables the employer to pay more without increasing costs.

A **shop steward** is the union representative in the workplace who can be contacted if a problem occurs. This is known as a **grievance**, i.e. where an employee or union complains that management is violating some agreed provision.

Bad **industrial relations** often result in an unhappy workforce, sloppy work or even strikes.

The main types of **industrial action** are:

- **Work-to-rule**, which involves following every rule in such a way as to slow the work down.

- **Go-slow** is where the employees deliberately work slowly.

- **Overtime Ban** is a situation where employees refuse to do any overtime

- **Sabotage** is where employees deliberately damage machinery and equipment belonging to the firm.

- **Boycott** is a situation where union members refuse to handle certain goods or materials or refuse to work with other employees.

- **Strikes** are normally the last resort and can be **official** (called by the union) or **unofficial** (not backed by the union). A **lightning** or **wildcat strike** is a sudden walkout as an expression of workers anger. **Picketing** involves workers standing at the entrance of the workplace carrying placards stating that a strike is in progress.

- **Lockout** is where the employers literally lock out the employees from entering the premises

When employers or unions cannot agree in a dispute an independent or government agency may be called in to arrange **conciliation** to get the two parties talking together again. **Arbitration** is where an independent third party listens to all the arguments and then makes a binding agreement, which both sides must accept. **Mediation** is non-binding where a third party listens and puts forward proposals for a solution, which both sides can accept or ignore.

  a. How does the cooperation between employers and employees work?
  b. What is meant by industrial action?

Discussion Forum

  a. Trade unions are no longer important. They often even hamper positive economic development. Discuss.
  b. Would you be willing to place job satisfaction ahead of high pay?
  c. What non-monetary types of remuneration could be regarded as acceptable?
  d. Discuss the changing aspects of work from the employer's and employee's point of view.
  e. What questions would you ask as an interviewer to prospective candidates. And as the interviewee?

VOCABULARY

A	
absenteeism	Fernbleiben (vom Arbeitsplatz), Abwesenheit
acquaintance	Bekannte(r)
affirmative action	aktive Förderungsmaßnahmen
aptitude	Eignung
arbitration	Regelung durch ein Schiedsgericht
at will	auf Widerruf
attrition	Arbeitskräfteabgang
B	
bonus	Prämie

C	
to cease	aufhören, beenden
clerical ability	Schreibfähigkeit
collective bargaining	Tarifverhandlungen
commencement	(Feier zur) Verleihung von akadem. Graden; Beginn
commission	Provision
to compensate	vergüten
compensation (AE)	Gehalt, Vergütung
conciliation	Schlichtung, Versöhnung
contingency worker	Bedarfskraft, Zeitarbeitskraft
D	
demotion	Zurückstufung
development	Weiterbildung
dismissal	Entlassung
E	
employee benefits	Arbeitnehmervergünstigungen
employee leasing	Arbeitskräfte- Leasing
employment agency	Stellenvermittlungsagentur
eternity	Ewigkeit
F	
filth	Schmutz
fringe benefits	zusätzliche Leistungen, Lohnnebenleistungen
G	
garbage	Müll
grievance	Beschwerde
I	
to impose	auferlegen
incentive	Anreiz
industrial relations	Arbeitgeber-/Arbeitnehmer-Beziehung
innate	angeboren
J	
job advertisement	Stellenanzeige
job interview	Bewerbungsgespräch
L	
layoff	Entlassung
lightning strike	Blitzstreik
lobster	Hummer
lockout	Aussperrung
to lounge around	herumliegen
M	
manual dexterity	manuelles Geschick, manuelle Fähigkeiten
marginal	hier: Grenzfall

mediation	Mediation, Vermittlung, Schlichtung
to miss out	zu kurz kommen
N	
natural wastage	natürlicher Abgang von Arbeitskräften (Rente, Tod)
notification	Benachrichtigung
O	
occupation	Tätigkeit
on the job training	innerbetriebliche Ausbildung am Arbeitsplatz
onus	Pflicht, Last
P	
performance appraisal	Leistungsbeurteilung
performance related payment	leistungsabhängige Vergütung
period of notice	Kündigungsfrist
perks, perquisites	Sondervergünstigungen
picketing	Streikposten stehen
proactive approach	proaktives (Initiative ergreifendes) Verhalten
probation period	Probezeit
productivity agreement	Produktivitätsvereinbarung
promotion	Beförderung
provision	Bestimmung, Vorschrift
R	
to redisign	neu-/umgestalten
redundancy	Entlassung (wegen Arbeitsmangel)
referral,	Verweisung an, Angabe
remuneration	Vergütung, Bezahlung, Bezüge
to retain	behalten
retirement	Ruhestand
S	
salary	Gehalt
settlement	Vereinbarung; Schlichtung
shop steward	gewerkschaftlicher Vertrauensmann, Personalvertreter
sloppy	nachlässig
staff assessment	Personalbeurteilung
statutory	gesetzlich
stock option	Aktienbezugsrecht
streamline	rationalisieren
succession	Nachfolge
T	
temporary worker	Aushilfe, befristete Arbeitskraft

to terminate	beenden
trade union	Gewerkschaft
training	Âusbildung
transfer	Umsetzung
turnover	Fluktuation
U	
unemployment assistance	Arbeitslosenhilfe
unemployment benefit	Arbeitslosengeld
V	
vacancy	freie Stelle
to violate	verletzen
voluntary	freiwillig
W	
wage	Lohn
welfare	Wohlbefinden, Wohlergehen
welfare/income support	Sozialhilfe
wildcat strike	wilder Streik

BREAKING DOWN THE BORDERS – FOREIGN TRADE

> *I'm opposed to millionaires, but it would be dangerous to offer me the position*
>
> *Mark Twain*

FOCUS This unit is divided into two sections. The first section considers the importance of international trade while the second section covers the various documentation involved.

In a special vocabulary section at the end of this unit you will find a grouped overview of types of orders, methods and terms of payment and delivery as well as export documentation.

SECTION I: INTERNATIONAL TRADE

1.0 Introduction
2.0 Movement Towards Free Trade
3.0 Methods of Selling Goods Abroad
4.0 The Difficulties Facing Exporters
5.0 Transport

SECTION II: DOCUMENTATION IN DOMESTIC AND FOREIGN TRADE

1.0 Standard Business Documents
2.0 Export Documentation
3.0 Methods and Terms of Payment and Delivery
4.0 Grouped Overview of Important Commercial Terms

SECTION I: INTERNATIONAL TRADE

1.0   INTRODUCTION

All the countries of the world are interdependent upon each other to a large extent due to different climatic, natural resources and geographic conditions.

Trade helps a country to earn **foreign exchange** and to create higher standards of living. It also increases specialization and results in greater **economies of scale** (reductions in unit costs and higher profits when goods are produced in large quantities), which in turn allow firms to grow to their optimal, or best, size. Another result is that there is more international co-operation.

Because of these advantages many countries around the world are members of organizations or are parties to agreements which have as their main aim the growth of world trade and the elimination of trade barriers.

Foreign trade can be defined as international trade carried on between firms in different countries consisting of both **visible** (physical goods) and **invisible** trade (banking, insurance, tourism, transport, loans, investments, etc) of goods and services in the form of exports and imports.

Multilateral trade describes the situation where a country is involved in foreign trade with many countries, with **bilateral trade** it transacts most of its foreign trade with only one country.

Terms of Trade refers to how many foreign goods a country can receive for one unit of its own production. More specifically the terms of trade represent the import purchasing power of one unit of exports.

If the terms of trade are **favourable** then the same amount of exports is able to pay for a greater quantity of imports than before; if not, the terms of trade have become **unfavourable**.

Balance of Trade is the comparison of the value of a country's total exports with the total value of its imports during the same period.

If the total value of exports is less than the total value of imports there is a **deficit** (adverse or unfavourable situation), the opposite is a favourable or **surplus** Balance of Trade.

Balance of Payments is the difference between the amount of money that has flowed into a country and the amount that has flowed out of it during the year - i.e. the income and expenditure of a country. It includes the balance of trade and all transfers of money for other reasons. The balance can be either a surplus or a deficit.

A state can interfere in trade in different ways in order to help its economy.

A **tariff** (import or customs duty) is a tax imposed on imported goods in order to make them more expensive, while a **quota** is a physical restriction on the amount of particular goods which can be imported into a country in order to protect home-produced goods.

Other methods of controlling trade include **embargoes** (the complete banning of trade between one country and another), **subsidies** (government financial support to enable domestic goods to be sold at a lower price thus reducing demand for imported goods) and **exchange control** (restricting the supply of foreign currency available for imports).

Gross Domestic Product (GDP) is a measure of income within a country that excludes foreign earnings while **Gross National Product** (GNP) is a measure of the sum of all goods and services produced by a country's nationals both living in the country and abroad.

   a. Why do countries trade?
   b. Explain terms of trade, balance of trade and balance of payments.
   c. Differentiate between GDP and GNP.

2.0   MOVEMENT TOWARDS FREE TRADE

The worldwide trend today is towards a more liberal trading environment through strategic intervention in the process of international trade. Organizations that promote this include:

* The **International Monetary Fund (IMF)** which was established in 1944 at the Bretton Woods Conference. Its main aim is to encourage trade by using the Fund to provide short-term loans to members with a Balance of Payments deficit.
* The **World Trade Organization (WTO)** which is the principal international organization dealing with the global rules of trade between nations. Its main function is to ensure that trade flows as smoothly, predictably and freely as possible.

The **European Union (EU)** is an example of a **trading bloc** which arises when a number of countries agree to form themselves into one trading area for business purposes and end all forms of tariffs and quotas on trade among themselves. They also agree to operate a standard rate of tariffs and quotas on dealing with non-member countries. Trading blocs of this nature are known as customs unions. The EU began life in this form but has now integrated social and political aspects. Agreements such as the **North American Free Trade Agreement (NAFTA)** and the **Association of South East Asian Nations (ASEAN)** are other examples, which, however, do not have the social and political direction which the EU has.

Free trade policies include:

- opening closed foreign markets, e.g. as Japan has in the recent past
- government support for strategic industries, e.g. the steel or coal industry, so that a country does not become too dependent on other states.
- targeting and penalizing trading partners who are involved in unfair trading practices, e.g. those involved in subsidizing exports of certain products when it is not allowed or engaging in **dumping**, i.e. the unloading of surplus stock in a foreign country at a very low price.

Some economists advocate managed **fair trade**, where countries involved agree to give each other similar concessions and/or restrictions in trade by imposing duties or not imposing restrictions on certain agreed items. Fair trade is a contrast to **free trade**, which refers to trade between states absolutely free from any restrictions.

Advantages of Free Trade	Potential problems of Free Trade
• It improves the efficiency of firms and can lead to reduced prices for consumers.	• It results in job losses, for example, the transfer of blue collar jobs from industrialized to industrializing (developing) countries that have cheaper labour costs.
• It gives firms the possibility of increasing output and profits.	
• A country can specialize in producing those goods it has an advantage in relative to other countries, i.e. it can satisfy the law of comparative advantage.	• It increases the rate of deindustrialization where companies move steadily to, for example, developing countries, offering lower taxes and more flexible environmental laws.

- It promotes a greater choice of goods and pushes innovation.

- There is a lack of protection for strategic industries.
- It speeds up the process of globalization, which is not seen as positive by everyone (see Unit 12).
- It can hinder the creation of a cleaner environment.
- It is claimed that it encourages violations of human and worker's rights.

To counteract the negative consequences of free trade, countries take measures to protect their own economy. This is referred to as **protectionism (protected trade)**, which exists in the form of retaliatory tariffs. It is deemed necessary in order to:

- enable domestic firms to compete with foreign low wage rate producers
- stimulate home employment
- provide for some measure of self-sufficiency and protect industries deemed to be in the national interest
- protect young firms or infant industries which are just starting up.
- provide revenue in the form of customs duties for the government
- protect the Balance of Trade and the Balance of Payments
- prevent dumping

    a. Differentiate between free trade and fair trade.
    b. What are the pros and cons of free trade?
    c. What is protectionism?

3.0   METHODS OF SELLING GOODS ABROAD

Some of the standard ways of getting goods to foreign markets are:

- **Direct sales**

   This involves running an export sales department and sending representatives abroad to meet foreign buyers

- **Foreign Distributors**

   Sometimes goods can be sold in bulk to foreign buyers who will sell and distribute them in their own country.

- **Overseas Agents**

  These agents are appointed abroad to represent the firm and sell goods on their behalf and are usually paid on a commission basis. A **Del Credere** agent will, for a higher commission, guarantee the creditworthiness of the clients he/she is dealing with.

- **Export Houses**

  These are specialist organizations which assist a firm in two main areas:

  1. They act as merchants, buying a company's products and selling them overseas on their own account.

  2. They act as agents responsible for handling all or part of a firm's overseas marketing such as promotion, transport and distribution.

- **Overseas Subsidiaries**

  Instead of exporting, a firm may choose to set up its own factory in a foreign country.

- **Licencing Agreement**

  A firm may decide to allow a foreign producer to manufacture its goods under licence. In return the licencing firm receives a special royalty payment. Coca-Cola is sold worldwide on this basis.

4.0   THE DIFFICULTIES FACING EXPORTERS

Exporters are often faced with a number of difficulties when selling abroad. This was one reason for introducing the euro which has brought many advantages to firms trading in the EU.

Typical problems include the following:

1. The **language barrier**, which is an important factor in terms of general communications, packaging and advertising.
2. **Standardization problems** concerning different units of length, weight, voltage, safety standards, etc.
3. **Payment problems** with overseas clients.
4. **Cultural differences** concerning punctuality, deadlines, etc
5. **Pilferage** during transportation.
6. **Political upheavals** cause constant problems to business people engaged in international trading.
7. **Legal problems** where the exporter must be aware of foreign rules and regulations.

8. **Marketing problems** concerning the tastes and customs of the exporting country.
9. The **cost of breaking into** the overseas market may be prohibitive.
10. **Currency difficulties** due to fluctuations. There are various ways of reducing the risk associated with fluctuating currencies including entering a **foreign exchange forward contract** (whereby a bank or financial institution agrees to buy or sell a certain amount of currency for the customer at a fixed rate on a specific date in the future). Using a **hedge market** means buying a currency for a future date in order to smooth out possible fluctuations.

Governments and financial institutes also recognize the difficulties that exporters experience. Services made available to alleviate some of these problems include:

1. **State export trade boards**, which provide information and advice on foreign markets and financial support for export marketing. They also organize stands at foreign fairs and exhibitions, instore promotions and the setting up of trade missions.
2. The provision of **export credit insurance schemes** (very often by the state, which may guarantee loans and overdrafts taken out to finance exports) to provide exporters with cover against a range of commercial and political risks that may result in non-payment of goods abroad on credit terms.
3. **Consulate and diplomatic services**, which collect information to assist exporters and also promote a country's trade.
4. **Export finance schemes** operated by banks and other financial institutions of a country who provide credit facilities to buyers of products from that country at lower interest rates.
5. The domestic **Chamber of Commerce** and the **International Chamber of Commerce (ICC)** provide information about overseas markets and help with export procedures and documentation. The ICC is actively involved with the **Incoterms** (**In**ternational Rules for the Interpretation of Commercial **Terms**).

    a. What are the main methods of selling goods abroad?
    b. What difficulties do exporters face?
    c. How are these difficulties overcome?
    d. Differentiate between export credit insurance and an export finance scheme.

5.0 TRANSPORT

> *The shortest connection between two places is usually closed because of road works.*
>
> *Anon*

Goods may be exported throughout the world by air, sea, road, rail and pipeline. Transport is concerned with the movement of materials, goods or people from one place to another and is therefore a vital part of marketing and trade. The essential factors, which determine the effectiveness and efficiency of a transport system are:

1. **Cost**
2. **Safety** - This is obvious where people are concerned but in relation to goods it involves care in handling, loading and unloading and theft.
3. **Speed**
4. **Convenience** - especially to manufacturers, warehouses, wholesalers, retailers and customers with appropriate loading and unloading terminals.
5. **Flexibility** - for both large and small consignments of goods.
6. **Reliability** - being both regular and punctual.

Essential elements are

1. **The Unit of Carriage**, i.e. vehicles
2. **Highways** - these may be roads, railways, water, air or pipelines.
3. **Terminals** - for loading and unloading.

Forms of Transport

1. Road

Road transport is the most important mode of transport in most countries.

Many toll roads are being built in Europe - mainly developed by private enterprise where users pay a travelling charge.

Road haulage is divided between 'hire and reward' and 'own account' transport. In the former a transport system is hired and paid for by an individual or firm while in the latter a business owns its own system and carries its own goods in its own vehicles.

A ***common carrier*** is a person offering to transport goods for anyone who will employ him/her. Most common carriers work as road carriers.

2. Rail

Rail transport is suitable both for passenger and freight transport. Freight business handled by railways can be listed under the following headings:

Unit load - where goods are carried in a container, which is loaded onto a train specially constructed to receive it.

Palletized - where certain goods, such as bagged cement and bagged fertilizer, are placed on pallets and mechanically loaded onto special trains.

Bulk cargoes - such as iron-ore, fuel oil, sugar, cement, chemicals are carried on special wagons.

3. Air

Necessary facilities for air transport are

- land
- technology
- skilled workers

Air transport is quick, suitable for rush orders and perishable goods. It is also, however, expensive, subject to weather conditions, tied to fixed timetables and not suitable for bulk cargoes.

The size of aircraft and number of airports is steadily increasing.

4. Water

The advantages of sea transport are that it is suitable for bulk cargoes, relatively cheap and facilitates long distance trading. The downsides are that it is slow, fixed to timetables, and is more subject to weather than other modes.

The following ships are used:

Specialized vessels including refrigerated ships, oil tankers and bulk grain carriers.

Coastal, river and canal vessels with fairly low tonnages.

Liners for carrying passengers and freight across the oceans of the world.

Container vessels carry large containers, which are loaded and unloaded by means of special gantries. A firm wishing to use a container, but without sufficient cargo to fill one, can hire space in one through a groupage service.

Roll on, roll off (Ro-Ro) traffic where the belly of the ship acts as an extension of the road system.

Ship Chartering

A businessperson can hire a ship for a voyage, which is known as a voyage charter, or for a period of time, known as a time charter. If the hirer provides his/her own crew and officers and controls the vessel, the charter is known as a demise charter.

5. **Pipeline**

These are used for transporting oil and natural gas. They are cheap to maintain and are not generally affected by weather conditions or industrial problems so an ongoing supply of the product is guaranteed. In comparison with road and water transport there are few pollution problems or environmental accidents.

a. What factors determine the effectiveness and efficiency of a transport system?
b. Compare road and rail transport.
c. What is ship chartering?

SECTION II: DOCUMENTATION IN DOMESTIC AND FOREIGN TRADE

> *Happiness is a very small desk and a very big wastebasket.*
> *Robert Orben*

Correct (and as little as possible!) documentation is the lubricant of national and international trade and its importance cannot be overstated.

1.0   STANDARD BUSINESS DOCUMENTS

There are a number of documents whose use is standard in domestic or foreign trade transactions. These are explained below in order of natural occurrence.

Normally, potential customers will send in a **letter of enquiry**, which is a letter seeking information about goods or services, which the sender is interested in. An **offer** is then sent, being something that is put forward to be accepted or refused. A **price list**, which is a list of the goods offered for sale showing current prices, may also be sent, together with a **catalogue** containing a list of goods that is both illustrative and descriptive.

For the customer who already knows exactly what he or she requires a **quotation** (an offer to sell certain goods at a price under certain conditions that are stated) is sent. This may take the form of a **tender** which is a written offer given in answer to an **invitation to tender** or advertisement inviting quotations for large construction projects, e.g. a motorway or bridge.

An **estimate,** on the other hand, is a written offer to do certain work or to supply certain commodities at a stated cost in a specified way and under specified conditions, e.g. repairing a roof.

An **order** may then follow, this can be in oral or written format and is an instruction to supply certain goods at the price and upon the terms mentioned.

A **credit enquiry** is information sought by the seller from a bank or credit reference agency regarding the creditworthiness and reliability of a buyer.

A **consignment note** is used when a firm does not deliver goods itself but sends them by road or rail transport while a **delivery/despatch note** is used when goods are delivered in the supplier's _own_ vehicle and contains details of the quantity, number and description of the goods.

The **invoice** is a document sent by the seller of the goods listing the goods supplied and stating the sum of money due plus the conditions of sale and delivery while a **proforma invoice** is an invoice that is sent in advance before goods are supplied and is often used for goods sent on approval or by the foreign buyer to apply for an import licence or for opening a letter of credit.

A **statement of account** is a document sent by a firm to its customers showing the balance due on that date.

A **reminder/collection** letter is sent by the seller when goods are not paid for or by the buyer in the event of delay in delivery. A **receipt** is a written acknowledgement of money received.

The seller sends a **credit note** after the invoice has been paid indicating that the invoice was too high. It can also be sent when the buyer returns goods while a **debit note** is generally sent by the seller showing the buyer that the amount(s) he owes is greater than that shown on the invoice and the outstanding balance must be paid.

Dissatisfied customers may send a **complaint,** which is made when wrong, defective, inferior quality or the wrong quantity of goods are received or supplied.

Explain the steps from an enquiry to a sale.

2.0   EXPORT DOCUMENTATION

Lack of awareness of overseas customs procedures will cause delays at ports, resulting in extra costs, late delivery of goods and dissatisfied customers. Important documents in foreign trade consist of the following:

The following two documents are directly concerned with the **transportation** aspect.

- **Air Waybill/Air Consignment Note (ACN)**: When goods are despatched by air this document is issued by the carrier as a receipt and as a contract of affreightment (to hire space). It is, however, unlike the bill of lading not a document of title. Details included on the ACN are the airports of departure and arrival, the consignor (sender) and consignee (receiver), the name of the carrier and a general description of the goods.
- **Bill of Lading**: This is a document issued when goods are entrusted to a shipping company for transport by sea or via inland waterways. It is evidence of a contract of carriage, a receipt for the goods, and a document of title to the goods (which allows another party to claim the goods specified on it). Bills are normally issued in sets of two or three.

The next set are concerned with the **customs authorities** of the importing country.

- **Certificate of Origin**: This is issued by the Chamber of Commerce in the exporting country testifying as to the *origin* of the goods. It is required by the customs authorities to assist in the charging of import duties, to prevent dumping and to enforce embargoes against certain countries.
- **Commercial Invoice**: This is a special invoice used in foreign trade issued by the exporter stating the name and address of the consignor and consignee, details of the goods, their origin, terms of delivery and payment and their destination.

- **Consular Invoice**: Some countries require a copy of the export invoice, which must be stamped and signed by their consulate situated in the exporting country. It is issued in varying numbers of copies and is required for the purpose of charging import duties when the Certificate of Origin is not seen as reliable.
- **Customs Declaration**: This states the type and value of the goods and is used to compile monthly trade figures for statistical purposes.
- **Customs Invoice**: This is a special invoice showing the value of the goods and is required for customs purposes. It is prepared by the exporter on a prescribed official form, which is obtainable from the customs authority of the importing country. (see Invoice and Proforma Invoice in Section 1.0).

The above documentation can involve a lot of time and work. The following is **making life easier** for exporters and importers.

- **Electronic Data Interchange (EDI)**: This involves the transmission of export documentation by electronic messages.
- **Single Administration Document (SAD)**: Trade between EU and non-EU member states has been considerably simplified with the use of one standardized international document referred to as the Single Administrative Document. It has helped to save time and money for companies and transporters, and has made the procedures of understanding and collecting computerized statistics easier.

The **exporter** is often required to present the following documents.

- **Export Licence**: This is prepared by an exporter giving detailed descriptions of goods being sent. It is especially important concerning the weapons industry, works of art, etc.
- **Export Packing List**: This is required by governments before goods can be exported or, in some cases, imported.

And of course both the exporter and the importer will have to agree on who pays for the **protection** of the goods.

- **Insurance Policy**: This is the document which evidence that the goods are insured against loss or damage and shows the contract between the **insurer** (insurance company) and the **insured** (person or firm requiring insurance cover) for goods covering all stated risks.

a. *Explain the two documents directly concerned with the transportation aspect.*
b. *Explain three documents connected with the customs authorities.*
c. *What is the SAD?*
d. *What is an export licence?*

3.0 METHODS AND TERMS OF PAYMENT AND DELIVERY

The importer and the exporter will also have to agree on the methods and the terms of payment and delivery. This can involve a lot of negotiation and the payment form very often depends on how well the two parties involved know each other and the creditworthiness and reliability of the importer.

The most common Methods of Payment are:

1. **Cash with Order (CWO):** This method is for absolutely unknown customers, i.e. first time dealings. The buyer sends payment together with the order.

2. **Letter of Credit (L/C) or Documentary Credit (D/C):** The importer's bank guarantees that exporter receives payment after exporter carries out his/her side of the agreement satisfactorily. With this document both importer and exporter are protected as their contract is guaranteed by their banks as long as the importer and exporter fulfil the conditions of that contract.

3. **Documents against Payment (D/P) or Cash against Documents (CAD):** Here the buyer receives the relevant documentation after making payment and upon signing a sight draft, which is a type of *bill of exchange* that has to be signed by the debtor and paid on first presentation. The goods can then be collected.

> A *Bill of Exchange* (sometimes referred to as a bank draft) is an order in writing from the creditor to the debtor to pay a certain sum of money on a certain date.

4. **Documents against Acceptance (D/A):** Here the buyer receives the relevant documentation after signing i.e. acceptance of after-sight draft. The goods can then be collected. After a period of time, i.e. on maturity the buyer pays. An after-sight draft is a type of *bill of exchange* that has to be signed

and accepted by the debtor on <u>first</u> presentation and paid on <u>second</u> presentation, i.e. after sight.

5. **Open Account Terms**: This is an arrangement for regular and reliable customers who are allowed pay on a monthly or on a quarterly basis instead of paying by invoice for each separate delivery.

The Terms of Payment include:

Cash in Advance: Here no discounts are granted. The buyer has to pay for the goods before they are sent.

Cash on Delivery (COD): Forwarding agents, i.e., The Post Office or a courier like United Parcels Service (UPS) collect the payment due on the invoice at the time of delivery.

Payment on Receipt of Goods: Under this term the buyer pays when the goods are received.

30 Days Net: No discount is allowed but the buyer has 30 days to pay.

2 Months' Credit: The buyer should pay within 2 months.

2% for Cash: A 2% discount is given if the goods are paid for in cash.

10 Days 2%: A 2% discount is given if goods are paid for within 10 days.

Strictly Net: The buyer has to pay the net price. No discounts are allowed.

Against 3 Months' Acceptance: The goods will be delivered if the customer accepts a draft where payment becomes due after a period of 3 months.

Hire Purchase (HP): This is a method of buying goods where the customer pays a deposit and the balance is then paid over an agreed time period in the form of regular instalments.

Leasing: Here the leaseholder (lessee) is allowed by the lessor (owner) to use a product for a specified time in return for a rent.

Payment on Receipt of Invoice: Customer pays when (s)he receives an invoice.

The Terms of Delivery (INCOTERMS)

Like the methods and terms of payment, the terms of delivery agreed on between the importer and exporter are also the result of a negotiated outcome.

The basis of agreement on delivery in modern trade is the **Incoterms** (**In**ternational Rules for the Interpretation of **Commercial Terms**). These were first agreed and published in Paris in 1936 by the International Chamber of Commerce (ICC). Amendments and additions were made over the years to take into account changes in transportation techniques - and to render them compatible with new developments in EDI (Electronic Data Interchange). The latest changes were made in 2000.

Thirteen now exist which are standard in defining the responsibilities of the buyer and the seller with regard to the costs and risks of transporting goods i.e. who has to pay for freight, organise the insurance, prepare the documents, etc.

They have been grouped into four different categories.

- **The E Group**

EXW Ex Works + named place

This means that the seller only has to have the goods ready at his/her premises, the buyer is then responsible for all transportation and insurance necessary.

- **The F Group**

FCA Free Carrier + named place
FAS Free Alongside Ship + named port of shipment
FOB Free on Board + named port of shipment

Here the seller has to bring the goods to a location where a carrier or transport company appointed by the buyer will undertake the main transportation to the buyer's premises. The buyer pays for the main transport and insurance.

The F Group is very common because it is normally easier for the exporter to arrange transport in his/her own country.

- **The C Group**

CFR Cost and Freight + named port of destination
CIF Cost, Insurance and Freight + named port of destination
CPT Carriage Paid to + named place of destination
CIP Carriage and Insurance Paid to + named place of destination

This is where the seller has to organise and pay for the main transportation. Note that in CIF and CIP the seller also pays for the insurance but the policy is in the buyer's name who has to process any claims that may occur. CPT and CIP can be used for any mode of transport including multimodal transport.

- **The D Group**

The seller has to bear all costs and risks and bring the goods to the agreed place or point in the country of destination

DAF Delivered at Frontier + named place
DES Delivered ex Ship + named port of destination *i.e. buyer must pay for the unloading costs*
DEQ Delivered at Quay + named port of destination *i.e. seller pays the unloading costs*
DDU Delivered Duty Unpaid + named place of destination
DDP Delivered Duty Paid + named place of destination.

- *Other terms of delivery include:*

Franco Domicile, which means that the seller pays the delivery costs.
Carriage/Freight Paid, which is the opposite to **Carriage/Freight Forward** and means that the seller pays the main freight costs.

    a. What are the most common methods of payment?
    b. Explain some common terms of payment.
    c. What are the Incoterms?
    d. Differentiate between the E and D Group in the terms of delivery.

 Discussion Forum

    a. Is fair trade possible?
    b. The role of the WTO - why is it often seen critically?

4.0   GROUPED OVERVIEW OF IMPORTANT COMMERCIAL TERMS

TYPES OF ORDERS

advance order	Vorausbestellung
bulk order	Mengenbestellung
repeat/follow-up order	Nachbestellung
firm order	Festauftrag
first/initial order	Erstauftrag
merchandise at call	Abrufauftrag
standing order	Dauerauftrag
trial order	Probeauftrag

METHODS AND TERMS OF PAYMENT

Against 3 months' acceptance	gegen Dreimonatsakzeptanz
Cash with order	Barzahlung bei Auftragserteilung
Cash in advance	Vorauszahlung
Cash on delivery (COD)	gegen Nachnahme
Documents against payment (D/P)/Cash against documents (CAD)	Kasse gegen Dokumente
Documents against acceptance(D/A)	Dokumente gegen Akzeptanz
Hire purchase/HP	Mietkauf, Abzahlungsgeschäft (Deutschl.)
Leasing	Leasing
Letter of credit (L/C)/Documentary Credit (DC)	Akkreditiv
Open-account terms	Kontokorrentbedinungen
Payment on receipt of goods	Zahlung bei Erhalt der Waren
Payment on receipt of invoice	Zahlung bei Rechnungserhalt
Strictly net	rein netto
30 days net	30 Tage netto
2 months' credit	2 Monate Ziel
2% for cash	2% Skonto bei Barzahlung
10 days 2%	Zahlung innerhalb 10 Tagen abzüglich 2% Skonto

PAYMENT-RELATED TERMS

bank transfer	Überweisung
bill of exchange	Wechsel
sight draft (BE)/sight bill (AE)	Sichtwechsel
after sight draft/time draft (BE)/time bill (AE)	Nachsichtwechsel/ Zielwechsel
deposit	Anzahlung
discount (a discount is deducted <u>in advance</u>, i.e. <u>before</u> payment is made, cf. rebate)	Rabatt, Preisnachlass
- quantity/bulk discount	Mengenrabatt
- cash discount	Skonto, Barzahlungsnachlass
- trade discount	Händlerrabatt, Nachlass, Skonto
instalment	Rate
price reduction (the seller may offer a price reduction if the goods have minor deficiencies)	Preisnachlass

rebate (an amount of money, which is returned to you after payment has been made, e.g. when you have paid too much tax, cf. discount) — Nachlass, Rabatt, Rückvergütung

TERMS OF DELIVERY (INCOTERMS)

CFR (Cost and Freight + named port of destination) — Kosten und Fracht + Bestimmungshafen

CIF (Cost, Insurance and Freight + named port of destination) — Kosten, Versicherung, Fracht + Bestimmungshafen

CIP (Carriage and Insurance Paid to + named place of destination) — frachtfrei versichert + Bestimmungsort

CPT (Carriage Paid to + named place of destination) — frachtfrei + Bestimmungsort

DAF (Delivered at Frontier + named place) — geliefert Grenze + Ort

DDP (Delivered Duty Paid + named place of destination) — geliefert verzollt + Bestimmungsort

DDU (Delivered Duty Unpaid + named place of destination) — geliefert unverzollt

DES (Delivered ex Ship + named port of destination) — geliefert ab Schiff + Bestimmungshafen

DEQ (Delivered ex Quay + named port destination) — geliefert ab Kai + Bestimmungshafen

EXW (Ex Works + named place) — ab Werk + Ort

FAS (Free Alongside Ship + named port of shipment) — frei Längsseite Seeschiff +Versandhafen

FCA (Free Carrier + named place) — frei Frachtführer + Ort

FOB (Free on Board + named port of shipment) — frei an Bord + Versandhafen

OTHER COMMERCIAL TERMS

Franco domicile — frei Haus

Carriage/Freight paid — frachtfrei

Carriage/Freight forward — unfrei

EXPORT DOCUMENTATION

Air Waybill/Air Consignment Note — Luftfrachtbrief

Bill of Lading — Konnossement

Certificate of Insurance — Vesicherungszertifikat

Certificate of Origin — Ursprungszeugnis

Consular Invoice — Konsulatsfaktura

Customs Declaration — Zollerklärung

Export Packing List — Exportpackliste

Import/Export Licence — Import-/Exportlizens

Insurance Policy — Versicherungspolice

Letter of Credit — Akkreditiv

Revocable/Irrevocable Letter of Credit — Widerrufliches/ Unwiderrufliches Akkreditiv

Single Administration Document — Standarddokument (EG)

VOCABULARY

A	
account	Rechnung; Konto
adverse	negativ, ungünstig
advice note	Versandanzeige, Avis
affreightment	Befrachtung (eines Schiffes)
after sight draft/time draft (BE)/time bill (AE)	Nachsichtwechsel/Zielwechsel
Against 3 Months' Acceptance	gegen Dreimonatsakzeptanz
Air Waybill/Air Consignment Note	Luftfrachtbrief
amendment	Änderung, Ergänzung
B	
balance of trade	Handelsbilanz
bank transfer	Überweisung
bill	Rechnung
bill of exchange	Wechsel
Bill of Lading	Konnossement
bulk cargo	Schüttladung, Massenfrachtgut
C	
Carriage/Freight paid	frachtfrei
Carriage/Freight Forward	unfrei
common carrier	Spediteur
cash discount	Skonto, Barzahlungsnachlass
Cash in Advance	Vorauszahlung
Cash on Delivery (COD)	gegen Nachnahme
Cash with Order	Barzahlung bei Auftragserteilung
catalogue	Katalog
Certificate of Insurance	Versicherungszertifikat
Certificate of Origin	Ursprungszeugnis
CFR (Cost and Freight + named port of destination)	Kosten und Fracht + Bestimmungshafen
CIF (Cost, Insurance and Freight+ named port of destination)	Kosten, Versicherung, Fracht + Bestimmungshafen
CIP (Carriage and Insurance Paid to + named place of destination)	frachtfrei versichert + Bestimmungsort
Chamber of Commerce	Handelskammer
complaint	Beschwerde, Reklamation
commission	Provision
consignment note, waybill	Frachtbrief
consignee	Empfänger, Konsignatar

consignor	Versender, Konsignant
Consular Invoice	Konsulatsfaktura
convenience	Annehmlichkeit, Zweckmäßigkeit
CPT (Carriage Paid to + named place of destination)	frachtfrei + Bestimmungsort
credit enquiry	Kreditauskunft
credit note	Gutschrift(anzeige)
credit reference agency	Kreditauskunftei
Customs Declaration	Zollerklärung
customs duty	Zollgebühr

D

DAF (Delivered at Frontier + named place)	geliefert Grenze + Bestimmungsort
DDP (Delivered Duty Paid + named place of destination)	geliefert verzollt + Bestimmungsort)
DDU (Delivered Duty Unpaid + name of destination)	geliefert unverzollt +Bestimmungsort
debit note	Lastschrift(anzeige)
Del Credere agent	Delkanfevertreter
to deem	erachten für
delivery/dispatch note	Lieferschein
demise charter	Mietvertrag
deposit	Anzahlung
DEQ (Delivered ex Quay + named port destination)	geliefert ab Kai + Bestimmungshafen
DES (Delivered ex Ship + named port destination)	geliefert ab Schiff + Bestimmungshafen
discount	Rabatt, Preisnachlass
Documentary Credit (DC)= Letter of Credit	Dokumenten-Akkreditiv
Documents against Acceptance(D/A)	Dokumente gegen Akzeptanz
Documents against Payment (D/P)/Cash against Documents (CAD)	Kasse gegen Dokumente
duty	Zoll, Abgabe

E

economies of scale	Größenvorteile, Größeneffekt
electronic data interchange	elektronischer Datenaustausch
to entrust	anvertrauen
to enforce	durchsetzen
estimate	Angebot, Kostenvoranschlag
Export Packing List	Exportpackliste
EXW (Ex Works + named place)	ab Werk + Ort

F

FAS (Free Alongside Ship + named port of shipment)	frei Längsseite Seeschiff + Versandhafen
FCA (Free Carrier + named place)	frei Frachtführer + Ort
FOB (Free on Board + named port of shipment	frei an Bord + Versandhafen
foreign exchange	Devisen
forward contract	Terminkontrakt
Franco Domicile	frei Haus

G

Gross Domestic Product	Bruttoinlandsprodukt
Gross National Product	Bruttosozialprodukt

H

haulage	Transport
hedge	Sicherungsgeschäft, Hedge
hire and reward	mieten (und bezahlen)
hire purchase/HP	Mietkauf, Abzahlungsgeschäft (Deutschland)

I

Import/Export License	Import-/Exportlizenz
installment	Rate
instore promotion	Promotion in der Verkaufsstelle
invoice	(Waren-) Rechnung

L

leasing	Leasing
Letter of Credit (L/C)	Akkreditiv
letter of enquiry	Anfrage(brief)

O

offer	Angebot
Open-Account Terms	Kontokorrentbedingungen
order	Auftrag, Bestellung;
overdraft	Überziehung (Bankkonto; Kredit)

P

to palletize	palettisierenl
Payment on Receipt of Goods	Zahlung bei Erhalt der Waren
Payment on Receipt of Invoice	Zahlung bei Rechnungserhalt
price list	Preisliste
price reduction	Preisnachlass
proforma invoice	Proforma-Rechnung

Q

quantity/bulk discount	Mengenrabatt
quotation	Preisangabe, Angebot

R	
rebate	Nachlass, Rabatt, Rückvergütung
receipt	Quittung
reminder/collection letter	Mahnung, Mahnschreiben
retaliatory	Vergeltungs-, Konter-
Revocable/Irrevocable Letter of Credit	Widerrufliches/ Unwiderrufliches Akkreditiv
S	
self-sufficient	autark, selbständig
sight draft (BE)/sight bill (AE)	Sichtwechsel
Single Administration Document	Standarddokument (EU)
statement of account	Kontoauszug, Abrechnung
Strictly Net	rein netto
subsidies	Subventionen
T	
tender	Ausschreibung, Angebot
terms of trade	Terms of Trade; Austauschverhältnis
trade discount	Händlerrabatt, Nachlas, Skonto
tariff	Zoll
U	
unit costs	Stückkosten
V	
vessel	Schiff
voyage charter	Reisecharter
10 Days 2%	Zahlung innerhalb 10 Tagen abzüglich 2 % Skonto
2 Months' Credit	2 Monate Ziel
2% for Cash	2 % Skonto bei Barzahlung
30 Days Net	30 Tage netto

THE QUARTET – TECHNOLOGY, GLOBALIZATION, ETHICS & THE ENVIRONMENT

FOCUS Here we examine four aspects of importance to the world of business that are all closely inter-related.

1.0   TECHNOLOGY

> *My interest is in the future ... because I'm going to spend the rest of my life there.*
>
> *Charles Kettering*

Thanks to technology the pace of change has never been faster. Information is available anywhere, anytime to anyone at close to no cost. Products and services are sold anywhere, anytime to anyone at rapidly declining costs. Parts of our society are ageing rapidly, accumulating enormous savings and living off their past achievements; others are young, learning and investing aggressively into their future. These are times of upheaval.

The last hundred years have resulted in huge discoveries and advances in areas such as transport, engineering, medicine, and communication.

Technology in business involves the application of knowledge based on discoveries in science, inventions and innovations with enormous positive effects. On the negative side it has given an increasing number of countries the capacity to destroy the planet - not least with the fruits of nuclear technology.

It was the development of the microprocessor chip in the early 1970s that was responsible for bringing about truly revolutionary changes in the world of business, education, government and in people's personal lives. New markets and industries have grown out of this, such as the Internet and interactive multimedia industries. Today innovation is accelerating in all industries from biotechnology to computers to satellites on an absolutely irreversible scale.

Current innovation in networked computers and telecommunications is not only on a par with the breakthroughs of the last century but is greater and more far-reaching.

1.1   Information Technology (IT)

It is clear that IT and the Internet are generating rapid change in homes, in businesses and in organizations of all kinds. Just as finance and accounting are integrated into all other departments' activities, IT has become an enabler for virtually all of the organization and there is increasing reliance on it to address challenges, issues and opportunities for synergy.

New economy or TMT (technology, media and telecoms) shares play an important role in stock markets

The Internet in the 21st century has changed businesses forever, not only in the way they are organised but also regarding management qualities and approaches and the importance of IT literacy. (see E-Business and the E-Manager in Unit 9, Section 2.4) The Internet is not simply a new way of communication and a new type of distribution channel. It is also a market place, an information system and a tool for manufacturing goods and services. It makes an important difference in a manager's daily activities such as locating new suppliers, collecting and managing customer data, interacting with clients and co-ordinating projects.

With the Internet firms can link their systems on the Information Superhighway directly to those of their suppliers and partners, do business online 24 hours a day, and learn more about their customers.

Key IT Terms

Electronic commerce or **e-commerce**, which refers in general to trade that actually takes place over the Internet, usually through the process of a buyer visiting a seller's website and closing a transaction there.

Electronic data interchange (EDI) is one of the oldest forms of e-commerce and is a computer-to-computer based exchange of quotations, orders, invoices and other business documentation between business partners.

Business-to-business (B2B) is where only businesses rather than standard consumers can access or buy products from a B2B website. One purpose of such a service is to streamline operations between businesses that already enjoy a commercial relationship. Transactions in this particular area currently outweigh the number of transactions between businesses and consumers.

B2B e-commerce comprises electronic data interchange and Internet based commerce which may include the use of extranets.

An **extranet** is an efficient secure network that is used by businesses to do business via the firm's website for external customers and other users and can be viewed as an extended intranet. **Intranet** is a private network that is contained within an enterprise. It may consist of many interlinked local area networks (LAN) and also use leased lines in the wide area network (WAN). The main purpose of an intranet is to share company information and computing resources among employees. An intranet can also be used to facilitate working in groups and for teleconferences.

The **World Wide Web (WWW)** refers to all the resources and users on the Internet that are using the Hypertext Transfer Protocol (HTTP), i.e. the set of rules for exchanging files (text, graphic images, sound, video, and other multimedia files).

Using a website even the tiniest firm can sell products and in a matter of seconds reach customers all over the world – this defines the **business-to-consumer (B2C)** relationship.

The versatility of the Internet has also allowed the **consumer-to-consumer (C2C)** to develop. This serves the purpose of allowing consumers to pass on their views concerning goods and services. **C2C Auction** is a customer to customer based auction on the Internet of an A-Z list of products.

Benefits and Pitfalls of IT

Benefits	Pitfalls
• Cost savings in a wide range of activities	• Initial cost outlay can be prohibitive
• Improved productivity	• Time delay before benefits to come through
• Enhanced customer service	• Effectiveness, i.e. reliability of Internet concerning security in information and payments
• Improved quality of work life	
• Access to company knowledge base	
• Creation of new jobs	• Workforce cutbacks
• More efficient global trading	• Isolation and alienation of workforce and/or consumers through loss of face-to-face contact
	• Electronic mugging, i.e. hacking, fraud and other criminal activities
	• The global nature of the Internet has made regulation extremely difficult as it takes time for formulation and implementation while technology moves on apace

 How has IT changed the business world?

1.2   Biotechnology

This refers to the use in science and industry of living things such as cells and bacteria to produce drugs or chemicals, to destroy waste matter, etc. Biotechnology has not been without controversy. Many people have expressed reservations regarding issues such as cloning, embryo stem cell research and genetically engineered or modified food.

The huge profits of pharmaceutical firms from the production of drugs and medicine are also discussed more frequently. Some African states have even threatened to ignore patents and allow the illegal production of cheap 'pirate' drugs for use in preventing or hindering diseases such as AIDS because their citizens cannot afford to buy the drugs produced by the big multinationals.

There is also frequent debate on whether enough research has been carried out in areas such as the artificial transfer of genes between species of plants and animals and potential harmful consequences.

 What is biotechnology?

 Discussion Forum

Should the Internet be subject to censorship?

2.0 GLOBALIZATION

> *Globalization is the compression of time and space that questions boundaries.*
>
> Dr. William Coleman

Globalization is a relatively new term, a popular term in the lexicon of bureaucrats, consultants, journalists and policy analysts. The reality of this concept is not new because ever since extensive trade developed between countries from the early eighteenth century onwards economists have pondered the effects of an increasingly global interdependency.

There are many broad-based definitions of globalization, and it is often used interchangeably with *interdependence*, such as the globalization or interdependency of economies (in a *think global, act local* = *glocalization* approach), of security arrangements, of communications, of the media, etc.

Globalization, aside from its use in political, military or other related fields refers primarily in business terms to a phenomenon that involves a fast international spread of two entities:

- The *development of new technologies* such as computers and telecommunications.
- A *spread of finance capital* through multinational corporations which is seen as necessary for the internationalization of technology

At the core of globalization is a central question: If countries are engaged in trade with one another, does each side benefit, or does one come out ahead?

2.1   Effects of Globalization

The huge advances in communications and other technologies have made the world a much smaller place resulting in the appearance of a truly global market or 'global village' and an increasing number of globally integrated multinational corporations like Proctor & Gamble, General Electric (GE) and AT&T.

The global economy is essentially an information economy, enabling companies to work smarter than before. American companies are leading this information revolution, investing huge resources which have paid off by increasing their global competitiveness.

More and more of these multinational corporations consider their natural markets to be the entire globe due to the shrinking of geographical and cultural distances. With modern, highly organized systems of production and distribution, manufacturing plants can be located in countries which have low labour costs with sales being directed to those countries that represent the richest markets. Many companies are forming strategic alliances with foreign companies - even competitors – and huge mergers and acquisitions have taken place.

As a result national governments have less and less control over their individual economies. The globalization of finance, trade, investment and consumption, as well as transportation and communications, is reducing the abilities of governments to generate socially desirable outcomes in the interests of those they govern. GDP (see Unit 11, Section 1.0) and its distribution, levels of employment, interest rates and rates of economic growth and development are substantially impacted by the rapidly integrating global economy.

Hence countries are unable to manage a growing number of such critical variables within their own borders and often find it necessary to rush to freer trade to facilitate private investment.

The economic engine of globalization that is transforming the world in its own image is therefore one of the hottest issues around.

Globalization has (real and/or potential) positive and negative effects.

Positive Aspects:

- Free traders argue that globalization has resulted in unprecedented world growth that benefits everybody.
- Globalization represents vast new markets for efficient firms.
- Information technology with its frontiers being constantly pushed by globalization increases worker productivity and improves customer choice and service.
- Production costs in many industries are shrinking or are remaining constant.
- Globalization, far from endangering human rights, improves and highlights this important issue

Negative Aspects:

- The gap between rich and poor in **developed countries** is widening significantly as those with technological skills and talents have prospered while blue-collar workers have seen traditional labour-intensive manufacturing jobs disappear. The result is increased income and wealth inequalities between the unskilled or low-skilled and the more sophisticated 'knowledge' workers.
- In **developing countries**, which have grown poorer during the past few decades, the majority of the population have difficulties in receiving an education appropriate for the new information age, and are as a result falling even further behind.
- Unchecked globalization is accelerating the use of child labour, the destruction of rain forests and endangered species, global warming and other environmental threats.

2.2 Opponents and Supporters

Opponents of economic globalization have a wide diversity and their backgrounds are significant. Trade union members, protectionists and ecological activists have joined forces with religious groups and student groups. They share the view that the **International Monetary Fund (IMF)**, and the **World Bank** (see Unit 6) are supporting ecological destruction by sponsoring large development and energy projects without paying sufficient regard to environmental safety guidelines.

Another general contention is that both of the above-mentioned organizations are promoting the aims of multinational corporations by encouraging poor nations to curtail spending on environmental protection in return for aid and to pay lip-service to or simply ignore the rights of poor workers. Protestors also charge that the IMF is contributing to the continuing poverty of the poorest nations by forcing them into debt.

Riotous demonstrations by these protestors have been responsible for disrupting several **World Trade Organization** meetings. Although the WTO has the aim of encouraging free trade and thereby higher economic growth and rising standards of living it is often seen by various protest groups as a 'rich countries' club making macroeconomic decisions and leaving poorer countries struggling to cope with the impact of those decisions.

The IMF counters this accusation by claiming it disperses $30 billion each year in loans to poor and developing countries. The loans, however, do come at a price; the IMF insists that in order to be eligible for loans, the poor countries must open up their markets to foreign trade and adopt American free market principles.

A huge amount of publicity has arisen from these protests with the result that the World Bank, the IMF and the WTO, clearly stung by the level of public resentment towards them, have embarked on a more transparent policy even inviting previously taboo organizations for consultative meetings.

On the other end of the political spectrum, some conservatives charge that the IMF and the World Bank are actually too lenient in their lending practices, bailing out poor countries time and again without insisting that those countries institute more responsible and transparent economic practices. They believe that poverty will continue as long as those countries (can) depend on the IMF for help.

2.3   Conclusion

What is clear is that globalization presents a huge challenge. There is a desperate need internationally for the creation of a set of rules to ensure greater market based fairness through well-defined, transparent rules governing progressive trade liberalization. This should also be compatible with poverty alleviation and environmentally sustainability.

a. Define globalization.
b. What are its positive and negative effects?
c, Summarize the views/positions of the opponents and supporters of globalization.

Discussion Forum

a. Globalization is a necessary and unstoppable process, which cannot be checked. Discuss.
b. Will globalization advance democracy and human rights, or will corporate power triumph above all else?
c. How can thinking globally while acting morally and responsibly be achieved?'
d. Globalization and the free market are bad for poor nations and also create insecurity in the West. Discuss.

3.0 ETHICS IN BUSINESS

> *There is one and only one social responsibility of business – to use its resources and engage in activities designed to increase its profits.*
>
> *Milton Friedman*

As we all know, **ethics** refers to what is right and what is wrong. It focuses on moral consciousness or conscience. It is the philosophical study of the moral value of human conduct and of the rules and principles that ought to govern it. The exploitation of young children in the workplace or the pollution of the environment are regarded as examples of unethical behaviour.

Ethics within the business organization comprises:

- Issues of social responsibility, i.e. their responsibility not just to the shareholders, but also to employees, customers, suppliers and the general community, known collectively as stakeholders.
- Issues of business practices often enforced by law, e.g. labour, health and safety regulations.
- The personal ethics that each individual employee brings with him/her to the workplace.
- Professionally linked ethics, e.g. medical ethics.
- Cultural ethics of the organization, e.g. customers first.

3.1   Approaches to Ethics

To many people the concepts of business and ethics sit uneasily together. Yet almost every multinational American company is putting a package together that they believe constitutes ethical corporate behaviour and actively encouraging its employees to observe it. US business management schools teach courses on the subject. Business ethics is all the rage and this has led to the creation of a veritable ethics industry, complete with consultancies, conferences, journals and 'corporate conscience' awards.

Global accountancy firms such as PricewaterhouseCooper even offer to 'audit' the ethical performance of companies. Fashionable – definitely; vague – probably. And outside of America only limited lip-service is paid. But plenty of people believe that companies should not be in the business of worrying about social responsibility, morals or the environment at all. If society wants to put such issues ahead of shareholder value optimization, let governments regulate accordingly.

The problem with business ethics is that no universal set of ethical principles exists, leading very often to a reactive (after the event) rather than a proactive (before the event) approach from companies.

Globalization brings companies into contact with other countries, some with minimum democratic credentials, if not totalitarian, that do business under different rules. Different standards of right and wrong exist, and in many countries child labour and bribes are considered standard practice. Competitive pressure is fiercer than ever before forcing companies to bring more out of their employees than ever before.

In the face of such competition and the fact that standards on such issues as the environment differ among countries it follows - when considered strictly according to profits - that a global company should implement local environmental standards that are lower than back home. These lower standards can often have disastrous results both for the country and the corporation. A horrific example was the Bhopal disaster in 1984, when an explosion at a Union Carbide plant in India killed at least 8,000 people. Today companies are facing more ethical quandaries than ever before.

3.2 The NGOs & the Media

Technological change brings new debates, on issues ranging from genetically modified food to privacy on the Internet.

Add unprecedented scrutiny **from non-governmental organiza-tions (NGOs)** such as environmentalist groups (Greenpeace, World Wildlife Fund) and agencies (Amnesty International, Oxfam) and it is not surprising that ethics is figuring in every manager's mind.

In the US companies often have a special incentive to pursue an ethics policy in order to avoid legal penalties from the government.

But the fear of the NGOs and the media is an even bigger incentive. Witness the example of Shell, the oil multinational, which in the 1990s suffered two major setbacks. The first was their plan to dispose of the Brent Spar oil rig in the North Sea which met with fierce opposition from Greenpeace and other environmental groups. The second blow was the company's failure to oppose the Nigerian military regime's execution of Ken Saro-Wiwa, a human-rights activist in a part of Nigeria where Shell was especially active. Because these stories were widely reported in the media, Shell suffered a brief loss in sales and in share price and was pushed into rewriting its business principles and consulting with a number of NGOs.

NIKE, the sports and leisurewear organization, was also hurt in the United States when it was revealed that one of its supplier-factories in Vietnam was exploiting employees. This was an independent firm manufacturing NIKE products but NIKE was blamed.

Nestlé, one of the world's largest food manufacturers, faces the wrath of many NGOs over the sale of its powdered baby milk products in those African countries which have dirty or contaminated water supply systems.

3.3 Ethical Investment

Ethical investment is one opportunity for organizations and individuals to match investments with morals. Ethical fund managers initially excluded investments in businesses involved in armaments, gambling, alcohol, tobacco, violation of human rights, the destruction of the environment, pollution, intensive farming and pornography. Recently there has been a move away from avoidance and absolutism to supporting the positive aspects of a company's attitude towards environmental, ethical and social issues. This is often referred to as socially responsible investment (SRI).

Most academic studies of the association between responsible corporate ethics and profitability suggest that the two often go together. At least in America research has shown that more ethically sensitive sales staff perform better, that share prices of organizations decline after reports of ethical misconduct, that staff feel less discomfort working for an organization which has an ethical policy that they can trust in and that companies which display an ethical commitment to stakeholders in their annual reports do better financially. However, these tend to be large-sized firms, small firms sometimes pay less attention than bigger rivals to normalizing ethical issues and to worrying about their social responsibilities.

   a. What is ethics ?
   b. What does an organization's ethics comprise?
   c. What are typical ethical problems in business? Cite some examples.
   d. Explain ethical investment

 ## Discussion Forum

   a. What can consumers do to force firms to adapt a more ethical position?
   b. Should child labour be universally abolished?
   c. Discuss private education and private health care from an ethical point of view.
   d. You can teach business ethics but you cannot teach people to behave ethically correct. Discuss.
   e. Is human embryonic stem-cell research ethically acceptable?

4.0   ENVIRONMENT

> *Only when the last tree has died and the last river has been poisoned and the last fish has been caught will we realize that we cannot eat money.*
>
> > *Cree Indian comment on the environment and materialism.*
>
> *It is all too easy for us to forget that mankind is a part of Nature, and not apart from it.*
>
> > *Prince Charles*

The **environment** refers to the natural world of land, air, plants, animals, the atmosphere, climate – in other words, all physical surroundings and conditions.

Environmentalism refers to that movement of concerned persons which seeks to preserve and protect the natural environment especially those areas affected by human activity.

4.1   Current Environmental Issues

Current issues include:

- The rate of climatic change, e.g. the general rise in global temperatures caused by pumping too much carbon dioxide (CO2) into the earth's atmosphere
- The use of nuclear energy and alternative sources
- The rate of deforestation – especially in South America and Asia
- The production and disposal of hazardous waste, e.g. radioactive waste
- The protection of water and other natural resources
- Recycling
- The preservation of ethnic cultures
- The protection of the animal kingdom and habitats
- Increasing rates of air pollution
- The promoting of environmental education
- The overuse of insecticides in agriculture and the preservation of biodiversity

Where in the past there was a mild acknowledgement of environmental issues among global consumers, there is now growing concern. The appearance of such diseases as BSE or 'mad cow disease' in the EU, the development of genetically modified (GM) crops, the testing of animal cells worldwide and the effects of the burning of fossil fuels on global warming have now galvanized public opinion.

4.2   Environmentalism vs. Free Trade

Many environmentalists believe free trade will lead to only greater pollution as production moves to newly industrializing countries that have more relaxed environmental laws. They argue that only 'safe' or 'clean' industries should be allowed in these states and that trade policy should be linked to tough environmental control laws. In their opinion, unpaid environmental costs cannot remain unpaid forever.

These might be regarded as high ideals in the Western World but aid recipient developing countries (Third World) often object to being told to adjust to rich countries' environmental standards without any regard to their own economic circumstances. This is especially the case when these adjustments are backed or demanded by Western politicians who do not want to be caught on the wrong side of the 'green line' debate. Developing countries often cite the example that the USA is not only a superpower but also a super-polluter producing almost 30% of world pollution with only 4% of the world's population.

Supporters of free trade argue that market and private property rights have clearly led to economic development in the industrialized countries while simultaneously alleviating poverty.

Environmentalists dispute this maintaining that sustainable development is the only answer for the future. **Sustainable development** can be defined as economic development that is compatible with resolving environment and equity concerns within a democratic framework.

Environmental movements such as Greenpeace are putting stricter demands on companies resulting in major green marketing and public relations responses from multinationals. This is, however, often dismissed as 'greenwash'. **Greenwash** refers to environmentally responsible company propaganda and nothing more. **Green marketing**, on the other hand, is a marketing strategy that promotes an environmentally safe product.

The various groups in environmental movements which celebrate Earth Day every year often come in for criticism. Opponents argue that these movements contain elements that are fundamentally attacking the ideals of Western civilization by leading an anti-industrial revolution with their opposition to science, technology and economic development. They also believe that these groups hold that non-human life has more value than the human - that all human productivity is seen as an intrusion on the sanctity of nature and the rights of animals.

Furthermore, it is claimed they place both non-violent and violent blocks in the way of new innovation and economic development from local to international level with the ultimate aim of retarding and dismantling the industrial and technological society.

    a. What are the current issues concerning the environment?
    b. What is meant by 'greenwash'?
    c. Explain the connection between free trade and
       environmentalism.

Discussion Forum

    a. Is it appropriate to bring in measures against countries to change their environmental conduct? How should this be done?

    b. Discuss the necessity of nuclear power. Are there realistic alternative sources?

    c. What are the effects of globalization and technology for environmental and ethical issues?

    d. 'We're twenty years too late to save the environment.' (John Connolly, environmentalist) Do you agree?

VOCABULARY

A	
to accelerate	beschleunigen
accusation	Vorwurf, Anschuldigung
acquisition	Übernahme, Erwerb
to adjust	(sich) anpassen
alienation	Entfremdung
alleviation	Linderung, Erleichterung
armaments	(Auf)Rüstung
B	
to bail out	aus der Patsche helfen
bribe	Bestechung
boundary	Grenzen
broad-based	breit gefächert, vielseitig
C	
to close a transaction	ein Geschäft abschließen
conduct	Verhalten, Benehmen,
conscience	Gewissen
consciousness	(Pflicht)Bewusstsein
contention	Behauptung
credential	Empfehlung, Referenz
to curtail	kürzen
D	
depletion	Verringerung, Abnahme
desirable	wünschenswert
to dismantle	demontieren
to dismiss	hier: abtun
to disperse	verteilen , verstreuen
destruction	Zerstörung
E	
to be eligible	berechtigt sein
to embark on	beginnen mit

to endanger	gefährden
to enforce	durchsetzen
to enhance	verstärken
equity	Gerechtigkeit, Fairness
exploitation	Ausbeutung
F	
fraud	Betrug
G	
galvanize	einen Stoß geben, wachrütteln
gambling	Glücksspiel
H	
hence	daher
I	
to impact	beeinflussen, einwirken
incentive	Anreiz
indigestible	schwer verdaulich
to institute	einleiten (Maßnahmen)
intrusion	Störung, Eindringen
K	
kickback	Schmiergeld
L	
lenient	nachsichtig
(to pay) lip service	(ein) Lippenbekenntnis (ablegen)
literacy	Bildung, Aufgeklärtheit
to live off	auf Kosten von etw. leben
M	
merger	Fusion
misconduct	Verfehlung, Fehlverhalten
to mug	rauben
O	
to object to	Einwände haben gegen, dagegen sein
onwards	vorwärts, weiter
outlay	Aufwand
outweigh	überwiegen
P	
pace	Tempo
to be a par	auf gleicher Ebene liegen
penalty	Strafe
to ponder	erwägen, überlegen, nachdenken
prohibitive	unerschwinglich, untragbar
Q	
(ethical) quandary	(ethisches) Dilemma
quotation	Preisangebot

R	
(to be) all the rage	der letzte Schrei sein
recipient	Empfänger
reliance	Vertrauen
resentment	Ärger, Ressentiment
to retard	verzögern
to reveal	aufdecken, enthüllen
riotous	aufrührerisch, mit Ausschreitungen verbunden
rush	hasten, hetzen
S	
sanctity	Unverletzlichkeit, Unantastbarkeit
scrutiny	genaue (Über)Prüfung
setback	Rückschlag, Schlappe
to shrink	schrumpfen
stakeholder	Stakeholder, Interessengruppe
sustainable	nachhaltig, tragfähig
to streamline	rationalisieren
to be stung	getroffen/betroffen sein
U	
unprecedented	beispiellos, nie da gewesen
upheaval	Umwälzung
V	
vague	undeutlich, unklar, vage
vast	gewaltig, enorm
veritable	wahr
versatility	Vielseitigkeit
virtually	praktisch, so gut wie
W	
workforce cutback	Arbeitsplatzkürzung
wrath	Zorn

INTRODUCTION TO BUSINESS LAW

> *It is better that ten guilty persons escape than one innocent suffer.*
> *Sir William Blackstone*

FOCUS This unit serves to give the reader a broad knowledge of law as it affects commercial transactions plus a brief look at EU international law.

1.0   INTRODUCTION

Law is the body of rules imposed by a State upon its members, which is designed to regulate human conduct within that State. The courts interpret these rules of conduct, decide whether they have been broken or not and pass sentence or make an award of compensation.

Law is not static – it changes and develops, reflecting the values and institutions of each era. Not only does it define and safeguard rights of property and uphold public order, but it is also used to develop the national economy and to deal with social problems. It consists of history, culture and social values. The first known law, the Hammurabi Code, originated in Babylon around 2000 BC and was carried by traders into the Mediterranean world.

There are many different legal systems in the countries of the world. To understand a foreign legal system is to understand its society and its resulting legal attitudes.

In the Western World two major legal systems exist. These are the Anglo-American common law tradition (law mostly derived from custom and judicial precedent) and the Romano-Germanic civil law tradition (law derived from statutes).

Business Law is a term that has no exact legal significance - it is a phrase used in connection with the rights and obligations of those engaged in commerce and trade.

A similar term, used more frequently by the legal profession, is *commercial law* which is understood to be the law pertaining to transactions in the commercial world.

Commercial law relates to the following areas: tort, contract, negotiable instruments and agency. It is also concerned with unfair trading, competition (including intellectual property rights), business associations and product liability.

In Anglo-Saxon countries commercial law is mostly regulated by common law supplemented by statute law. Commercial law is not a distinct branch or source of law.

On the European Continent commercial law is very definite and separate from general law and is only applicable to those in commercial relationships (as e.g. German Commercial Code).

1.1   Sources of English Law

English law is the law on which many former British colonies legal systems are based, e.g. the USA, most African states, Canada, Australia, New Zealand, India, Ireland, Pakistan.

English law is derived from two main sources:

- **Historical:**

  Common law (ius commune), a rudimentary legal system began by the Normans in England in 1066. It was based on customs and decisions recorded over the centuries. The common law was also used later in Wales and Ireland.

- **Legal:**

  Legislation (Statute Law) as laid down by the UK Parliament

  Judicial precedent or **judge-made law** based on judges decisions and their reports

  International law, e.g. from the UN

  EU law which is today of ever increasing importance.

Each country in the UK today has its own slightly different legal system. Wales and Northern Ireland follow the English system, but Scotland has different laws and courts, which are historically more closely connected to Continental law.

1.2   Sources of US Law

The laws regulating the conduct of business in the United States , originate from English law. They have naturally developed in their own distinct way since colonial independence, and flow from three basic sources: federal, i.e. United States, state, e.g. California, and municipal, e.g. San Francisco.

Federal law derives from the United States Constitution and from statutes enacted by the United States Congress and approved by the President. Federal law applies everywhere in the US, and prevails over conflicting state or municipal law, but federal and state law often co-exist without conflict, and in those cases both laws may apply.

State law derives from each state's constitution, and from statutes enacted by the state legislature and approved by the Governor. State law only applies in that particular state or jurisdiction. It prevails over conflicting municipal regulation.

Municipal law derives ultimately from state statutes conferring special powers on cities and towns, and is usually expressed in by-laws, ordinances, or regulations adopted by any of a variety of municipal bodies. It is most significant in the areas of land-use planning and public health and safety enforcement.

NOTE

The bulk of the remainder of the unit focuses on the various constituent parts of law as it affects commercial transactions and should help the reader to be aware of the need to consider the legal implications in the decision-making process of a business organization. It should be emphasized that this is only a general, and not an exhaustive, guide to business law.

2.0   CIVIL AND CRIMINAL PROCEEDINGS

Civil proceedings or actions exist to deal with civil, or private, wrongs. The object of civil law is the resolution or solving of disputes over the rights and obligations of individuals dealing with each other. The State has no role in such disputes and it is therefore up to the injured parties to commence a civil action to seek compensation for a loss they have suffered.

In most civil cases, there will be a **plaintiff** (the aggrieved party) and a **defendant** (the offending party). The plaintiff sues the defendant and the names are placed in this order, e.g. *Ryan v(ersus) Jones (2001)*. The burden of proof shifts between both parties until the judge or appropriate person makes a judgement.

Criminal laws exist to deal with criminal, or public wrongs. It is a set of standards imposed by a society on its individuals and if they are breached (broken) can result in sanctions to punish the offender, e.g. prison.

Criminal proceedings are started by the State against the accused who is presumed innocent until proven to be guilty.

Some situations represent both a civil action and a criminal offence, e.g. a passenger of a taxi is injured in an accident caused by a careless taxi driver. Here the passenger sues for compensation caused by pain and suffering and the State prosecutes the driver for the offence of dangerous driving.

The **court system (judiciary)** consist of **judges** and **juries**. The parties in court can be represented by a **solicitor** (AE **lawyer**) and a **barrister** (BE) who is a specialist in important court cases.

In America lawyers are also referred to as attorney, counsel or counselor – the use of these names does not reflect any formal differences in status or speciality.

    a. Explain business law.
    b. What is the English legal system based on?
    c. What is the difference between civil and criminal proceedings?
    d. Explain the laws regarding the conduct of business in the UK and USA.

3.0   ELEMENTS OF THE LAW OF TORT

3.1   Definition of a Tort

A **tort** (French for *wrong)* is a civil, and not a criminal, wrong for which the normal remedy is a common law action for unliquidated damages (i.e. damages determined by the court).

Wrongs dealt with by the law of tort include:

- causing physical injury to another person or persons intentionally or negligently
- interfering with another's land or goods
- making a false statement about another person (Libel and Slander – see Section 3.4)

3.2   Remedies

The most common remedies available from the courts are **damages** or an **injunction.**

Damages can be of three types:

- **Real damages**, i.e. full monetary compensation
- **Nominal damages** where a nominal (small) sum is awarded for minor cases.
- **Exemplary (punitive AE) damages** where in addition to compensating the plaintiff an additional sum is awarded

Injunction is an order of the court which commands a party *to do* something (a 'mandatory injunction') or *to refrain from doing* something (a 'prohibitive injunction') e.g. a trade union is refrained from unlawful picketing at the gates of a factory where a strike has occurred.

What wrongs are dealt with by the law of tort and what remedies are available?

3.3   Negligence

Negligence is the breach of a legal duty of care which causes loss or injury to the person to whom the duty is owed. The duty of care may arise in a number of ways. It is owed, for example, by a manufacturer to the consumers of a product (that the product is safe and reliable) or by a lawyer to his client (that the client is properly represented).

The degree of duty of care varies from country to country. The USA, for example, is probably the only country in the world where a toner pack has a warning on it not to eat the contents.

Types of Negligence

Contributory negligence, in common law, means that if the plaintiff was guilty of any negligent actions which contributed to the incident, then the defendant could escape liability for negligence.

Occupiers' liability is where occupiers have a duty to exercise care towards persons who enter their premises, regardless of any contractual relationship between them.

Vicarious liability is where a person may be held liable by law by authorizing another person, either expressly (directly) or implicitly (indirectly), to commit an action which causes injury or damage to a third party.

Strict liability is where a person collects or stores non-natural things on their property, which are likely to do harm if they escape from the property. The defendant need not have acted either intentionally or negligently for strict liability to apply, e.g. overflow of chemicals into a river causing contamination of water supply.

3.4   Defamation

This is the publication of a false statement which injures the plaintiff's reputation or causes the plaintiff to be shunned by ordinary members of society.

There are two types of defamation recognized by the law: libel and slander.

Libel – Defamatory material is classified as libellous if it is in permanent form, or if it is for general reception, for example, in writing, pictures, films, recordings, television or radio.

A libel which does or is likely to cause a breach of the peace is a criminal offence as well as a tort.

Slander – Defamatory material is classified as slanderous if it is in a transient form, for example, in words or gestures. Slander is not a crime. In most cases, slander is not actionable *per se* (by or in itself), i.e. one cannot take any action. Plaintiffs must prove that they have suffered special damage, i.e. actual material loss capable of monetary evaluation, such as loss of employment.

Mitigation and aggravation of damages in defamation means that the defendant may mitigate, i.e. make milder, payment of damages by apologizing, by producing evidence of the plaintiff's bad reputation prior to this, or by counter-defamation charges.

The defendant may aggravate, i.e. increase payment of damages by the approach the defendant uses communicating the defamatory material or by his/her conduct throughout the trial.

    a. Explain what negligence is.
    b. Differentiate between libel and slander.
    c. How can a defendant mitigate or aggravate the payment of damages in a defamation case?

4.0   LAW OF CONTRACT

4.1   The Contract

A contract is a legal agreement between two or more parties whereby rights are acquired by one or more parties in return for certain acts on the part of the other or others.

Essentials

- there must be an agreement made as a result of an offer and an unequivocal or clear acceptance of that offer.
- there must be an intention to create legal relations, i.e. that the parties to a contract must intend or plan to create a legally binding transaction. Commercial (business) agreements, unlike domestic agreements (between members of the family) or collective agreements (e.g., between unions and employers) are examples.
- the parties must have the capacity (legal competence) to contract, e.g. be over 18
- there must be genuine consent to the terms by all parties to the contract
- the terms of the contract must be legal and capable of performance.

4.2   Offer

An offer is a definite promise to be bound on certain specific terms and can be made either by the seller offering to sell or by the buyer offering to buy. The **offeror** is the person making the offer and the **offeree** the person who receives the offer, which can be accepted or rejected by refusal or counter offer.

Revocation is where the offeror may revoke (withdraw) the offer at any time before it has been accepted.

Lapse of time means an offer will terminate at the end of the time specified in the offer, or if no time limit is specified, it will terminate after a reasonable time. What is reasonable depends on the nature of the contract and the circumstances of a particular case.

4.3   Terms of a Contract

Express terms are the words used and clearly stated by the parties, either written or spoken, during the negotiations leading up to a contract, and by which they intended to be bound.

Implied terms cover where the parties may not expressly state each term of the contract, but they agree to the main purpose of the contract and some basic terms, leaving the rest to be implied from the situation or circumstances.

Terms in a contract may be conditions, warranties or exemption clauses.

A **condition** is a vital or fundamental term of a contract, breach of which entitles the injured party to rescind (annul or cancel) the contract, but allows the injured party the option to affirm it. In either case, the injured party may also recover damages for losses incurred (caused).

A **warranty** is a minor term connected to the main purpose of a contract, breach of which only entitles the injured party to claim damages. The injured party is still bound by the contract.

An **exemption clause** is a term of a contract which exempts one of the parties from a liability which may arise.

4.4   Misrepresentation

A **misrepresentation** is a false statement of material fact, made innocently or otherwise, by one party to the other before the contract is made, in order to induce or entice the latter to enter into the contract.

The misled party may rescind the contract (since it is voidable), refuse to perform his/her part of the contract and/or recover damages in tort for any loss suffered.

4.5   Duress and Undue Influence

Duress is the actual use or threatened use of violence to, or the false imprisonment of, the contracting party, their spouse or partner, parents or children. Its effects, if proved, are that the contract is voidable.

The doctrine of **undue influence** enables a court to annul contracts where an agreement has been reached by excessive pressure, but which falls short of duress.

Undue influence often occurs in contracts between a parent and a child, a trustee and a beneficiary or between a guardian and a ward.

4.6   Contracts in Restraint of Trade

A contract in restraint of trade on the freedom of an individual to trade will be upheld if it is shown to be in the interest of both parties and the public.

A restraint of trade clause may be justified and enforceable if the person or firm who impose it have a genuine commercial interest to protect. An example are restrictions imposed by a firm on an ex-employees to work for another firm in a similar industry or to set up a similar business.

Other examples include *solus (exclusive) agreements* to use goods only from one manufacturer or *resale price maintenance agreements* between producers or retailers keeping prices of goods and services at a certain level

4.7   Termination/Discharge of a Contract

There are five ways by which the rights and obligations of the parties to a valid contract may be terminated or discharged.

These are:

*   discharge by performance, i.e. the obligations have been carried out.
*   discharge by agreement

- discharge by bankruptcy, i.e. one or more of the parties are bankrupt.
- discharge by frustration, e.g. a music venue is burnt down so the owner is not liable for compensation to groups whose concerts are cancelled.
- discharge by breach, i.e. where a party breaks a condition.

?
    a. Explain the fundamentals or prerequisites for contracts.
    b. What is an offer?
    c. Differentiate between condition, warranty and exemption clause.
    d. Briefly explain misrepresentation.
    e. Differentiate between duress and undue influence.
    f. How may a contract be discharged?

5.0   NEGOTIABLE INSTRUMENTS AND AGENCY

5.1   Negotiable Instruments

Negotiable instruments are transferable commercial documents between individuals and/or businesses giving the holder(s) a title to money or property. They are of crucial importance to business, as they are widely used in international sales as well as in foreign trade.

They must be signed by the drawer or maker and be payable on demand or at a definite time.

Typical negotiable instruments include:

- bills of exchange
- cheques
- promissory notes, (a document containing a signed promise to pay)
- share warrants, i.e. securities giving the holder a right to subscribe to a share or a bond at a given price and from a certain date.
- banker's drafts, (or bank draft) i.e. a draft drawn on a bank where payment is guaranteed by the bank.

There are two main parties involved. One is the **transferor** (person transferring on something) the other is the **transferee** (person receiving something) who has a right to payment of the full amount on the negotiable instrument, e.g. cheque. Transferees are entitled (have the right) to sue in their own name.

The essential characteristic of a negotiable instrument is that the **title** (right to ownership) can be passed on *by delivery* (handing over), *plus endorsement* (signature) of the transferor on the reverse side of the instrument, e.g. in the case of a cheque payable to Mr X, Mr X can pass it on to Ms Y by signing on the back. Ms Y is then the new holder.

    a. What is a negotiable instrument?
    b. Explain the two main parties involved.
    c. What is title and how is it passed on to another party?

5.2 Agency

Agency is the relationship which arises when one person, called a *principal*, appoints another party, called the *agent*, to enter into contracts with third parties on the principal's behalf, i.e. for the principal.

Classification of Agents

- **General agent** – has implied authority to enter into any contracts which are normally within the scope of the trade, business or profession the agent has been appointed to by the principal, e.g. an agent appointed to manage a public house would have implied authority to buy alcohol, tobacco, etc
- **Special agent** – has authority to enter into any contracts relating to one specific purpose; an estate agent may be appointed to find a purchaser for the principal's house.
- **Universal agent** – has unlimited authority to enter into any contracts for which the principal has contracted capacity. A universal agent is appointed by a deed known as a 'power of attorney'. An example is where you give someone permission to access your bank a/c to pay bills while you are abroad.

Special types of agents include:

- auctioneer
- broker
- factor, i.e. an agent entrusted with goods or documents of title for the purpose of sale in either their own name or their principal's name.
- estate agent
- *Del Credere* agent, i.e. a person who undertakes to indemnify their principal should the third party purchasers of the principal's goods fail to pay. This agent charges a higher commission than normal.

a. *Explain agency.*
    b. *What are the main types of agent?*

NOTE

Business law concerning types of business organizations and insurance are dealt with under the appropriate units in the book.

6.0 INTERNATIONAL LAW

On an international level, the development of the law on international treaties in the area of business is most important, and, as yet, unfinished. Laws are necessary to regulate international trade and investment and focus on foreign investment, taxation, joint ventures, real estate ownership, the environment, export controls and dumping, i.e. the unloading of surplus stock in a foreign country at a very low price.

Important treaties include:

- **The Paris Convention** with its collateral agreements
- **The World Copyright Convention**
- **Incoterms** (International Rules for the Interpretation of **Commercial Terms**) which were first published in Paris in 1936 by the International Chamber of Commerce (ICC). see unit on Foreign Trade.
- **Agreement on Trade Related Aspects of Intellectual Property Rights (TRIPs)** concluded by the World Trade Organization.

The International Institute for the Unification of Private Law or UNIDROIT (French for *one law*) has been working to develop uniform law guidelines on a global basis with the United Nations Commission on Uniform Trade Law (UNICITRAL) and the International Chamber of Commerce. It has a database called UNILAW that offers information on international trade, international dispute resolution and cultural property.

7.0 EUROPEAN UNION LAW

EU countries' national constitutions are no longer supreme in all respects.

The **primary law** of the European Union which consists of all the Treaties establishing the EU, including the annexes, schedules, and protocols attached to the Treaties, plus subsequent additions and amendments signed by the member states, today takes precedence over national or domestic law.

The **secondary law** of the European Union, made by the Council of Ministers or the European Commission, consists of regulations which apply to the member states and of directives which are made obligatory. Recommendations and opinions expressing the Council of Ministers and Commission's views may also be issued but these, however, are not binding, merely persuasive.

The **Court of Justice** has the task of interpreting, applying and developing EU law. Thus, it has jurisdiction in:

* actions brought by the European Commission or by Member States for infringements of Treaties by Member States.
* actions brought by Member States, corporate bodies or private individuals against EU institutions (see below).

While it is true that membership of the European Union does restrict the supremacy of the constitution or equivalent of the member states, the directives which must ultimately be conformed to are issued as a result of painstaking negotiations between the governments of the European Union.

Central Institutions of the EU include:

The **European Commission**, which is the executive body, or civil service of the EU. It acts as guardian of the Treaties, initiates EU policy, issues proceedings against Member States, makes proposals and fines individuals and companies.

The **Council of Ministers** consists of representatives of the governments of the Member States. It represents the sovereignty of the Member States, and considers and protects national interests, but is also obliged to take the EU interest into account.

The **European Council** is simply a meeting of political Heads of State of Member States. In recent years, such meetings have provided political impetus in areas such as economic and monetary union, reform of agricultural policy, social policy measures and the accession of new members.

The **European Parliament** is directly elected by the population of each Member State with the proportion of members being dependent on the population size of each Member State. It shares legislative power with the Council of Ministers, supervises the European Commission and adopts the annual budget of the EU.

 Explain the primary and secondary law of the EU.

> *If you read this unit too often you might get the feeling that there is*
> *something missing in your life - like your first case in court!*
>
> *Comment from Berit Jähnigen, Sandra Paschke and Jochen*
> *Schaefer who were kind enough to edit this unit.*

Discussion Forum

a. *You can break any law – all that is required is a brilliant*
   lawyer. Discuss.

b. *Should serious breaches of business law, e.g. destruction*
   of the environment or child slave labour, be punishable
   with the death penalty (capital punishment)? Discuss.

c. *The EU Court of Justice is just another step down the line*
   to a Brussels dictatorship. Discuss.

d. *Businesspersons who break the law are treated more*
   leniently than 'ordinary' criminals such as thieves and
   burglars.

e. *There is increasingly a discrepancy between common*
   sense and court decisions.

VOCABULARY

A	
act	Handlung, Tat; Gesetz
actionable	klagbar, belangbar
adultery	Ehebruch
to affirm	bekräftigen
agency	Vertretung, Bevollmächtigung, Vollmacht
agent	Bevollmächtigter
aggravation	Verschärfung, Erschwerung
aggrieved (party)	geschädigte/klagende Partei
award	Zuerkennung, Zubilligung
B	
banker's draft	Bankscheck
barrister	Barrister,(plädierender) Anwalt
be bond to	gebunden sein
beneficiary	Begünstigter
bill of exchange	Wechsel, Tratte
breach (of)	Verstoß (gegen), Bruch, Verletzung
to bring to bear	ausüben
burden of proof	Beweislast

C

capable of performance	erfüllbar
capacity to contract	Vertrags/Geschäftsfähigkeit
case	Rechtsstreit
charge	Anklage(schrift/punkt)
circumstances	Umstände
civil action	Zivilprozess
Civil Code	Bürgerliches Gesetzbuch
civil law	(auf römischem Recht basierendes) Rechtsystem mit kodifiziertem Recht
clause	Klausel, Absatz, Nebenbedingung
to commence	einleiten
Commercial Code	Handelsgesetzbuch
Commercial Law	Handelsrecht
to commit (an action; crime)	begehen
common law	Common Law; (anglo-amerikanisches Rechtsystem)
compensation	Entschädigung(sleistung); Abfindung
condition	wesentliche Vertragsbestimmung
conduct	Verhalten
to confer(a title)	(einen Titel) übertragen, verleihen
confidence	Vertrauen
consent	Einwilligung, Zustimmung
consideration	engl. Vertragsrecht: Gegenleistung (als Wirksamkeitsvoraussetzung eines formlosen Vertrages)
contractually bound	vertraglich gebunden
contributory negligence	Mitverschulden, mitwirkendes Verschulden
counter-	gegen-
court	Gericht
criminal law	Strafrecht
criminal proceedings	Strafprozess
custom	(Handels)Brauch

D

damage	Schadensersatz; Entschädigung
damages in tort	Schadensersatz wegen unerlaubter Handlung
decree	Verfügung, Erlass

deed	Tat, Handlung; auch Urkunde
defamation	Diffamierung, Ehrverletzung
defence(s)	Verteidigung(svorbringen), Einwand
defendant	Beklagter
Director of Public Prosecutions	Strafverfolger, Anklagebehörde (für schwere Straffälle)
discharge (of a contract)	Beendigung, (Vertragsende; auch: Vertragserfüllung)
dispute	Streitfall
domestic	häuslich; Innen-, Binnen-
duress	Zwang, Nötigung
duty	Sorge, Obhut
E	
to enforce	durchsetzen, geltend machen
enforceable (by law)	(rechtlich) erzwingbar, einklagbar, vollstreckbar
enforcement	Durchsetzung, Vollstreckung
to entice	verleiten, überreden
to entitle	berechtigen
equitable remedy	besonderer Rechtsbehelf nach equity Recht
to escape liability	der Haftung entgehen
essentials	wichtigste Punkte
exemplary damage	exemplarische Strafe
to exempt	freistellen, befreien
exemption clause	Haftungsauschlußklausel, Freistellungsklausel
expressly	ausdrücklich
F	
fair comment	sachliche Kritik
faith	Glaube, Vertrauen
to fall short	nicht ausreichen, nicht erfüllen
false imprisonment	Freiheitsberaubung
fault	Schuld, Verschulden
forbearance	Unterlassung; Stundung; Nachsicht
fraudulent	arglistig, betrügerisch
frustration	Vereitelung, (objektive) Unmöglichkeit der Vertragseinhaltung
G	
genuine	echt, ernsthaft
guilty	schuldig

I	
implicitly	stillschweigend
implied terms	nicht ausdrücklich erwähnte/stillschweigend eingeschlossene Vertragsbedingungen
to imply	mit einschließen, einbegreifen
to impose (restrictions on)	(jdm Beschränkungen) auferlegen
to impute	bezichtigen, zur Last legen
incident	Vorfall
to incur	nach/auf sich ziehen; sich aussetzen
to induce	veranlassen, überreden
inevitable	unvermeidbar
to infer	folgern, schließen, erkennen lassen
to infringe	(Recht) verletzen, verstoßen gegen
injunction	einstweilige Verfügung, gerichtliche Anordnung
to injure	verletzen
injured (party)	Geschädigter
injury (physical)	(Körper)Verletzung
innocent	unschuldig, schuldlos
innuendo	versteckte Anspielung/Andeutung
to intend, intention	beabsichtigen, Absicht, Wille
intentional(ly)	vorsätzlich, absichtlich
to interfere	beeinträchtigen, stören
international law	internationales Recht, Völkerrecht
invitation to treat	Aufforderung zur Abgabe eines Angebots
J	
judge	Richter
judicial precedent	Präzedenzfall, Präjudiz
jury	Geschworener, Schöffe; Schwurgericht, Jury
justification	Rechtfertigung
L	
lapse	Zeitablauf, Verjährung, Fristablauf
latter	letzterer, letztgenannter
law	Recht, Gesetz
Law of Contact	Vertragsrecht

Law of Torts	Deliktrecht, Recht der unerlaubten Handlungen
legal duty (of care)	Rechtspflicht, gesetzliche (Sorgfalts)Pflicht
legal relationship	Rechtverhältnis
legally binding	rechtsverbindlich
legislation	Legislatur, Gesetzgebung
liability	Haftung
libel	schriftliche (o.a. dauerhafte Form der) Verleumdung
libelous	verleumderisch
M	
mandatory injunction	einstweilige Verfügung zur Vornahme einer Handlung
merely	lediglich
minor	geringfügig
to mislead	irreführen
misrepresentation	falsche/unrichtige Darstellung
mitigation (of damages)	Milderung, (Herabsetzung des Schadensersatzes)
to mitigate	mildern, herabsetzen
N	
negligence	Fahrlässigkeit, Verschulden
negligent(ly)	fahrlässig
negotiable instrument	(durch Indossament oder Übergabe) begebbares/ übertragbares Wertpapier
nominal damage	nomineller (symbolischer) Schadensersatz
O	
object	Ziel, Zweck, Gegenstand
obligation	Verpflichtungen
occupier's liability	Haftpflicht des Besitzers (eines Grundstücks)
offence	strafbare Handlung
offending party	beklagte Partei
offerer/offeror; offeree	Anbieter, Offerent; Empfänger eines Angebots
onus of proof	Beweislast
to owe	schulden
P	
performance	Erfüllung
plaintiff	Kläger (in Zivilprozessen)
premises	Grundstück
pressure	Druck
presumption	Vermutung, Annahme

prima facie (at first sight)	beim ersten Anschein, auf den ersten Blick
prior (to)	vor
proceedings	(Gerichts)Verfahren, Prozess
prohibitive injunction	einstweilige Verfügung zur Unterlassung einer Handlung
to promise	sich verpflichten, zusagen, versprechen
promissory note	Schuldschein
property	Eigentum
to prove	beweisen
Public Prosecutor	öffentlicher Ankläger, Staatsanwalt
public	öffentlich
publication	Bekanntmachung, Zurkenntnisbringung
public order	öffentliche Ordnung
punitive damage	extrem hohe, exemplarische Strafe
to punish	bestrafen
R	
reasonable	angemessen
reckless	rücksichtslos
to refrain from	unterlassen (einer Handlung)
regardless	unabhängig von
remedy	Rechtsbehelf, Rechtsmittel
reputation	Ruf
resale price maintenance	Preisbindung bei Wiederverkauf
to rescind	auflösen, zurücktreten, aufheben
restraint of trade	Wettbewerbsbeschränkung
to revoke	widerrufen; zurücknehmen, anullieren, aufheben
revocation	Widerruf
S	
to safeguard	sichern
sanction	Strafmaßnahme
seal, under seal	Siegel, gesiegelt, versiegelt
sentence (to pass)	(Straf)Urteil (fällen, verkünden)
to set aside	aufheben, außer Kraft setzen
share warrant	(auf den Inhaber lautender) Aktienschein
to shift	wechseln
to shun	meiden

slander	mündliche (o.a. nicht dauerhafte Form der) Beleidigung, üble Nachrede
slanderous	beleidigend
solicitor	Anwalt
statute law	Gesetzesrecht, kodifiziertes Recht
statute	(vom Parlament geschaffenes, kodifiziertes) Gesetz
statutory	gesetzlich
strict liability	strenge Haftung, Gefährdungshaftung
subsidiary	untergeordnet
to sue	veklagen, (gegen jdn) klagen
to suffer (a loss)	(enen Verlust) erleiden
supervize	überwachen
T	
to terminate	beenden, enden
terminate	enden, erlöschen, ablaufen; beenden, kündigen
terms	vertragliche Bedingungen, Klauseln
to threaten	(an)drohen
tortiuos act	unerlaubte Handlung
to transfer	übertragen
transient	vorübergehend
trial	Gerichtsverhandlung, Verfahren
trustee	Treuhänder, Vermögensverwalter
U	
undue influence	ungebührliche Beeinflussung
unequivocal	unzweideutig, eindeutig
union	Gewerkschaft
unlawful picketing	gesetzwidrige Aufstellung von Streikposten
unliquidated damages	schätzungsbedürftiger, (noch) unbestimmter Schadensersatz
to uphold	aufrechterhalten, bestätigen
V	
valid	gültig
VD (venereal disease)	Geschlechtskrankheit
vicarious liability	stellvertretende Haftung, Haftung für Verhalten Dritter
void, to void	nichtig, ungültig, ungültig machen

voidable	annullierbar, aufhebbar, anfechtbar
W	
warranty	unwesentliche Vertragsbestimmung; Garantie (für Sach- und Rechtsmängel)
to withdraw	zurückziehen, zurücktreten
witness	Zeuge
wrong	Unrecht

SOURCES OF FINANCE & TAXATION

I think the necessity of being ready increases. Look to it.
Abraham Lincoln

FOCUS This unit is about the need for finance in a business, how it is obtained and employed. The second part looks at taxation, a very important source of finance for governments, and examines the different types of taxes in the world today.

SECTION I: SOURCES OF FINANCE

1.0 Introduction
    1.1 Assets
    1.2 Liabilities
2.0 Ratio Analysis
    2.1 Profitability Ratios
    2.2 Liquidity Ratios
    2.3 Solvency Ratios
3.0 The Sources of Finance
    3.1 Short-Term Sources
    3.2 Medium-Term Sources
    3.3 Long-Term Sources

SECTION II: TAXATION

1.0 Introduction to Taxation
2.0 Functions of Taxation
3.0 Canons of Taxation
4.0 Types of Tax
5.0 Other Forms of Revenue
6.0 Double Taxation Agreements (DTA)

SECTION I : SOURCES OF FINANCE

1.0 INTRODUCTION

When a businessperson sets up a firm **capital** is required to buy various things which are essential for running the business, be it a factory, machinery, vehicles, raw material, etc.

Goods will then be manufactured and traded or services offered and hopefully sold on a profitable basis. To encourage sales, credit is often given, which means that the firm will have debtors.

Profits, which are highly dependable on the level of competition in the market, will be ploughed back into the firm, if some of it is left after taxes have been paid.

Let us now look at some accounting terms which are important to the basics of Finance.

1.1 Assets

An asset is something of value that will bring in revenue to a business including cash, raw materials, premises, machinery, stock and debtors (persons or organization who owe money to other persons or organizations).

Assets are usually divided into two groups:

- **Current assets** are cash, raw materials, stock and debtors.
- **Fixed assets (fixed capital)** are machinery, factory buildings (plant), and strategic investments. It is important to stress that fixed assets cannot be converted into cash as quickly as current assets.

1.2 Liabilities

Liabilities are debts, the opposite to assets. **Current liabilities** include creditors (persons or organizations to whom money is owed to by other persons or organizations), tax due, and overdrafts (credits from a financial institution where the customer's current account can be overdrawn to a credit limit agreed), while **long-term** liabilities include loans.

The current assets less the current liabilities equals the working capital of a firm. **Working capital** is the capital used for working or running the business, i.e. for paying wages, salaries and other working expenses, raw materials, etc. Thus, the working capital represents a first approach to finding out a firm's liquidity.

2.0   RATIO ANALYSIS

Ratio Analysis is a method of analyzing the figures that appear on financial statements and helps to evaluate the strong and weak points in the financial performance of a business. Weaknesses that are detected can then be corrected. The process of identifying sources of certain financial needs normally results from implementing a ratio analysis.

A **financial ratio** is computed by taking selected figures from the financial statements and expressing one figure as a percentage of another figure or ratio.

2.1   Profitability Ratios

These attempt to show how well a firm has performed.

The **profit margin** is the net profit divided by its sales.

Return on Equity (ROE) is the net profit divided by the equity capital and shows the return on the owner's investment in the business. This represents a specific way to measure the return on investment. The problem with ROE is that it is too general.

2.2   Liquidity Ratios

Liquidity is the ability of a firm to meet its obligations in the near future. In this connection liquidity ratios attempt to assess whether a firm is maintaining an appropriate level of liquidity. A consequence of too little liquidity could be bankruptcy. In the case of too much liquidity strategic long-term investments have more than likely been missed.

Liquidity ratios can be assessed by the following formulae

- *Current ratio* = the current assets divided by the current liabilities. It answers the question whether the business has enough current assets to meet its current debts or liabilities.
- *Acid-test ratio* = the current assets minus the company stock (raw materials or finished goods) divided by the current liabilities. This shows whether a business could meet its current obligations with the available funds if all sales revenue should stop.

2.3   Solvency Ratios

In contrast to liquidity ratios, **solvency ratios** take a more long-run view. They attempt to determine whether the management of a firm has made too much use of financial leverage. Two common solvency ratios are:

- **Debt/equity ratio** = the total long-term debt, i.e. borrowed funds divided by the owners' (equity) capital. It shows the amount of borrowed money in the business compared with the equity capital.

  It follows that a firm with constant sales and earnings can afford to have more debt than a firm experiencing wide swings in its sales volume.

- **Capital gearing (leverage - AE) ratio**

  The capital of a company may consist of different classes of shares or debentures (see Unit 5 on the Stock Exchange) which carry different rights. Investors will not be interested in purchasing shares (ordinary or preference) or offering finance through a debenture bond (in reality a loan) unless the company is a very safe one.

  The ratio by which the capital of a company is split between debt finance (preference shares and debentures) and the ordinary shares (equity capital) is called the capital gearing of a company.

  A large amount of preference shares means that a big preference dividend has to be paid before any dividend is paid to the ordinary shareholders. If a company has any debentures then the debenture interest must be paid before the preference and ordinary dividend.

  A firm with such a high proportion of fixed-interest loan debt, compared to its equity capital is said to be **high-geared**. It can mean high interest repayments, little or no dividends and difficulties in getting more loans. It can be favourable when a company uses the debt for expansion and investment.

  A high proportion of equity capital to fixed-interest debt means that a firm is **low-geared.** A lowly geared company with a constant profit and little risk-taking, i.e. expansion, is more in the interests of the ordinary shareholders. However, the firm may fail to reach its true potential.

Over-capitalization means that a firm has too much working capital <u>in relation</u> to the profit it is generating. This can be a result of poor sales, strong competitive pressures, sunk costs (i.e. the opportunity costs incurred on entering a market including R&D and advertising) or even poor management forecasting.

Under-capitalization is the term used when a firm has insufficient working capital. Typical problems would be that such a firm cannot avail of bulk-buying, there is a lack of resources to aid expansion and the firm is slow to pay creditors.

A firm that is under-capitalized is said to be **over-trading**.

Insolvency arises when a firm's total liabilities exceed a fair valuation of its total assets, which means the firm is legally **insolvent** or **bankrupt**. A less serious situation is when the current assets are not enough to meet the debts of the firm as they become payable. Then the firm is only **technically insolvent** or **illiquid,** on a technical point of law. An overdraft could solve this problem temporarily.

a. *Differentiate between assets and liabilities.*
b. *Explain over-capitalization and under-capitalization.*
c. *What is insolvency?*

3.0   THE SOURCES OF FINANCE

To build up a firm's assets a businessperson requires **finance**. There are three main sources - short, medium and long-term.

3.1   Short-Term Sources

These consist of:

- **Accrued expenses**, which refers to money not yet paid out, for example, tax due, wages in arrears.
- **Trade credit (accounts payable)**, which refers to the period of time between buying goods and paying for them.
- **Overdrafts**
- **Inventory financing**, i.e. using stock as security for a loan.
- **Factoring** which is the sale of a company's debts (accounts receivable) to a factoring firm (factor) which accepts the responsibility of debt collection and credit risk. A fee is charged by the factor.
- **Commercial paper** issued by large firms, where the lender receives a loan from the firm by signing a **promissory note** (a promise to pay the lender within a stated time).

- **Accounts receivable** which is the form of financing involving borrowing money from a financial institution using the invoices of the firm as security.

3.2 Medium-Term Sources

These include:

- **Hire-purchase (HP)**
  which involves part payment of a good with a deposit and settling the balance by instalments. The ownership of the good passes from the buyer to the seller after the last payment has been made. The main object is to buy, this method is often used for the purchase of luxury goods, less so with capital goods.
- **Leasing**
  where the leaseholder (lessee) is allowed by the lessor (owner) to use a product for a specified time in return for a rent. The main objective of the leaseholder is to rent. It is normally used for capital goods, e.g. equipment, machinery.

  An **Operating Lease Contract** has no full amortization, i.e. payments by the lessee are not sufficient to cover the full cost. The contract is usually written for a period less than the expected economic life of the object being leased. The lessor also takes care of maintenance and the lease contains a cancellation clause.
- **Term loans**
  which are loans for up to seven years, with standard monthly repayments.

3.3 Long-Term Sources

Long term sources of finance are:

- **Owner's capital** - i.e. the funds invested by the entrepreneur.
- **Shares** (see Unit 5 on Stock Exchange).
- **Debentures** (see Unit 5 on Stock Exchange).
- **Retained profits** or **earnings (reserve capital)** - which are the unpaid dividends ploughed back into the company for expansion.
- **Finance Leasing** - a contract with full amortization which cannot be cancelled and where the lessor is not responsible for maintenance of the object leased. **Sale and leaseback** is a special kind of finance leasing which involves a firm selling its

premises in order to gain an injection of finance, and then leasing it back from the buyer.

- **Project finance** - funding for large projects from a financial institution or group of financial institutions.
- **Government finance** - funding in the form of grants (non-repayable) and loans.
- **Venture capital** - which is 'risk' capital provided by venture capital companies who are willing to give 'seed' or start-up capital and future development capital.

     a. Give examples of short term and long term sources of finance.
     b. Differentiate between HP and leasing.

SECTION II: TAXATION

> Q: *What is the difference between a taxidermist and a tax collector?*
>
> A: *The taxidermist takes only your skin.*
>
>   *Mark Twain*

1.0   INTRODUCTION TO TAXATION

Governments have two main economic tools in order to implement their policies:

a. **Monetary policy**, which involves the control of the supply of money circulating in an economy by altering interest rates, exchange rates and the availability of credit.

b. **Fiscal policy**, which is the government policy concerning the relation between taxes collected and public expenditure made.

Tax is what is paid to the government in order to enable it to finance economic and social objectives. Everyone pays it in one form or another, either directly or indirectly.

The three original uses of tax were to:

- support military spending for attack and defence
- fund the justice system
- finance public buildings, roads, bridges and harbours.

In the past tax used to be payable in kind (payment in the form of goods and services rather than cash), or by personal service (as in the feudal system). Nowadays all tax is assessed and paid in the form of money.

The greatest elements of expenditure in a modern government's budget are social welfare, public health, education, agriculture and the promotion of business enterprise.

2.0 FUNCTIONS OF TAXATION

The functions of taxation nowadays are to:

- raise revenue (along with borrowing) for the running of a country.
- provide services and social benefits, thereby redistributing wealth from the richer sections of the community to the poorer.
- construct essential infrastructure, for example, motorways or bridges.
- finance employment, e.g. civil servants.
- service the national debt, i.e. pay the government's total outstanding debts plus the interest.

3.0 CANONS OF TAXATION

The principles or canons of taxation, which were originally suggested by the economist Adam Smith in his book *The Wealth of Nations (1776),* are still valid today.

They are:

- The **Principle of Equity**, which means that taxes should be levied on the population in accordance with their ability to pay. Taxes which do this are referred to as *progressive taxes* which take a greater percentage of income as tax as income rises. The government takes proportionately more from the rich than from the poor. The opposite are *regressive taxes* which take a lower proportion of income in tax as income rises. This tax takes proportionately less from the rich. An example of the latter is Value Added Tax because it is charged at a uniform rate irrespective of the purchaser's income. High rates of tax are, of course, a disincentive and can reduce the savings and work effect.
- The **Principle of Certainty** where the amount payable and the time when they must be paid by should be clear.
- The **Principle of Convenience** which means that taxes should be convenient from the point of view of both collection and payment.

- The **Principle of Economy** means that taxes should not cost the tax authorities too much to collect.

    a. What economic tools do governments use to implement their policies?
    b. What is tax?
    c. Explain the functions of taxation.
    d. What are the canons of taxation?

4.0 TYPES OF TAX

Nowadays taxes are often divided into four main categories.

    A. Direct Taxes
    B. Indirect Taxes
    C. Local Taxes
    D. Capital Taxes

A. Direct Taxes

Direct taxes are mostly taxes on income, examples include income tax and corporation tax.

The advantages are that both the government and the taxpayer can work out the amount of tax due.

Because of its progressive nature (the more you earn the more you pay) it may be a disincentive for people to work, to save money, or to invest. This is particularly true when taxes are at a high level.

A.1 Income Tax

Income tax can be derived from a variety of sources, e.g. from rent, from investment or from employment. Income tax is therefore divided into a series of categories, or schedules depending on the types of professions or types of business activity.

Each category has its own rules which reflect the problems met in trying to tax that form of income.

Basic Facts:

The **income tax year** in most countries runs in a yearly January to December time period.

Taxable income is normally divided into two **tax bands**, i.e. single person and married person and each band is taxed at a different rate.

Married persons can be taxed as single people or under a **joint assessment** or separate assessment.

In some countries very low wage earners are **exempt** from tax in order to ensure a certain amount of tax free income that guarantees a minimum standard of living.

Tax-(free) allowances can include mortgage interest relief and private health insurance which are deducted from gross income to give taxable income. For example, Jane earns £30,000 per year less £3,700 mortgage relief and £2,000 private health. This means her taxable income is £24,300.

In the USA pension contributions to Individual Retirement Accounts (IRA) can be deducted from taxable income.

The self-employed normally have to pay **preliminary tax**, which is an estimate of income tax. Normally this is done several times a year. At the end of the financial year a tax return has to be made.

Because income tax is progressive, the dictum follows the more you earn, the more you pay. Combined with allowances, this can lead to a significant difference between the **average rate of tax** paid and the **marginal rate**. The latter is the rate of tax paid on extra units of income earned which has the effect of bringing the taxpayer into the highest tax band. For example, a person may only pay 20% on his first $5000 income but he has to pay 35% on all income earned after $5000.

Employed people do not pay annual tax bills in one go, instead their employers deduct tax at source from their weekly pay or monthly salary and pay it over to the tax authorities or *Revenue Commissioners (Internal Revenue Service or IRS in the USA)*. This system is usually known as **Pay As You Earn (PAYE)** or **Pay As You Go (PAYG)** in the USA. Other levies such as social insurance for unemployment and sickness are also deducted.

At the end of the tax year the employer must furnish each employee with a **statement** of all tax and other deductions. This can then be sent to the Revenue Commissioner's (Tax Office) if a review of a taxpayer's tax liability is demanded.

Every citizen is obliged to send in or file an **annual tax return** - sometimes a tax rebate is due.

A.2   Corporation Tax (Corporate Income Tax - AE)

Corporation tax is a tax levied on a company's profits. A form of **double tax** exists for private and public limited companies which are obliged to pay tax on their earnings and in addition to that the shareholders or owners of the corporation or company pay personal income tax on their dividend income. In some cases they pay capital gains tax when they sell their shares.

B.   Indirect Taxes

Indirect taxes are taxes on goods and services, not on income, and are passed from the entrepreneur to the final consumer. He/she is the one who finally has to bear these taxes. For that reason they are referred to as indirect taxes.

There are three main types:

- **Customs duties**, which are taxes on imported and exported goods.
- **Excise duties** are taxes levied on the consumption of certain home-produced goods in order to yield revenue for the state. These goods are normally selective ones such as cigarettes, petrol and alcohol which cause social costs. Raising excise duties is often justified by a budget deficit which has to be reduced.
- **Ad valorem taxation** is a percentage tax - a good example is Value Added Tax (VAT).

C.   Local Taxes

Local taxes are imposed by local authorities for services rendered such as police and fire services, refuse collection, water supply, etc.

D.   Capital Taxes

Capital taxes are charged on assets such as land, cash, property, shares or other valuables such as paintings and silverware. Personal assets such as a person's home are usually exempt from this tax. There are two types:

Capital gains tax is charged on the profits made when something is sold for a higher price than it was bought for.

Capital acquisitions tax is levied when wealth is transferred to another person in the form of a gift or as an inheritance.

5.0   OTHER FORMS OF REVENUE

A common example is motor vehicle duty (road tax/car tax) which is charged on owners of vehicles.

Other forms of public revenues include **national** or **state insurance** where pay related contributions are made by both the employer and employee. This is used to pay for health contributions, employment training for the unemployed, etc.

Employers often object as they see it as a tax on jobs which makes employing a person more expensive.

6.0 DOUBLE TAXATION AGREEMENTS (DTA)

These are agreements made by countries for the avoidance of double taxation. This means that profits earned in the country of residence will not be liable in the tax in the mother country of the firm or person in question.

a. Differentiate between direct and indirect taxes.
b. Explain how income tax works.
c. What is capital gains tax?
d. Explain double taxation and double taxation agreements.

 Discussion Forum

a. Are taxes too high in your country?
b. Is tax reform necessary? Why? What has to be changed?
c. Tax evasion is not a crime. Discuss.
d. Discuss whether tax havens should be permitted to exist.

VOCABULARY

A	
accounts payable	Verbindlichkeiten
accounts receivable	Forderungen, Außenstände
accounts receivable financing	Finanzierung durch Vorausabtretung von Geschäftsforderungen
accrued expenses	entstehende Ausgaben, anticipative Passiva
acid test ratio	Liquidität ersten Grades
ad valorem (tax)	dem Wert nach
to aid	helfen; fördern
allowance	Ermäßigung; Steuerfreibetrag
to alter	verändern
amortization	Tilgung, Amortisierung, Abschreibung
to assess	veranschlagen, bemessen
assessment	Steuerveranlagung
assets	Vermögen
- current	- Umlaufvermögen
- fixed	- Anlagevermögen
to avail oneself of	Gebrauch machen von, nutzen
average rate of tax	Durchschnittssteuersatz

B

| budget deficit | Haushaltsdefizit |
| bulk-buying | Kauf großer Mengen |

C

cancellation clause	Kündigungs-/ Aufhebungsklausel
canons/(of taxation)	(Besteuerungs-) Grundsätze
capital acquisitions tax	'Kapitalerwerbssteuer', Schenkungs-u. Erbschaftssteuer
capital gains tax	Kapitalgewinnsteuer, Kapitalertragssteuer
capital gearing	Kapitalstruktur, Leverage Effekt
capital gearing ratio	Nettofremdkapitalquote
to charge	berechnen; auferlegen
commercial paper	kurzfristige Geldmarktverschreibung, Handelspapier
convenience	Angemessenheit
corporation tax	Körperschaftsteuer
creditors	Kreditoren; Gläubiger
current ratio	Liquidität dritten Grades
customs duty	Zoll

D

debenture	Schuldverschreibung, Anleihe, Obligation (langfristig)
debt equity ratio	Verschuldungskoeffizient, Verschuldungsgrad
debtors	Debitoren; Schuldner
to deduct	abziehen, einbehalten
deposit	Anzahlung; Pfand
derive from	herleiten aus, gewinnen aus
dividends	Ausschüttung
to be due	fällig sein
Double Taxation Agreement (DTA)	Doppelbesteuerungsabkommen (DBA)

E

to enable	ermöglichen
equity capital	Eigenkapital
estimate	Schätzung
excise duty	Verbrauch-und Aufwandsteuer
to exempt sb. from sth.	jmd. von etwas befreien/ausnehmen
expenditure	Ausgaben
expenses	Aufwendungen, Auslagen

F

| factoring | Factoring |

finance leasing	Finanz(ierungs)-Leasing
G	
gearing	Fremdkapitalaufnahme, Verschuldungsgrad, Verhältnis Fremdkapital/Eigenkapital
gross/net income	Brutto-/Nettoeinkommen
H	
hire-purchase	Ratenkauf
I	
in arrears	im Rückstand
incentive, disincentive	Anreiz, kein Anreiz, Demotivation
income tax	Einkommensteuer
inheritance tax	Erbschaftsteuer
(il)liquidity	Zahlungs(un)fähigkeit
insolvency	Insolvenz, Konkurs, Zahlungsunfähigkeit
(in)sufficient	(un)genügeng
instalment	Rate; Ratenzahlung
K	
kind, in kind	(in) Naturalien
L	
land tax	Grundsteuer
latter	letztgenannte(r,s)
lessee	Leasingnehmer, Mieter
lessor	Leasinggeber, Vermieter
leverage	Leverage, Hebelwirkung; Kreditaufnahme
levy	Abgabe, Steuer
to levy (tax)	erheben, einziehen
liabilities	Schulden, Verbindlichkeiten
- current	- kurzfristige Verbindlichkeiten
- long term	- langfristige Verbindlichkeiten
loan	Darlehen
loan capital	Fremdkapital
local tax	Kommunalsteuern
M	
maintenance	Wartung
marginal rate of tax	Grenzsteuersatz
to moot	zur Debatte stellen
mortgage interest	Hypothekenzinsen
motor vehicle duty	Kraftfahrzeugsteuer
O	
objective	Ziel(vorstellung)
operating lease contract	(meist) kurzfristiger Leasingvertrag

opportunity cost	Opportunitätskosten
overcapitalization	Überkapitalisierung
overdraft	Kontokorrentkredit, Überziehungskredit
overtrading	Liquiditätsklemme trotz hoher Rendite
to owe sb. sth.	jmd. etwas schulden
P	
pay as you earn/go	Quellenabzug (Lohnsteuer)
plant	(technische) Anlage
to plough back into	thesaurieren, einbehalten, reinvestieren
preliminary tax	Steuervorauszahlung
premise	(Geschäfts)Grundstück; Gebäude
principle of economy	Wirtschaftlichkeitsprinzip
principle of equity	Gerechtigkeitsprinzip
profit margin	Gewinnspanne, Gewinnmarge
promissory note	Eigenwechsel, Schuldschein, Schuldanerkenntnis
R	
ratio analysis	Kennziffernanalyse
to redistribute	umverteilen
refuse collection	Müllabfuhr
relief	Entlastung
residence	Wohnsitz, (ständiger) Aufenthalt
retained profits/earnings	(Gewinn)Rücklagen, einbehaltene/thesaurierte Gewinne
return	Umsatzerlöse, Ertrag, Rendite
return on equity	Eigenkapitalrendite
return on investment	Kapitalrendite
revenue	Einnahmen; Steueraufkommen
revenue commissioners, internal Revenue Service (AE)	Finanzamt, Steuerbehörde
S	
security	Sicherheit
seed capital	Startkapital
solvency ratio	Solvenzkennzahl,
to spur	vorantreiben
statement	Erklärung, Aufstellung
stock	Vorräte, Lagerbestand
T	
tax (free) allowances	Steuerfreibetrag
tax assessment notice	Steuerbescheid
tax authority	Steuerbehörde
tax band	Steuerkategorie/-stufe

tax due	fällige Steuer
tax liability	Steuerschuld
tax office	Finanzamt
tax rebate	Steuererstattung, -rückzahlung
tax relief	Steuervergünstigung
tax return	Steuererklärung
tax threshold	Steuereingangsstufe
taxation	Besteuerung
taxidermist	Präparator (von Tieren)
tenet	Grundsatz
term loan	mittelfristiger Kredit
trade credit	Warenkredit, Lieferantenkredit, Kauf auf Ziel
V	
venture capital	Risikokapital
W	
working capital	Betriebskapital

Bibliography

- Armstrong, G., Kotler, P.
  Marketing
  (Prentice-Hall, London, 2000)

- Blanchard, K., Schewe, C., Nelson, R., Hiam A.
  Exploring the World of Business
  (Worth Publishers , New York, 1996)

- Boone, L., Kurtz, D.
  Contemporary Business
  (The Dryden Press, Toronto, 1999)

- Buckley, M.
  The Structure of Business
  (3rd Ed., Longman, Harlow, 1997)

- Cole, G.
  Management Theory and Practice
  (5th Ed. Letts, London, 1999)

- Economist Newspaper Limited
  (London, 25 October 1997)

- Fischer, S., Dornbrush, R.
  Economics
  (5th Ed. McGraw-Hill, London & New York, 1997)

- O'Connor, J.
  Business Organisation
  (Folens, Dublin & London, 1992)

- Schäfer, W.
  Wirtschaftswörterbuch - Englisch-Deutsch, Deutsch-Englisch
  (Verlag Vahlen, München, 1992)

- Terrell, P., Schnorr, V., Morris, W., Breitsprecher, R.
  Collins German-English, English-German Dictionary
  (HarperCollins Publishers, Glasgow, 1997)